Also by Jesse Ventura

*I Ain't Got Time to Bleed: Reworking the
Body Politic from the Bottom Up*

*Do I Stand Alone? Going to the Mat Against
Political Pawns and Media Jackals*

Don't Start the Revolution Wi

Don't Start the Revolution Without Me!

From the Minnesota Governor's Mansion to the Baja Outback

Reflections and Revisionings

By Jesse Ventura
with Dick Russell

A Herman Graf book
Skyhorse Publishing

Skyhorse Publishing books may be purchased in bulk at special discounts for sales promotion, corporate gifts, fund raising, or educational purposes. Special editions can also be created to specifications. For details, contact Special Sales Department, Skyhorse Publishing, 555 Eighth Avenue, Suite 903, New York, NY 10018 or info@ skyhorsepublishing.com.

www.skyhorsepublishing.com

10 9 8 7 6 5 4 3 2 1

Library of Congress Cataloging-in-Publication Data

Ventura, Jesse.
    Don't start the revolution without me! : from the Minnesota governor's mansion to the Baja outback : reflections and revisionings / Jesse Ventura ; with Dick Russell.
        p. cm.
    ISBN 978-1-60239-273-1 (hardcover : alk. paper)
1. Ventura, Jesse. 2. Ventura, Terry. 3. Governors—Minnesota—Biography.
4. Governors' spouses—Minnesota—Biography. 5. United States—Politics and government—1989– 6. Minnesota—Politics and government—1951– 7. Ventura, Jesse—Travel—Southwest, New. 8. Ventura, Terry—Travel—Southwest, New.
9. Southwest, New—Description and travel. 10. Baja California (Mexico: Peninsula)—Description and travel. I. Russell, Dick. II. Title.

F610.3.V46A3 2008
977.6'053092—dc22
[B]

                                          2007048884

Printed in the United States of America

To Doug Friedline,

A man who worked endlessly and ultimately gave his life trying to elect honest people to public office.

—Jesse Ventura

and

To our son, Tyrel, and our daughter, Jade, and to all the children of the future: Your freedom is at risk. Be wary.

—Terry Ventura

"I can't be a politician. I don't know how. I love the truth. I love to speak it, to recognize it. And that's why many people criticize me behind my back. To be a politician, you have to take many factors into account, manipulate them, lie if it's necessary. I'm no good at that. I'll never be good at any of that."

—Ernesto (Che) Guevara

Contents

CHAPTER 1

The Need for a New Adventure

"The first Westerners known to have landed on Baja were a ship's crew dispatched by Hernan Cortés, looking for an 'island of pearls' that the Spanish conquistador had heard about from the Aztec ruler Moctezuma. During the 1500s a popular chivalric romance narrative also mentioned a race of Amazon women who ruled a gold-filled island. Their queen was called Califia, the place California. The early Spanish expeditioners apparently believed that the Baja terrain resembled that of the fictional island. Indeed, Baja was widely thought to be an island until the end of the seventeenth century. This was the first California. The peninsula would later be called Lower California, as differentiated from its neighboring American territory. (The Spanish adjective baja means 'geographically lower.')"

—Dick Russell, *Eye of the Whale*

When you're at a crossroads, sometimes all you can do is take a reprieve from the fast lane. As I begin to write this book, I'm facing probably the most monumental decision of my fifty-six years on this planet. Will I run for president of the United States, as an independent, in 2008? Or will I stay as far away from the fray as possible, in a place with no electricity, on a remote beach in Mexico?

Right now I'm leaving Minnesota, where I was born and raised, been a pro wrestler and a radio talk-show host, and have served as both a mayor and a governor. I don't know how much of an expatriate I'll become. Looking at the political landscape of America today, my outrage knows few bounds.

We're losing our constitutional rights because of the so-called "war on terror." It reminds me of that line from the movie *Full Metal Jacket*: "Guess they'd rather be alive than free—poor dumb bastards!" Not me—once America is no longer what our country has stood for since 1776. We've gone backwards. When you look at how religious fanatics and corporate America are teaming up, we today are on the brink of fascism.

What infuriates me more than anything is that it's my generation that is now in charge. We came out of the sixties, the Vietnam era. I served over there, but it's now a historical fact that we were duped into that war by our leaders. Now, we've let it happen again with Iraq—a war based on lies and deceit that's costing thousands of lives.

We're also the generation that experimented more than any other with recreational drugs. If anybody should understand how wrongheaded the "war on drugs" is, it's us. Marijuana should be legalized and regulated the same way as alcohol and tobacco. Bill Maher recently put it in this context: the Beatles took LSD and wrote *Sgt. Pepper's*. Anna Nicole Smith's autopsy turned up nine prescription drugs and she couldn't dial 911. Yet the first drug is outlawed and you'll go to jail for it, while all the others are given to you legally. I don't get it.

And thirdly, we—"the free love generation"—are now telling our children to abstain from sex? When I spoke at Carleton College, I told the young people: "Unless they were a virgin on their wedding day, anyone who preaches abstinence to you is a hypocrite." Two weeks later, Ann Coulter showed up at the same school, and one of the students raised his hand and asked her whether she'd been a virgin! It made the papers—and made me laugh. You know what Coulter did? Attacked the kid and changed the subject.

What also makes me so angry about America is that 50 percent or more of us don't vote. Yet we're out supposedly spreading democracy and spending billions of dollars to give it to Iraq—when half of us don't even bother?

We've allowed our media to be turned into entertainment, rather than facts, enlightenment, and knowledge. We've gone from Woodward and Bernstein to Bill O'Reilly. From Walter Cronkite to Katie Couric. The death of Anna Nicole Smith received more coverage, for a longer period, than the assassination of President Kennedy did at the time.

Why is our government so secretive? If we are indeed a nation of the people, by the people, and for the people, how come they insist upon keeping us in the dark as much possible? I call it the dumbing-down of America, by both the media and the government. But the tragic fact is that we, the people, are becoming like lemmings racing in a suicidal pack toward the sea. And most of us won't even face the fact that, because of our neglect, the seas are dying.

If you want good government, you must have an involved citizenry. Yet it seems like apathy is a contagious disease. People don't pay attention to government because they don't think it affects them. Well, you work five days a week. Why wouldn't you pay attention to an entity that's taking the fruits of your labor two of those days?

Wouldn't that be enough motivation to pay heed to what your tax dollars are being used for?

Today, the special interests have a stranglehold on our reality. Nobody is being told the truth. We've bought a bill of goods. I can't believe everyone is so asleep. I achieved the impossible once—a wrestler becoming governor of one of our fifty states. Why is nobody else coming forward?

Or do I have to throw myself into the political ring again? And, if I do, is it worth the price that my family and I will have to pay?

This is the dilemma I'm facing. I can't live with this apathy. I can't tell myself it's not happening. I have to stand up and talk about it. I love my country and what it was founded for. I believe deeply in its inherent freedoms. And we're losing them. We're losing more of them every day. I can't just ignore it. . . . I don't know about you. . . .

Psychologically, I needed to break away from the United States. I also felt it was time in my life to go on an adventure. I was still young enough, but I knew the window of opportunity was closing. From watching my parents pass on, I knew that your health becomes an issue at some point and eventually you're not going to be able to travel. As you get older and older, you revert back to a childlike existence, where your little house and neighborhood are about the extent of your world. So, an adventure was important for me—not only physically, but mentally.

I needed to refocus, to do something that really went back to basics. And I found that, even in the twenty-first century, you can still be something of a Kit Carson. There are frontiers left to explore that are relatively untouched by humans. Some of these are located along the Mexican peninsula known as Baja California, almost a thousand miles of desert, mountains, and sea.

My wife Terry and I left Minnesota in the middle of winter, planning to drive our truck-camper, pulling a trailer with two wave runners, all the way across America and then over the border into Mexico. This was also an opportunity to renew our relationship. After playing the game of governor and First Lady for four years, in the public eye constantly, with our fully scheduled agendas, we'd often been like ships passing in the night.

Our two kids were grown up now, and had their own lives to lead. Tyrel was out in Hollywood, where he was working at becoming a screenwriter. Jade still lived in Minnesota, and was making plans to get married. So Terry and I were free in a way we'd really never been during all those years I'd spent in the limelight—as a pro wrestler, a movie actor, a radio personality, and finally as the improbable governor of the thirty-second state.

I'd have a lot of time along this journey to reflect.

At first, it feels strange leaving all the comforts of home behind. The three-story place we moved into after I decided not to seek a second term as governor is really my dream house. Built on a lake, the house is also right next to a railroad track. Even though I might be fishing and in complete solitude when a train goes by, it always awakensed me to the fact that the rest of the world is still moving. It's a beautiful sight actually, when you're out on the lake. Maybe that's what helped put the wanderlust in me, too.

I live north of St. Paul, and it's the first time I've ever lived east of the Mississippi River. As we pull out of our gate and head down along the shoreline of nearby White Bear Lake, I recall to Terry a story that my dad told me long ago. "This was a very famous lake back in the twenties and thirties. Back then, most of the laws were state-to-state, and if you hadn't committed a crime in one particular state, the authorities there wouldn't bother you. The folklore was,

Al Capone and his gangsters had kind of a working agreement with Minnesota law enforcement—they wouldn't do anything illegal if they could go on vacation to White Bear Lake. We were their home away from home."

Terry laughed. "Your dad's stories," she said, "were amazing."

TERRY: When we started doing the family holiday thing, it was unbelievable. His whole family had the best time sitting around arguing politics. I would just sit there, because my own family was really non-political. In southern Minnesota, when you went to some-one's home or a gathering, you didn't talk about your religion, you didn't ask how much anything cost that they owned, and you never mentioned politics! But his family would sound like they were beating the living heck out of each other mentally, and at the end they'd say, "Wow, what a great time we had!"

My dad George only got as far as the eighth grade, and worked as a laborer for the Minneapolis street department. He was ten years older than my mom, Bernice, who survived the Great Depression growing up on an Iowa farm and somehow put herself through nursing school. They both served in Africa during World War Two. He was an enlisted man, and she was a lieutenant. I remember when they'd get into an argument sometimes, he'd say, "Ah, the lieutenant's on my case again. What the hell is them officers' problem, anyway?"

I was born on July 15, 1951. My older brother Jan and I grew up in a two-story house in a lower-middle-class neighborhood of south Minneapolis. When I was in sixth grade, I used to set up a ring in our basement and stage different fights among my classmates. Sometimes I'd referee, sometimes I'd jump in there myself. Pro boxing was pretty big then in Minneapolis, and Jan and I loved listening to the bouts on the radio. I was probably no more than nine when my elementary teacher asked what I wanted to be when I grew up. When I said, "a pro boxer," she told me that was a ridiculous idea.

Bernice was the disciplinarian in our family, and also handled all the finances, including our allowances. George was an easygoing type—except when it came to politics. We often watched the TV news while we ate dinner, and he argued back loudly whenever something pissed him off. He didn't have much good to say about any politician, or our government. Minnesota's own Senator Hubert Humphrey—whose son I eventually defeated in the governor's race—he called "Old Rubber-Lip." Richard Nixon was "The Tailless Rat."

Years later, I remember we were watching TV together the night Nixon gave his famous "I am not a crook" speech during Watergate. "Look, you can see the son of a bitch is lying," George said. I raised my eyebrows. "Come on, how do you know that?"

"Because anyone with sweat on their upper lip is lyin' to you," he said. I've thought of that a lot lately, watching George W. Bush and Dick Cheney.

Minnesota had quite a few people like my father, more than you find in most states. They liked straight shooters—politicians who weren't afraid to put themselves on the line for what they believed. Even if those beliefs went against the grain of American public opinion. A statewide poll once showed that Minnesota voters favored "independents" above either the Democratic-Farmer-Labor Party or the Republicans. The thing was, party didn't matter so much. The man was what counted.

Think about some of the unique politicians that Minnesotans went for. Harold Stassen—called the "Boy Governor" when he was elected in 1939—came out fiercely against the isolationists, who were pretty powerful just before World War Two started.

He actually stepped down as governor to join the Navy, ending up with the Pacific fleet fighting against the Japanese. Can you imagine any politician doing that today? For the most part, they wouldn't let their third cousins serve! After the war, Stassen was instrumental in creating NATO and the United Nations. He then became best known as a "perennial candidate" for president. He ran ten times between 1948 and 1992, and the media made a laughingstock out of him. But I admired this man so much that, when he passed away during my term as governor, I ordered that he lie in state.

During the 1970s and '80s, Rudy Perpich was elected governor twice. His detractors called him "Governor Goofy," and he did do some curious things. He'd personally stop speeders on the freeways, and go back to the ghost town where he was born to "talk" to his ancestors. But Rudy was all right. I actually think he was ahead of his time. He proposed selling off the governor's mansion to save money, and later I ended up shutting down the old mansion for a while after the legislature cut back on my budget. Rudy also worked hard to put Minnesota on the international map by traveling to many foreign countries, something I emulated with my trade missions to Mexico, Japan, China, and even Cuba.

Wendell Anderson was another remarkable governor, a former Olympic hockey player. After he found it necessary to raise people's taxes fairly steeply, he traveled to every county telling the voters his reasons—and he won all eighty-seven counties in the next election.

In 1978, another Rudy—last name of Boschwitz, known for doing these hokey TV commercials for his Plywood Minnesota company—successfully ran for the U.S. Senate. He was replaced after two terms by a former wrestler who had no political experience, and who no one thought had a chance. That was Paul Wellstone, a liberal professor from Carleton College.

Between 1964 and 1984, from Hubert Humphrey to Walter Mondale, five out of the six presidential elections had a Minnesota native on one of the major party tickets. No other state in the union could claim that distinction.

Not that I paid too much attention to all this when I was growing up, except for my father's political opinions. George had been a terrific swimmer—he could go across the Mississippi and back—and that gene apparently passed on to me. I was captain of the swim team at Roosevelt High, a district champion in the butterfly stroke. I also played defensive end on an unbeaten football team my senior year, got average grades, and ran with the same kids I had since grade school. We called ourselves the South Side Boys, and did a lot of camping, fishing, and drinking. I liked being a center of attention. And I liked being mischievous.

The one subject that grabbed me was "Mac" McInroy's American history class. I'd get in some heated discussions there. And his admonition to his students stayed with me. He'd say, if we didn't like the way things were, then stop bitching and start a petition and do something about it. America, he drilled into us, was a country where the individual could make a real difference.

My brother Jan had seen a Richard Widmark movie called *The Frogmen* and, after he graduated from high school in 1966, decided that's what he wanted to be. Three years later, when I graduated, my parents badly wanted me to go on to college. I tried for a swimming scholarship to Northern Illinois, but I was only in the upper half of my class and not the upper third, so academically I didn't qualify. I was working for the state highway department, repairing bridges, when I went along with a friend to hear what a Navy recruiter had to say. Even though Jan had come home on leave from Vietnam and tried to convince us this was a lousy idea, I ended up getting talked into enlisting. It was September 11, 1969.

My mom was especially upset about it. My dad opposed it, too. I think one of the driving forces, subconsciously, that led me to enlist was that every other member of my family was a war veteran. George had seven Bronze Stars for battles in World War Two. He fought in Normandy, Remagen Bridge, the Battle of the Bulge. He started off against Rommel in the North African desert, came up through Anzio in Italy, and finished in Berlin. Bernice was an Army nurse in North Africa. Jan was in Vietnam. Not that any of my family would have cared, but I must have wondered how I could sit down with them at the dinner table: three veterans and one non-veteran. Especially in a time of war.

So, I reported for boot camp with a buddy of mine named Steve. That was January 5, 1970. The date became relevant again for me in 1999: Steve would be there when I held a dinner party at the governor's mansion for a bunch of old friends, the night after my inauguration. When he raised his glass for a toast, Steve said, "You guys probably don't remember, but it was twenty-nine years to the day when Jesse and I went off to the Navy."

The Navy SEALs were created by President John F. Kennedy. SEAL stands for Sea-Air-Land, an elite special team trained to carry out clandestine missions abroad. Basic training is called BUD/S (Basic Underwater Demolition/SEAL). It lasted twenty-two weeks. It's set up so that, literally, only the strong survive. There was an 80 percent dropout rate.

My first phase instructor was Terry "Mother" Moy (I'll leave it to your imagination as to what the "mother" stood for). At my inauguration, he would stand behind me in full uniform, along with two others from my SEAL team. Later, "Mother" Moy told one of my biographers that, out of maybe 2,300 recruits who went through his training, he could only remember about a dozen. I was one of them. He recalled that I had a good sense of humor which, he said, "leaves you open to a little play, 'cause the instructors have a sense of humor, too."

He was the scariest guy I ever met. My first day, we went through an obstacle course that took me forty-five minutes. Eventually, we'd have to do it in about ten. I came away with torn blisters hanging from my hands. When "Mother" Moy asked if any of us had any such "flappers," I admitted that I did. He asked me to put out my right hand—and he ripped all the loose skin right off it. Then he had me do the same thing to my left hand, myself.

The first five weeks were all physical training—you ran everywhere you went—capped by what the instructors referred to as "Motivation Week" and we recruits called "Hell Week." Those who made it through the pits of hell then went through nine weeks of demolition, reconnaissance, and land-warfare training, with new instructors to teach us how to blow things up. After that came six more weeks of underwater diving—how to swim with attack boards, navigate underwater with a compass at night, and dive scuba and deeper with mixed gas. Our mainstay was using re-breathers that emitted no bubbles.

Then it was on to jump school, becoming a skydiver. I was deathly afraid of heights. One of the reasons I joined the SEALs was to overcome that fear in my psyche. It worked—in the course of thirty-four parachute jumps, fast-roping out of a helicopter, or rappelling down a mountain.

After jump school, it was a week with the other services in SERE School (Survival, Escape, Resistance, and Evasion). We started out in the desert around Warner Springs, California, where even lizards can't live, and ended up frying acorns for our meals. For the last twenty-four hours, you become a POW. They put me in a box so small that, given my size, they had to stand on it to close it. When they pulled me out—it may have been ten minutes, but it felt like ten hours—I couldn't stand because my legs and arms were completely asleep. The infamous Chinese waterboarding procedure was also employed. This is where a towel is wrapped around your head and water is poured over your face, giving the sensation that you're drowning. (It was recently deemed torture when the Americans applied it to the detainees in Iraq, but in SERE School they did it to our own soldiers!)

I moved on to SEAL Cadre, or SBI School, seven weeks of advanced guerrilla warfare in Niland, California. It was all in a jungle context, because we were being prepared for Vietnam. You learned it all, including how to conduct ambushes, kidnappings, and assassinations. And you fired every hand-held weapon known to man.

I was never the same after training, in a good way. Because then you truly know who you are, deep down inside. That would always be the scale, the measuring stick. No matter what I face in life, I always go back to my Underwater Demolition Team–SEAL training days and say to myself, "This is nothing, compared to that."

The UDTs would rotate on tours overseas in six-month shifts. On my first deployment, I ended up headquartered at Subic Bay in the Philippines. It was like being on the frontier, and my friends and I were a wild bunch. Lot of cheap beer, lot of easy, pretty girls. I wore a necklace made out of shark's teeth, sported an Australian bushman's hat, and grew a beard and a Fu Manchu mustache. That's when I started lifting weights, thinking maybe I'd play pro football after I got out.

From Subic Bay, our different detachments would be dispatched to Vietnam, Korea, Thailand, Hong Kong, and Guam. I spent time off the coast of Hanoi waiting with a Marine division for a

Normandy-type invasion. That never happened. It was supposed to speed up "Peace with Honor," Nixon's political sell job. I served seventeen months of overseas deployment. Being a frogman, you defy death on a weekly basis, in war or peace.

In between my two deployments in Southeast Asia, we were conducting massive war games back in California. One pitch-black night, I was sure I was going to die. We were running "ops" on a river that was flowing like hell. I was in the first of two boats. We figured, hey, we're going downstream and we don't even have to paddle. This is gonna be a piece of cake. I was strapped in with ammo, lying there studying the shorelines, when all of a sudden we began hearing a dull roar. You can't say anything, because on an op it's all hand signals; you don't want to give away the mission. Pretty soon the noise became deafening. My buddy, Rick, stood up in the front of the boat and said, "Oh my God, it's a dam!"

Rick jumped out of the boat, made it to shore, and was able to run down and signal the second group so they wouldn't go over. For us, it was too late. All six in my boat jumped into the river. Loaded down with ammo as I was, I landed in a churning mass of white water. I hit the side of the dam, desperately scratching for something to hang onto like the proverbial cat—but over the top I went.

When I landed, even though I was a championship swimmer, the current was so powerful that it spun me around like a pebble in a washing machine and kept sucking me under. I began accepting that I was not going to survive. Was I going to let my breath out and drown, or just hold it until I passed out? Those seemed like my only choices. I felt a sense of deep calm settle over me.

Then I had a crystal-clear vision of my parents. George and Bernice were bending over my casket, crying. I had the impression they were also angry—or maybe it was my own rage—that, after serving in Vietnam, now I was going to die in California! At the same time, I felt my boots scrape against the river bottom. And I shot up to the surface. After taking a few breaths, somehow I broke away from the washing-machine effect. Of the five guys who'd been with me, I was the one under the water longest, and the last one out.

For the first time, I began to think that there was a mysterious force guiding everyone's life, a destiny, something bigger than coincidence. Because at least one of us should have drowned, but we all made it back alive.

When they sent divers over the next day to retrieve all the lost weapons, it was considered too dangerous even to try. Initially, the brass were going to court-martial me for losing my weapons . It was my first big confrontation with wrongheaded authority. I said, "Oh really? Well, I will then seek justice toward whoever did not brief us that there was a dam we'd have to somehow negotiate around. Because of their negligence, this almost cost the lives of five Navy SEALs."

All of a sudden, the court-martial idea disappeared.

My last day of active duty, at the end of 1973, was close to the end of the American debacle in Vietnam. I was a naïve kid, and I didn't know any better than many of my peers what was really behind it. Except for watching the news with my father, who'd said that stopping the "domino" effect of Communism was a shuck and that it wasn't about anything other than money.

It was many years before certain painful truths about Vietnam became public. In 2004, when I was teaching at Harvard, Robert McNamara came to speak and show the documentary about himself, *The Fog of War*. That's where the former secretary of defense first admitted that the Gulf of Tonkin incident never happened. Our government and our media told us that the North Vietnamese had fired at two of our ships, basically a declaration of war. That was the invented catalyst that escalated into a war that cost 58,000 American lives.

I was pretty worked up the night McNamara came to the Harvard campus. I don't remember whether I threatened him or not, but certain faculty members told me they preferred that I not show up at his lecture. And I didn't. Being one of the veterans sent into the Vietnam War under false pretenses, I wouldn't have let him off the hook easily.

Leaving Minnesota . . . so many memories . . . I'd first moved back after my four years as a frogman ended had ridden rode for nine months with the South Bay Mongols motorcycle club. I was adrift then, with a whole host of choices before me, and really no clue about where I wanted to be or what I was going to do. Not so different, I suppose, than how I feel now, heading down a whole new road. But that was when Terry and I first met, in September of 1974.

I was working as a bouncer at the Rusty Nail, a bar in a Minneapolis suburb called Crystal. By day I was attending North Hennepin Junior College on the GI Bill. Even with a warning about how tough I'd find freshman English, I did discover a knack for it. In fact, I ended up with the highest grade in the class. I found I especially enjoyed the classroom discussions. And I ended up being recruited into a college play, *The Birds*. No, not the Hitchcock; the one by Aristophanes. It's a comedy about these two people from Athens trying to escape from the city because of all the corrupt politicians. I was cast as Hercules.

Terry showed up at the door of the Rusty Nail on a Ladies' Night. She was voluptuous, with long brown hair and the most amazingly beautiful eyes and smile. She'd already been carded by a cop at the door, and now she was headed my way, and I sure didn't feel like any Hercules in my sport jacket and turtleneck sweater. I had to say *something* to her.

"Can I see your ID please?" I blurted out.

"But I just showed *him*," she said, pointing at the cop.

"I don't care how old you are, I just want to know your name," I said, feeling kind of proud of such a good line. Well, she went through her purse until she found her ID again, presented it to me without a word, and kept right on going.

TERRY: This was the first time my two girlfriends and I had ever gone to a suburban bar. They were mostly full of softball players or used-car salesmen, we thought. But we did live in the suburbs, and we were all broke. I was a receptionist, holding down two jobs at the time, and they were going to school. So when we heard about this ladies' night at the Rusty Nail, we decided to go.

When I first saw Jesse, he appeared to be the biggest thing in the entire place. Downstairs was where the rock and roll was, so that's where we went first. But I couldn't get that fellow at the door out of my head. Finally I said, "I'm going upstairs." My girlfriend said, "You're gonna go flirt with that guy and leave us down here; real nice." But I couldn't help myself.

Later that night, we ended up talking. She was from a rural area in southern Minnesota. I wasn't calling myself Jesse Ventura yet, but I was already enamored of the world of wrestling. I'd gone to a pro bout at the Minnesota Armory featuring this huge, bleached-blond "bad guy" called "Superstar" Billy Graham. When I'd seen his total control of the crowd, I said to myself, "That's what I want to do." So I'd already gone into training just about every day at the Seventh Street Gym. I was big—six-foot-four and about 235 pounds—and I didn't scare easy. Except, of course, around someone like Terry.

Lo and behold, the first thing she said to me was: "God! You look just like 'Superstar' Billy Graham!" (As soon as I got out of the Navy, I'd grown my hair down to my shoulders and bleached it blond).

"I ought to," I said coolly. "He's my older brother."

Well, it turned out that she hated Graham. For being the villainous sort, always strutting around the ring and bragging to the crowd. Terry had started watching wrestling on TV with her dad, and still tuned in on Saturday nights before she went out. She gave me her work number and I called the next day to ask her on a date. I took her to a neighborhood bar called the Schooner. We hadn't been there long when several cops came bursting through the door, yanked a fellow off a bar stool, and beat the crap out of him when he resisted. Nevertheless, Terry agreed to go out a second time. We went to the movies, my choice being Charles Bronson in *Death Wish*.

I guess she saw something beyond my macho exterior. A quality, she once told me, that she found soft, even sweet. Plus she had a terrific sense of humor. And I can be a pretty amusing fellow. Before long, I was taking Teresa Masters around to the gym to meet the guys.

TERRY: There was no doubt in my mind, after two weeks of knowing him, that I was absolutely, totally infatuated. I thought about him all the time; he was like nobody I had ever met before in my life. He had a vision and he had drive—such charisma. I got so scared, I tried to break up with him. I said, why don't we also date other people. He said, nope, this is a one-way street, you're either on it or you're not.

We'd been dating for nine months when we got married, three days after my twenty-fourth birthday in July 1975. She was nineteen. And the best thing that ever happened to me.

November 3, 1998. Election night. Not all that long ago, but it seems like another lifetime. My family and I were driving down to Canterbury Park, a racetrack where we'd planned to hold our postelection party. I'd kept rising in the polls. That last weekend, the media had begun calling it a three-way horse race for the governorship. I knew I'd need some luck, that everything was going to have to fall into place. But I'd never doubted whether I could win. Otherwise, I would never have run in the first place.

The sun goes down early in November and the moon was very bright that night, with a fuzzy, broad ring around it like you see in Minnesota sometimes before it snows. There were several feathery ribbons of northern lights emanating from it, which drew our attention. I will never forget my son, Tyrel, suddenly saying from the back seat, very quietly: "Dad, something strange is going to happen tonight."

"Do you think so, Ty?" I said.

"I'm telling you, it's in the air. You can feel it."

There had definitely been signs, especially over the last three days of nonstop campaigning into every region of the state. Fifteen hundred miles, thirty-four stops, in some rented RVs. We called it our No-Doz "72-Hour Drive to Victory Tour." Kind of patterned after those whistle-stop train rides that candidates used to take.

Except we had an extra advantage called the Internet. My "Geek Squad" transmitted video clips and digital photos of all our rallies onto my Jesse Ventura website as soon as they happened, along with up-to-date information on where we were headed next. This was the first time any politician had really used the Internet; some of the pundits later compared it to JFK's use of television during his presidential race in 1960.

> *TERRY: When his staff came up with the Winnebago tour idea for that final weekend, they said they really wanted me to participate. I'd stayed away from the campaign; the whole thing terrified me. I said, "I'm not going unless my parents come along." My sister and my brother-in-law had just gotten a mobile home, and I rode with them. My brother-in-law drove, and most nights I stayed up, trying to keep him awake. In fact, I started singing cowboy songs to him. He finally told me if I sang any more he was going to crash the bus!*

We'd kicked things off at sports bars in the northern suburbs of St. Paul, places like the BeBop and the Mermaid. I'd do twenty-minute walk-throughs, and I was stunned at the size of the crowds. "There's an old saying: if you don't vote, don't bitch!" I told them. And I had people coming up and telling me they hadn't voted in twenty-five years, but they were turning out for me on Tuesday. I still see the face of this kid who approached me in the little town of Willmar. "Jesse," he said, "you are us." As the sun was setting one of those evenings, our caravan went past a sign painted in big orange letters on a bedsheet—"Ventura: Highway to the Future."

It was heady stuff, but I sure wasn't overconfident. I mean, it had been a fun ride, but I knew I could be back with my family soon on our thirty-two-acre horse ranch. And when this reporter asked, did I *really* think I could govern, I gave him a straight answer. I said, "I've jumped out of thirty-four airplanes in my life. I've dived 212 feet under the water. I've swum with sharks. I did things that would make Skip and Norm wet their pants." (Referring to my two opponents, Democrat Skip Humphrey and Republican Norm Coleman). Which made all the media types laugh. Then I added,

"This is simply governing and common sense and logic. Nothing more. Nothing less. I can do the job."

> *TERRY: As we continued moving across the state, I knew. When you would pull into a tiny town at 11 o'clock at night, and find about Seven hundredu people freezing in a parking lot, holding up babies and old Jesse Ventura wrestling figures, I knew it was going to happen. But I still couldn't fathom it. It was like saying we were going to get the Hope Diamond—but you have no clue what it looks like, feels like, or will be like when you own it.*

We were an hour or two late getting to Hutchinson, Minnesota, our last stop of the night. We didn't know what the turnout would be. It was a Sunday, and people had to go to work the next day. And there were all these people waiting! Hundreds of them! I'll always remember Terry turning to me and saying, "My God, you're going to win!"

We stole the headlines from the other two candidates at the most critical time of the election, the weekend before, when I think a lot of people make up their minds. A lot of the undecideds wait until virtually the eleventh hour. On that Tuesday, I heard rumors that people were flocking to the polls. Minnesota has a unique system where you don't have to preregister to vote; you can do so right on election day. Supposedly, there were five times the number of people standing in the registration lines as in the voting lines. Over in Todd County, where they'd planned on as high as an 80 percent turnout, so many folks showed up that they ran out of printed ballots. When the polls closed that night, Minnesota ended up leading the country with a 61 percent voter turnout. Shamefully, the national average was 37 percent.

Of course, I didn't know about these things until later. When I went to cast my ballot and the press asked me for interviews,

I said it would have to be quick because my favorite TV show—*The Young and the Restless*—was about to come on. That afternoon, I lay down on my bed and put Oliver Stone's brilliant movie *JFK* on the VCR.

Now, out at Canterbury Park, where the long shots sometimes come through, we started watching the returns. There was a feeling of electricity in the air. It looked more like a rock concert than anything, a partying crowd wearing blue jeans and ball caps and downing tap-beer. That was just the way I wanted it. When the first two exit polls were announced, I was, as everyone expected, in third place. Then, at 3 percent of the vote, I passed Coleman. And at 5 percent, I had a 120-vote edge over Humphrey. I figured, well, we could always say that, for one brief moment, we led. I went out and spoke to the crowd, and they whooped and hollered. Back in our private room, I noticed Terry's face had gone pale.

TERRY: As the results from different areas of the state started coming in, I got more scared. I kept hearing, so-and-so wants to interview you. All these security people surround you and drag you through this crush of people, everybody's hands out and touching you as you go. They were nice, but it was just so bizarre. No one cared before. No one was at the farm trying to grab onto me. I was out there going, "Please, someone, help me bail hay!"

It was five minutes to midnight. About 60 percent of the vote had been counted. I had 37 percent, Coleman stood at 34, and Humphrey was at 28. Out in the public area, kids were getting wild. They had several mosh pits going, passing bodies over their heads. I was asked to go out again and calm them down a bit. As I stood up, on the TV the local CBS affiliate put a check mark beside my name. Declaring me the winner!

I envisioned that famous headline from the 1948 presidential election: "Dewey Defeats Truman." I quieted my people down, saying, "Wait a minute, how can they do that? Four out of ten Minnesotans haven't even been counted yet. I'm not going out there and claiming victory, I'll look like an idiot."

Then the other two networks followed suit with check marks. Bill Hillsman, a true genius, who'd put together the TV and radio ads that many people felt pushed us over the top, walked over to me. He said, "Jesse, you trusted me with the ads, didn't you?" I said yes. He said, quietly, "Then will you believe me on this?" "What?" I said. I felt numb, more than anything. "Trust me, Jesse. You're the governor. They know. They haven't been wrong since Dewey."

TERRY: All of a sudden we looked and there was this check mark on the screen by his name. I was so terrified, I couldn't think; I was hyperventilating. I went in the bathroom with two of my friends, because we were getting ready to go out onto a big stage. "What am I gonna do?" I asked them. "Oh, you're the First Lady!" they shouted at me.

I went in the stall, sat down, and said, "Okay, nothing has changed. Even when you're the First Lady, you still don't get the stall with the toilet paper!" And my girlfriends just busted up.

I went out and told the crowd that nothing was official until I received those calls of concession from my two opponents. Forty-five minutes later, the phone rang twice. At the racetrack, the Rolling Stones were blaring. The people were splashing beer and high-fiving and chanting like they do after a touchdown at pro football games: "Na-na-na-na, na-na-na-na, hey-hey-yeah, goooooood-bye!"

In a private room, Terry was curled up in her mother's lap. She was crying. "I don't know to handle this," she said. "I wear leather and jeans. And I'm supposed to be Minnesota's First Lady? I don't think I can do it!"

I stood at a microphone and gazed out at the people. "Thank you for renewing my faith that the American Dream still lives," I said.

"I didn't make a lot of promises," I told them. "I'm gonna do the best job I can do. I'm human. I'll probably make mistakes. And let's remember that we all make 'em. And if they're mistakes from the heart, then you don't have to apologize for them."

I thanked my wife and kids, who, about a before year ago, had said to me, "Are you NUTS?!" With my voice trembling I thanked my parents, who were buried not far away in the Fort Snelling National Cemetery.

It was about three in the morning when the state troopers shuttled Terry and me over to a hotel about five hundred yards away. Somehow, Terry had the presence of mind to bring along some champagne. I popped the cork, we each took a swig and smiled at each other. "You're the governor!" she said.

I could feel her excitement for me, but I also knew that she was terrified.

"And you're the First Lady!" I said, and raised my glass to the woman who still means more to me than anything.

Headline: THE NATION: NOW, PRESIDENTIAL 'BODY' POLITICS; BUT SERIOUSLY, MR. VENTURA

Neither Vice President Al Gore nor Gov. George W. Bush of Texas is ripping his shirt off and wrapping a feather boa around his neck in the style of Gov. Jesse Ventura of Minnesota. But barely one year after Mr. Ventura's unlikely election on the Reform Party ticket unnerved Democrats and Republicans, politicians have generally stopped joking about the professional wrestler turned politician.

Now they are scrutinizing Mr. Ventura's every pronouncement, assembling focus groups and even making pilgrimages to St. Paul, Minnesota's capital, searching for clues to a mystery that confounds even the most savvy politicians: How does a candidate excite the electorate and galvanize new voters when the public does not seem to be paying attention to politics?"

—The New York Times, *September 19, 1999*

Now, leaving Minnesota, all the tumult and the shouting seemed almost like another lifetime. The State Capitol dome faded into the skyline as dusk descended over our camper. We were heading south, way south, on a new adventure whose outcome was equally uncertain, equally unpredictable.

CHAPTER 2

The Road to the Arena

"There can hardly have been a weirder sight in this country's political history: Minnesota governor-elect Jesse 'The Body' Ventura standing before a whooping crowd at his 1999 inaugural ball, sporting a garish, tasseled jacket, biker's headscarf, shades, and a psychedelic Jimi Hendrix T-shirt, a pyrotechnical display fizzing behind him. That night, Ventura paraded and pumped his fists as if his prize were not the leadership of the nation's 32nd state but a WWF smackdown victory, his head thrown back, his enormous mouth bisecting his enormous face, in the midst of a warrior's cry that would make Howard Dean's notorious howl look like a lullaby."

—Boston Phoenix, *March 2004*

When I taught at Harvard's Kennedy School of Government in 2004, I called my last class "Wrestling, Then Politics: The Perfect Preparation for Serving." People thought it was a joke but, when the class was over, they realized it hit the nail right on the head.

First of all, in wrestling you have to be able to ad-lib and think on your feet. In politics, you'll have questions fired at you and situations where you can't run to your handlers. You need to be able to come up with an answer that doesn't destroy you, and you're going to learn the hard way that some of them will. Wrestling taught me that, because no matter how much you talk over what you're going to do in a match, anything that can go wrong usually will.

The second thing I told the students was about how you had to sell yourself as a wrestler. I had to convince people to pay their hard-earned dollars to see me get my butt kicked, because I was billed as a villain. Well, in politics, you have to sell yourself similarly to convince people to vote for you, allow you to take their tax dollars, and run their government.

In both wrestling and politics, you travel a lot—especially to small towns. Wrestling is the only pro sport that goes to those places. We call them spot shows. It lets you get the message right out to the people. Because so much of it is visual today, wrestling makes you learn how to be very comfortable in front of a television camera. In that way, too, it's a great stepping-stone to politics.

Finally, the wrestler is often not in public the same person he is in private, and I think it's the same with the politician. Was I really Jesse "The Body" Ventura, a guy who struts around with bleached blond hair, six earrings, and feather boas around his neck? Of course not. That's a total creation. So was the politically fabricated life of Mark Foley, the now-disgraced Republican Congressman from Florida who railed against gay marriage at the same time he was writing lurid e-mails to page boys.

Interstate 35, where I maneuvered our camper straight south out of Minneapolis on a gray, cold winter's evening, was the identical road I'd driven thirty years earlier to begin my wrestling career. Back then, I'd been sending out pictures to different promoters around the country. One day I got a call from Bob Geigel in Kansas City, which was then one of the twenty-six wrestling territories in the U.S. He said my trainer had told him I had great potential and did I want to come for a tryout? Terry and I had started dating, and we were already pretty crazy about each other. But how could I pass up this opportunity? I hopped into my old Chevy, carrying a couple hundred bucks in my wallet, and took off.

"I missed you so bad," I recall, glancing over at Terry as she jots a few notes into her travel journal. "I remember when you came to visit me once, after I'd been in Kansas City for a couple months, you cried when you saw how I was living."

"Well," Terry says, not looking up, "you were staying in basically a flophouse."

"Twenty-three dollars a week," I marvel, and shake my head. "But I'd seen worse in the service. Didn't bother me."

Pro wrestling had heroes and villains, and I'd already decided I was going to be a "bad guy" like "Superstar" Billy Graham. That's why I grew the blond mane, to look like a California beach bum. I knew people in the Midwest would hate that. In a sport where Gorgeous George, Gorilla Monsoon, and The Crusher were some of the big names, I knew that plain old Jim Janos wasn't going to cut the mustard. I'd always liked the name Jesse, maybe because of Jesse James. I looked on a map of California and my eyes landed on a highway that ran north of L.A. called Ventura. Jesse Ventura, the Surfer. Now that had a ring to it.

Besides Kansas City, on this trip we'd be passing right through Wichita, Kansas, where I made my debut against a "good guy" called Omar Atlas. Beforehand, Bob Geigel called us together and sketched out the plan. If the match was going well, I was to pick Omar up and throw him over the top rope. In those days, that was cause for automatic disqualification. So I went strutting out there, bragging and making fun of Omar, climbing up on the ropes and insulting the crowd when they booed me. And when I tossed Omar at them, and he landed with a thud and came up, I paraded around while the people got what they came for: They hated my guts. I spent two months around Kansas City earning peanuts for my matches, between thirty-five and sixty-five dollars per night.

"I knew then that I wanted to spend the rest of my life with you," I said, turning again to Terry. "But I was still your typical noncommittal bachelor. Remember what you told me over the phone?"

"I said, I ain't leavin' up here unless I get a bigger commitment than 'come on down and live with me.'"

"And I said, 'Well, I guess I'll just have to say 'Will you marry me?' You started crying, and said yes."

By the time we got married that summer of 1975, I was moving on to Oregon, where the money was a little better. I traveled to towns all over the state for the next two years, at one point wrestling for sixty-three consecutive nights. I put 128,000 miles on the first car I ever owned, a '75 Mercury Cougar, and often I was carpooling! For a while I billed myself as The Great Ventura and wore a mask—"to hide my good looks"—so tearing it off became a new gimmick. I fought a "battle royal" one time, where the promoters told everybody that the winner would get $50,000. I won all right, and probably got a little over a hundred bucks for my trouble. That's the un-glorious part of the sport.

Other wrestlers went out carousing after their matches, while I went back to my hotel room alone and called Terry. This was tough on both of us, until she moved up.

TERRY: In Oregon, we lived in an apartment way off the beaten path, alongside an unpaved road that had a strip mall with wooden sidewalks. We only had one car, I didn't know anybody, and I often just sat in an apartment with our dog for three or four days. I got in trouble with Jesse when I ran up a hundred dollar phone bill calling my mom, because I was so lonely.

In 1978, when an announcer started referring to me as Jesse "The Body" and the nickname stuck, I joined one of the bigger leagues, the American Wrestling Association, and went home to Minnesota. That's where Adrian "Golden Boy" Adonis and I first became an unpopular tag team. There's an old saying in the world of wrestling: "They gotta hate ya before they can love ya."

I've often referred to pro wrestling as "ballet with violence." Yes, it's staged, as far as who's going to be the winner, but it's not fake. It's really an art form, and one that requires careful discipline. When you smash your opponent with a folding chair, you've got to know how *not* to hurt him. When you get body-slammed, it's painful, no way around it. But you get used to it.

At my induction into the WWE Hall of Fame a few years ago, I had a conversation with Ric Flair about backdrops. That's a wrestling term that means getting thrown into the rope, flipping up in the air, and landing flat on your back. Ric would take at least three backdrops a night. He wrestles 300 nights a year, so that's 900 backdrops. And he's been wrestling thirty years—so that's 27,000 backdrops. And that's a minimal estimate! I find it amazing that Ric is still walking around, but he is.

In this particular dance, it's the bad guy who leads—and who gets to be the most creative. I wore a flamboyant costume—starting with the wildly colored sunglasses and the big earrings, on to the bright colored tights, and the feather boas around my neck. I loved riling up the crowds. I'd pose in the ring and shout out things like, "Take a look at this body, all you women out there, and then take a look at that fat guy sitting next to you who's eating pretzels and drinking beer. Who would you *really* rather be with? IT'S JESSE THE BODY EVERYWHERE!"

I developed a move called "The Body-breaker," where I'd pick the other guy up across my shoulder and shake him relentlessly while I jumped up and down. "The most brutal man in wrestling!" I'd yell at the crowds. "The sickest man in wrestling! Mr. Money! Mr. Charisma! Mr. Show Business! Win if you can! Lose if you must! But always cheat!"

When the St. Paul Civic Center was sold out for one of my matches in 1980, I looked out upon thousands of fans, all yelling in a near-deafening chorus for a full five minutes: "Jes-SEE SUCKS! Jes-SEE SUCKS! Jes-SEE SUCKS!" I took it as a compliment, meaning I'd mastered my role as a ring villain. When I won the election in 1998, I recalled that night during my acceptance speech and told the celebrating crowd: "And you're *still* cheering me!"

Well, in the eighties, the sport of wrestling became huge. I accepted an offer from Vince McMahon, Jr., to bid farewell to the old regional system and become part of a new World Wrestling Federation. Vince was a brilliant promoter, as well as being a smart and ruthless businessman. Before long, we were accepted by main-stream America. The first WrestleMania, in 1985, sold out Madison Square Garden. Terry and I arrived in a limousine. I was called "wrestling's Goldilocks" by *Sports Illustrated* and featured alongside superstars from baseball and basketball. My tag-team events with Adrian were earning $3,000 a match. Adding it to the royalties from a Jesse Ventura action figure, I bought myself a Porsche Carrera.

One time, I was wrestling Hulk Hogan, and early in the match he kicked me in the jaw. I was supposed to go down first and then he'd wait. Except, as I started to fall, he kicked me a second time—and dislocated my jaw, only four minutes into a thirty-minute match.

So we both had to ad-lib our way around this. Fortunately Hogan, being the professional that he was, allowed me to virtually beat him up for the next twenty minutes so he wouldn't be touching my jaw. Afterward, I went immediately to the hospital so the doctors could yank it back into place.

Maybe it was a sign. I was due to wrestle Hogan for the world title in L.A.—the Sports Arena was already sold out—followed by bouts between us all over the country. I was destined to make millions, I was sure. Then, during a match in Phoenix, I couldn't seem to catch my breath. I figured it was probably the hot autumn air of Arizona. But the next night in Oakland, it happened again. After flying on to San Diego the following morning, I went to bed instead of doing my customary workout. When I awoke at about one in the afternoon, I was drenched in sweat and my lungs were absolutely killing me. I thought it must be another bout of the pneumonia I'd suffered a few years earlier.

I checked myself into a hospital, where they did some preliminary tests. These showed blood clots in my lungs. If one of those broke loose and traveled to my heart or brain, I could have a heart attack or stroke. I was placed in intensive care, on intravenous heparin to try to dissolve the clots. The specialist called Terry and told her she'd better fly out, that I could die at any moment.

I spent six days in the hospital with Terry at my bedside. They put me on a blood thinner to prevent more clots from forming, but it also makes you a bleeder. I had to be on the medication for sixty days. There was no way I could go back in the ring during that period. My tour with Hogan was canceled.

I did return to wrestling, but only briefly. My last match was in Winnipeg, Canada, in the spring of 1986. My opponent was Tony Atlas, and I tossed him out of the ring. So I began and ended my career with an Atlas and a disqualification.

By then, Vince McMahon had called with another idea. "There's never been a bad guy on the microphone," he said. "Somebody who will do color commentating and side with the villains. Do you think you can do it?"

"Sure, I can," I told him. And so, out of my latest round of adversity, began a new life as a broadcaster.

On the surface, farm country never seems to change. Driving down through southern Minnesota—where much of the farming takes place in our state—and then on past the endless cornfields of Iowa, it had all looked pretty much the same as a generation ago. Kansas, with its vast wheat fields, was as flat as ever.

But driving an interstate can be deceiving. Agribusiness keeps the big "factory farms," livestock operations with thousands of cattle, hogs, and poultry, just far enough off the freeway so you can't usually see or smell them. In the area closest to the feedlots, you can barely breathe even if you roll up your windows and shut off the outside air.

TERRY: When I was a kid, I thought the air in southern Minnesota was the most refreshing in the world. Today, the area where I grew up is so full of chemicals that I cannot go down there at certain times of the year (when they spray their fertilizers and weed killers) without getting terrible allergic reactions. When my daughter, Jade, and I were showing our horses, our eyes would water and our noses would run whenever we drove by the feedlots.

As First Lady I tried hard to work on the problems of feedlots because I also think they only produce toxic food. How can something good come from animals living in severe stress, fed nothing but chemicals and antibiotics and who knows what? None of that kind of meat can have the amount of protein, vitamins, and minerals that animals raised humanely on a normal diet could yield.

We'd bought a thirty-two-acre ranch in Maple Grove in the mid-1990s, because Terry wanted a place where she could have her horses on our own land, instead of boarding them. We hadn't been living there long when I had to fight the county tax assessors to keep our farm status. They claimed I had another job. Well, many farm families have dual occupations. I remember my uncle farmed and my aunt worked for the county. Now they're telling me that Terry could only be a housewife? It was she who baled the hay and fed the horses. I was going to sue them over that premise, until the county attorney told the assessor's office to forget it.

The truth was, the government wanted to drive us out—because of pressure from developers. Eventually they succeeded.

TERRY: We sold the farm when it turned out I'd become allergic to everything in the barn, but mostly because of the development going on all around us. We were basically being surrounded, as the small family-owned farms sold off to contractors, because the owners were getting old or had died and the kids did not want the place. At Jade's graduation party, right after Jesse left office, the farm land directly adjacent to us was being bulldozed, and the dust rolled over our property like a desert storm. We were told by our neighbors that the city council had said they would not look kindly at any farmland owners trying to hold onto their property as this area was being developed. We'd fought so hard to get the farm built and at that point just couldn't see involving ourselves in another fight to hold onto it. Our home state has never been too kind to us in this regard.

It's personal battles like this that got me involved in politics in the first place. I had no political intentions until I ran for mayor of Brooklyn Park, Minnesota, in 1990. I did it because I was outraged about developers coming into the area where we lived then, aiming to make housing subdivisions out of the few remaining potato fields. Rubber-stamped by the good old boys on the city council, they demanded that our neighborhood pay for curbs, gutters, and storm sewers through assessments—none of which we needed because we all already captured rain runoff in ditches. Where they planned to put the runoff water only added insult to injury: Since pollution laws forbade the developers from draining it into the Mississippi, they decided to pump the polluted storm water into a beautiful wetland about a block from my house. This would have completely destroyed the wetland.

It was supposed to be a nonpartisan election, meaning there are no parties, you run as who you are. But when it came down to the last week of the campaign, the heads of the state Democratic and Republican parties came together and wrote a joint letter to every citizen in Brooklyn Park, urging them to vote for the twenty-five-year incumbent. They called me "the most dangerous man in the city." For a moment I took offense at that, but then I thought, well, as a professional wrestler and a Navy SEAL, they might be telling the truth here.

Anyway, I won, 65 percent to 35 percent, taking all twenty-four precincts of the city, including the one the incumbent lived in. A few weeks after the election, both parties independently came courting me to join them. I said, "But why would you want the most dangerous man in the city? Three weeks ago, you thought I was horrible. Now you're welcoming me with open arms. You know what? I got elected pretty substantially on my own, so please explain why I would need you now."

TERRY: I'd campaigned for him when he was running for mayor. Back then I thought politics was a really grand and noble thing to do. And I found out quickly, in the little town of Brooklyn Park, that it's just dog-eat-dog, and stab everybody in the back. After he got elected, suddenly all these politicians were treating us like the best thing since sliced bread. It just seemed like everything was so underhanded and deceitful and dishonest. It was about who has power, who gets money, and what makes one side win.

Early in 1992, I began seeing these signs in people's yards: "Independence Party—Dean Barkley for Congress." I decided to check it out. Many of the people involved were centrists like me, disgruntled Democrats or Republicans who couldn't stand what the two parties had turned into. The Independence Party of Minnesota wasn't a wing like the Libertarians, who tend to want anarchy, or the Green Party, which was too far left to be my cup of tea. The Independence folks were all very passionate. It wasn't about money, but about ideas. It wasn't about power and control, but about the Constitution and "we the people," and what government should be, in my opinion. And their charter stated unequivocally that, within the Independence Party, you only had to agree on 70 percent of the issues. That meant, if they could handle it, pro-choice and pro-life people could both be part of it; they could actually coexist with each other around other important issues.

So I affiliated with the Independence Party, which is where I met Dean Barkley and Doug Friedline and all of the people who eventually worked on my campaign for governor. Dean was a lawyer and small businessman who got inspired by Ross Perot's third-party presidential campaign and decided to run for Congress. With a blend of fiscal conservatism and social liberalism, Dean gathered a healthy 16 percent of the vote in 1992.

Dean really is the hero of the third-party movement in Minnesota, more so than I am. He paved the way, and made my victory possible. In 1994, he ran for the U.S. Senate and got more than 5 percent of the vote, just the amount you need to achieve major party status under Minnesota law. That was my final year as mayor. I started working for talk radio, and had no inclinations for any further life in politics.

But in 1996, Dean decided to try for the Senate again and I agreed to become honorary chair of his campaign. His hometown of Annandale, Minnesota, is only eight miles away from my summer lake cabin. I was going to be up there over the Fourth of July anyway, and Dean asked me if I'd walk with him in the Annandale parade, because everyone knew me as the pro wrestler who'd served a term as mayor. As we started down Main Street in this little Midwestern town, all of a sudden the whole crowd started chanting: "Jesse! Jesse!"

Dean, smiling, leaned over to me and said, "See? The wrong candidate is running." I smiled back at Dean and made what I thought was a joke. "Dean, I don't want to go to Washington, but I'll tell you what—I'll run for governor of the state of Minnesota."

Unfortunately or fortunately, whatever shoe you want to wear, Dean didn't forget what I'd said off-the-cuff that day in the parade. He kept the pressure on me and, two years later, he'd be my campaign chair. My running was really thanks to Dean, who retained our major party status by getting 7 percent of the vote in 1996.

At the time I was doing a radio show called "Sports Talk," but I couldn't do just sports for three hours. What are you going to do, dissect every single statistic of last night's basketball game? So I would always devote an hour to politics, because it was natural for me. Besides, politics are in sports; they're in everything.

Minnesota had just seen its first major budget surplus—and they spent it, about $4 billion! The governor and the legislature didn't care one iota. They had all this extra money and, by God, they could fund all these pet projects they'd dreamed of—they were like kids in a candy store. I started explaining to people over the radio how this represented overtaxation. I spoke about how, in Minnesota, you do a two-year budget. Now, because the tax system was bringing them more money than they'd budgeted for since the economy was so strong, I felt that money ought to be returned to the people. Let's remember also that state budgets, by law, do not run on deficit like the federal government. If you had a situation where you applied that additional money to a debt, maybe I could have lived with it more. As it was, I started complaining vehemently on the air about how wrong our supposed leaders were for doing this. After all, this is *our* money!

Then, again in passing, I started stating that maybe I should run for governor. Well, it caught on like wildfire with many of the listeners. It got to where I felt I'd boxed myself into a corner—if I didn't attempt to do this, I would lose my credibility. And in the world of talk radio, once that happens, you're finished.

In the rural hinterlands of Kansas, the emptiness is enveloped by a vast, cloud-filled sky, Terry and I glimpse an old stone barn over the horizon and simultaneously think back to the afternoon that I invited Barkley and Friedline out to our ranch. It was September 1997, a little over a year before the next election. By then, we'd affiliated our independent state party with the national Reform Party that Ross Perot had begun. I told Dean I'd like to see if a citizen could become governor, instead of somebody who's worked their way up through the two-party system by holding various offices until they're basically hand-picked. I asked what he thought it would cost, and he figured at least $400,000, to make a credible run. We talked about all the turned-off voters we wanted to reach.

Finally I said, "I think I want to give it a shot. But I'm the easy sell. Now we've got to go out to the barn and convince Terry."

She had a pitchfork in her hand. She looked at Dean and said, "You'd have to clean the barn barefoot before I'd ever say yes to this."

I stop reminiscing to ask Terry if she remembered that.

"Hey, we had a great thing going," she reflects. "I had my horse business and my riding lesson business; I was finally in the black. I liked our life the way it was. It was quiet and it was good. I didn't want our family exposed like that to public life."

"And I agreed with you. But I also asked you, 'If I don't do it, who will?'"

TERRY: I could see the fire in his eyes. Remember when George W. Bush said he's 'The Decider?' Well, Jesse's 'The Persuader.' I understood how strongly he felt about this. If it meant that much to him—being married and loving him as I do—I didn't see how I could stand in his way. This is a guy who didn't like or know anything about farming, and yet he let me get the farm, and have horses, and he bailed hay with me. For better or for worse.

I told Terry, when I decided to run, that she would not be needed. I said, this has got nothing to do with you or the kids. I want to change politics and turn it into what it truly is, and that's the business of running government. Your private life is your business. I went down to the Capitol on a cold January day and stood on the steps, by myself, and made the announcement. The first thing the media asked was, "Where's your family?" I said to them, "What do they have to do with this?" The media didn't appreciate that, but too bad. We weren't off to a good start. And it would get a lot worse.

The unique thing about our campaign is that, while people might was have thought we were some big piece of machinery, it was totally fly-by-the-seat-of-your-pants. I remember being booked in parades where I would drive for four hours across the state, and get to some small town where the parade lasted all of ten minutes. And I was the only candidate dumb enough to go there.

You know how millionaires will use their money to run for public office. I told Doug and Dean from the very minute they approached me, "Look, I will not put one penny of my own into this." In the end, I did. But in a way that I felt was honorable. The entire campaign year, I drove to every event in my own car and I paid for my own gas. I never charged it back to the party. So that was my contribution.

Everyone on my staff was unpaid except for Doug Friedline, and he only received a salary from the primary onward when he left his job to become my full-time campaign manager. My volunteer secretary, scheduler, and advance woman was Mavis Huddle, a sixty-four-year-old retired secretary from Brooklyn Park who walked around spryly with a cane. Barkley brought in his ex-campaign press secretary, Gerry Drewery, sixty-eight, a semi-retired PR consultant and part-time reporter for the *Farmington Independent*. I told the staff we had only one rule: this is going to be fun.

To me, ours was what a campaign should be. It wasn't a campaign of money, but of ideals. A campaign of belief. I refused to take any corporate PAC money, and most of my individual contributions were for $50. We thought about money only because you need it to do certain things, like advertise on television, for legitimacy. When I found out that you could set up a website for about $45, that fit right into our budget. I didn't even know how to send an e-mail, but I had an old Army vet named Phil Madsen who could design a great Internet site. Since I knew that education was big in the minds of voters, I decided to choose a schoolteacher, sixty-four-year-old Mae Schunk, for my running mate as lieutenant governor. Her top priority was improving the teacher-to-student ratio in Minnesota.

I enjoyed being out among the people, and I wasn't bad with the one-liners like: "Elections and politics are pretty much like war without guns, and I'm pretty good at it." One time, a reporter asked how fast my light-blue Porsche with the NAVY SEAL plates could go. I said, "You know that high stretch of road leaving town out of Two Harbors? I've had it up to 140 there." It was true, but I only hoped that not too many cops were listening.

Nobody took me seriously at first. I mean, no third-party candidate had won a statewide election in more than half a century. The Minneapolis *Star Tribune* didn't bother putting a full-time reporter on my campaign. When the big East Coast papers came out to cover the race, I wasn't even mentioned. Their stories focused on "My Three Sons," the boys raised by Hubert Humphrey, Orville Freeman, and Walter Mondale who were squaring off for the nomination in the Democratic-Farmer-Labor primary.

Sure enough, by early February, those candidates had already raised more than a million dollars. I'd received a little over a thousand. In the spring, I briefly resumed an acting career that had started ten years before when I played Blain alongside Arnold Schwarzenegger in *Predator*. This time, I was cast in an independent film being made in Minnesota. It was called *20/20 Vision* and I played Buddy "One-Arm" Sanchez, a disturbed marriage counselor who goes nuts at the end and becomes violent. I hoped this wouldn't get aired over the next few months.

That June, when the Reform Party held its convention at my alma mater—North Hennepin Community College—I told the 109 delegates not to worry about the polls. My opponents' numbers could only go down, and mine could only go up. "Fifty percent of Minnesotans don't vote!" I told them. "That's disgusting!" Those were the people we had to tap into.

My talk radio job was still my main source of income, and I tried to convince the bosses at KFAN to let me stay on the air at least until the primaries in mid-September. But they were afraid of retribution from the Federal Communications Commission. So the day I formally filed as a candidate, July 21, was my last morning at the station. I didn't think that was fair. Here the professional politicians could continue being paid their salaries. How come they didn't take an unpaid leave of absence to run for office?

Things started to get interesting at the State Fair in August, when people took almost 50,000 of the Ventura/Schunk brochures and bought $26,000 worth of my "Retaliate in '98" T-shirts. "I don't care if a bill is Democrat or Republican," I said to folks. "If it's good for Minnesota, I'll sign it. If it's bad, I'll veto it." The polls showed my support to be growing, even though, by late August, I'd only raised a little over $60,000. The Republican candidate, Norm Coleman, now had $1.4 million, and the two leading Democratic contenders almost as much, between them.

At the Governor's Economic Summit, in the middle of September, I wasn't invited to speak. But Roger Moe, who was running for lieutenant governor with Skip Humphrey, graciously gave half his time to me. Everybody else was wearing suits and ties. I had on black Levi's, a camouflage shirt, boots, and an Australian outback hat not unlike the one I'd worn in *Predator*. "You're going to find me a little different," I said to the audience seated around tables with white linen and flowers. "If the thought process were the same as it is today 150 years ago in this country," I went on, "you would not have had Abraham Lincoln up here to talk to you. Because Abraham Lincoln was a third-party candidate. At that point in time the Republicans were the growing, new party."

For the first gubernatorial debate, I wore a sport coat over a golf shirt, and my sneakers. I was always casual. There were something like four Democrats and four Republicans still in the running. I was sitting at the end of the table, since they had us in alphabetical order and Ventura came last. I looked around and every other candidate had stacks of books, spin documents; you can't imagine all the paper. I had nothing. A lady came over and sat down, brought out a legal pad and pen, and started to hand them to me.

"What's that for?" I said.

"Don't you think you'll need these?" she asked.

I said, "No."

She said, "Really? Why not?"

I passed the pad and pen back and said, "Because, ma'am, when you tell the truth, you don't have to have a good memory." She sat there a moment, then smiled and said, "I understand."

During the final debates, Humphrey and Coleman were at each other's throats about family farmers. When the moderator finally let me get a word in, I said, "I figure this obviously shows who's above all this." Everybody in the room laughed.

I suited up for the final debates. A navy-blue suit with a diamond-patterned tie and a white button-down shirt that Terry starched. The primaries were over, and it had come down to just Humphrey, Coleman, and me. The candidates were asked if they were behind a government plan to support various economic development projects. Both of them thought this was very important. I said I didn't know a thing about it, but nowhere in the Constitution did it describe government's business being to create jobs. To me, that was the responsibility of the private sector. Coleman called my response absurd "and actually very frightening." But the audience went wild with applause.

Later, I was driving home, thinking about my Republican opponent. Norm Coleman was so polished. For one fleeting moment I said to myself, "This guy is beyond me. I can't possibly compete with him." Then it dawned on me a few minutes later that I didn't *want* to be like him. There are thousands of Norm Coleman wannabes out there, who've all been to Political Science 101 class on how to get elected. They're so predictable. If you were only allowed a three-minute stage to give your response, I wouldn't take up that time with double-talk rhetoric. We all know what that is—when the candidate is done, you turn to the person next to you and ask, "What did he *say*? He wasn't answering the question!" I gave truthful, simple answers. And it seemed to work.

Sometimes, of course, speaking my mind proved a bit controversial. I told the veterans gathered at an American Legion post that I opposed any constitutional amendment to outlaw flag-burning. The point was that we have the freedom to do something like that in America, and the flag is only a symbol. Besides, I told them, flag-burners usually get the crap kicked out of them by construction workers, anyhow.

Another time I got asked whether I favored legalizing prostitution. I replied no, but it was legal in Nevada, and they didn't seem to have any huge problems with it. So I'd rather imprison the people who really deserve it. Besides, isn't it easier to control something when it's legal? I mean, why not put all the porno shops in one place? My opponents responded that such remarks ought to outrage and frighten the good people of Minnesota, and the media made a big deal out of attacking me, too. (Not one newspaper in the state endorsed my candidacy.) I guess they figured I was self-destructing but, somehow, my popularity kept building.

At the same time, my campaign was just about flat broke. In Minnesota, there's a system where you check off some money on your taxes to go into a general fund that gets distributed to candidates for office. My two opponents were entitled to a larger percentage, but I was supposed to be allotted more than $325,000 in campaign financing. However, to get the funds, you first had to procure a loan from a bank. Then, after the election, the government would repay the bank. The only stipulation was that you had to get at least five percent of the vote and, by the time of the primary, I was already polling at ten percent.

Anyway, with only a month to go before the election, my campaign's loan applications had been turned down by a half dozen banks. The head of the Republican Party at that time happened to be Bill Cooper, the head of the Minnesota Banking Association. Coincidence? You tell me. The law said you could not put up your own collateral. I was in a real bind.

Then Steve Minn, a member of our Reform Party who'd been elected to the Minneapolis City Council, happened to talk to his neighbor one day over the backyard fence. The neighbor was vice president of the Franklin Avenue Bank, in what was basically the Minneapolis ghetto. Giving high-risk loans was their specialty. "Send Jesse down to us, we'll do it," he said.

It's safe to say I would not have become governor had it not been for the Franklin Avenue Bank. Within twenty-four hours, they wrote up our loan. That $325,000 then went to Bill Hillsman, with the Northwoods Advertising Agency. His TV ads were ready, and all he was waiting for was the check. One of Bill's ideas was a Jesse Ventura Action Figure, being used by these two kids to do battle with an Evil Special Interest Man doll. Another ad had me sitting there, posed like Rodin's famous sculpture of "The Thinker," not quite naked but almost. (Truth be told, a body double did the filming, not me). The idea was, "The Body" had morphed into "The Mind."

TERRY: This was where I had to eat crow. When they came to me with that last commercial, I said to Jesse, "You can't run this, everybody's going to hate it! They're even going to question whether you're wearing any clothes! I don't see how this makes you a serious candidate!" I thought the "little-guy ads" were frivolous. I remember arguing with Bill Hillsman in our living room. Bill kept saying, "Trust me, trust me." Well, these turned out to be killer ads that people just loved! I went to Bill later and said, "Man, it's a good thing there was somebody smarter than me running that campaign!"

Bill has a sixth sense about how to communicate to the people. He'd put Paul Wellstone over the top with his ads in 1990. By the time of the last debate, which was televised statewide, I'd shot up to 23 percent in the polls. Once again, Humphrey and Coleman were jabbing at each other, this time about how they would reduce health-care costs for low-income senior citizens. Norm accused Skip of making the same promises ten years ago. I chimed in, "Ten years ago, Norm was a Democrat." Which was true—he'd switched parties. "And working in my office!" Skip cried, taking my bait. When I challenged their budget and tax-cut notions, they got so hot against each other that the moderator tried to cut them off. I stood up and pretended to hold them apart, in this political boxing-ring.

That last weekend of our 72-Hour Drive to Victory tour, a new TV ad appeared that featured my animated action figure driving a huge RV down the highway to the tune of "Yankee Doodle

Dandy." A voice-over talked about another six-foot-four-inch wrestler from a third party—Honest Abe—who the people voted in because they believed in what he stood for.

Farm country ends after you cross the border into northern Oklahoma, and you soon enter a lush area filled with trees and beautiful rolling hills. Our dog, Dexter, a Belgian Malinois—they're the original shepherds—sits quietly in the seat behind us, looking out the truck-camper window. Terry and I are talking about stopping before long, when we come to a good truck stop.

"Hey, honey," I say, "remember when we all met in our kitchen at the ranch, the day after the election?"

"I thought it was pretty impressive," Terry says, "that there were my girlfriends and my mom, kinda running the show with all your big political people."

"But do you remember the first thing we said?"

"Never forget it. Everybody was sitting there looking around at each other, and it was: 'What in the hell do we do *now*?'"

CHAPTER 3

Down That Texas Trail

"The Christian church in all its freakish ramifications and efflorescence's is as dead as a doornail; it will pass away utterly when the political and social systems in which it is now embedded collapse. The new religion will be based on deeds, not beliefs."

—*Henry Miller,* The Air-Conditioned Nightmare, *1945*

We always spend the night in truck stops. These are real Americana, a truly unique part of blue-collar America. We pull into the back and expand the camper out, among all the 18-wheelers. The drivers tend to leave their trucks on a low idle, a kind of soothing hum that lulls you to sleep. I never have any trouble sleeping in the truck stops. Usually we get there before a lot of the truckers arrive and, by morning when we wake up, the lot will be jammed.

You can stay there for free, and you get a feeling of security parking among them. I'm not ever recognized. I've grown my hair out and cut off my beard, and I haven't been clean-shaven probably since the military. Maybe a couple of times in wrestling, but I had the bleached-blond hair back then.

The friendliness we generally encounter on the road is wonderful. Except on one particular night in Denny's. They have a big-screen TV in the corner, and everybody is glued to it. All watching Fox News. It doesn't take me long to get sick of it, and I ask if they can change the channel. But they won't. It's stuck on Fox News!

TERRY: Most of the truck drivers are these huge, burly guys. And there's Jesse, sitting there complaining about Fox News and talking loudly about Bush. I mean, he's big too, but it scared the heck out of me!

Why do I react like this? The media today are controlled by the big corporations. It's all about ratings and money. Believe it or not, I think the downfall of our press today was the show *60 Minutes*. Up until it came along, news during the Walter Cronkite era was expected to lose money. The networks wrote it off, in order to bring the people fair reporting and the truth. But when *60 Minutes* became the top-rated program on television, the light went on. The corporate honchos said, "Wait a minute, you mean if we *entertain* with the news, we can make money?" It was the realization that, just like any sitcom or drama series, if packaged the correct way, the news could make you big bucks. No longer was it a matter of scooping somebody else on a story, but whether *20/20*'s ratings this week were better than *Dateline*'s. I'm not knocking *60 Minutes*. It was tremendously well done and hugely successful, but in the long run it could end up being a detriment to society.

My major criticism of today's media is, they're no longer reporting the news, they're creating it. When that happens, you're in deep trouble. Here's an example from the sports world: Not long ago, after the Vikings lost a football game, the press went to a Minneapolis bar wanting people to trash the team. I heard this from somebody who was there that night. Instead of arbitrarily seeing what a certain table's opinion was of the game, they kept going around the room until they found the right person to say what they were looking for. That's who got on TV. To me, that's dishonest reporting. Creating the news.

I went through something similar after I appeared on David Letterman's show. I guess Letterman wanted to get a little spark going, so he said: "Now you're governor of Minnesota, home of the Twin Cities. If you had to pick one, which city do you like better?" Well, back home, that was a death sentence waiting to happen. So I figured, rather than avoid the question, I'd be honest. "Well, David," I said, "I was born in Minneapolis. So naturally, if push comes to shove, I'm gonna choose my hometown. I went to Minneapolis Roosevelt, not St. Paul Central."

Then I thought I'd have some fun. I made a mistake, though. In my position, I wasn't allowed to make jokes, even on Letterman or Leno. (Even though, last time I checked, mostly what they do on those shows is entertain people and say funny things.) Anyway, I said, "My biggest criticism of St. Paul is their streets. In Minneapolis, all the streets are either numerical or alphabetical, so you've got a good idea where you are. In St. Paul, there's no rhyme or reason to them."

I added this: "Dave, you know that St. Paul's got a huge Irish population. And when they were naming them streets, well, you know them Irishmen." I made the motion of drinking a beer. Now correct me if I'm wrong but, on St. Patty's Day, what do they do? They drink—not water, right? When I go to see the Timberwolves play, right across the street is so-and-so's Irish Pub. So I kind of viewed the two as synonymous with each other.

Here's what the Minnesota media did with that: They went out until they found an Irishman who was angered and offended. I heard they went through about ten people first, who all laughed and said, "Of course, who cares, that's what the Irish are known for." That last angry Irishman was the one who got on TV.

I was greeted home by hordes of reporters at the airport, demanding an apology to the Irish community. At that point I realized that, from now on, I could only tell Slovak jokes. See, if you tell them you're that nationality, then you're off the hook because you're talking about yourself.

I came back to Letterman's show a year or two later. The first line out of David's mouth was, "Well, what have you been up to, and what have you learned in the last year, being governor?" I looked over at him and said, "Well, David, I've learned that I can get in trouble without *you*!" Because I'd been in hot water for a half dozen other things I said or did by then. Letterman roared.

I had some fun with Tim Russert, too, on *Meet the Press*. Our first exchange, soon after I became governor, went like this:

Tim: "If I call you Jesse 'The Mind' Ventura, will you call me Tim 'The Body' Russert?"

Me: "Take off your shirt right now, Tim. Let's see what you've got."

Shows like Russert's would often display a picture of me wearing my pink feathered boa from my wrestling days and say, "Look, there's the governor of Minnesota!" Well, one day an old college classmate of Tim's sent us a picture of him from those years, wearing a beard and shoulder-length hair and looking a lot like Meathead from *All in the Family*. So when I went on *Meet the Press* the next time and he started remarking about old photos of me, I said, "Speaking of photos, Tim"—and I whipped this one out and asked the cameraman to zoom in—"I want people to see the real Tim

Russert!" He looked kind of embarrassed, but he was a good sport about it.

I got a fair shake from Chris Matthews on *Hardball*, even from Geraldo Rivera. They didn't take cheap shots and they asked good questions. The thing about most of the media is that they want to reduce everybody to the lowest common denominator. They don't want people to have any heroes. I've got nothing against criticism of political figures, but that's different from a personal attack. It's easier to do sensationalism and character assassination than focus on the real issues. And they're obsessed, it seems, with portraying the ugliest side of humanity—the dishonesty, hypocrisy, ego battles, and fights.

How dare Fox, CNN, and MSNBC call themselves news stations? They're entertainment stations. Think about Anna Nicole Smith. A live feed to the hotel where she died? Why would she deserve this type of coverage? She's nothing but a silicone-breasted gold digger who married an old guy to get his money. I wouldn't even list her as the poorest poor man's Marilyn Monroe. Yet the woman warrants weeks of our attention? At the very same moment, a group of scientists came out and said unequivocally that global warming *is* being caused by human beings. Did you hear that mentioned on the "news"? No, that day Britney Spears shaved her head. People would rather hear about this than what's happening in Iraq? Or are we simply being dumbed-down to that point? The people of the United States should demand more than this!

Which is why I go ballistic in a truck stop that can't manage to switch away from Fox News.

The famous Route 66 out of Oklahoma City doesn't get traveled much anymore. There's even grass growing over parts of it. John

Steinbeck, when he described the westward migration of the Dust Bowl farmers to California in *The Grapes of Wrath*, called Route 66 the "Mother Road," a nickname it still retains. As a kid, I remember Nat King Cole, and later Chuck Berry and the Rolling Stones, singing about how you could "Get Your Kicks on Route 66." Then there was the TV show *Route 66*, featuring these two young guys in a Corvette looking for adventure on the highways of America.

So the road became part of our auto culture mythology. The first drive-through restaurant sprang up along Route 66—Red's Giant Hamburgs in Springfield, Missouri. And yes, the first McDonald's, out in San Bernardino, California, also appeared in the mid-1950s on 66. Later, you found restaurants like the Big Texan, which advertised a seventy-two-ounce steak dinner that was free of charge to anybody who could down the whole thing in an hour!

Given all this history, Terry and I had to check it out for a while. She's a real sucker for roadside attractions, and Route 66 had always boasted plenty of these—from Dairy Queens to reptile farms. (Our standard operating procedure was to start the day with a hefty breakfast, grab an afternoon ice cream, and then stop for dinner.) When we came to our first "Authentic Indian Trading Post," Terry got all excited. But when we pulled into the village, we got out and saw that all the "authentic" teepees were painted on plywood boards. There were "authentic moccasins," but they were made by the Minnetonkan Moccasin Company back up in Minnesota! I didn't figure our Indians had gotten as far south as Oklahoma.

A day later, after we'd driven by a dozen more of these "authentic trading posts," I realized these were the McDonald's of Native Americans. I understand commercialism, but it's disheartening to realize that even American history has suffered a corporate takeover. It was actually kind of heartbreaking for Terry, because she thought we'd stumbled onto something unique. And it isn't at all.

Road signs noted in Terry's journal:

Native American Cherokee Trading Post—24-Hour Restaurant and a Subway.
Rattlesnakes Exit Now.
Pumpkin Maize and Pizza Farm.
Dinosaur Park and Petrified Forest—free polished petrified wood, meteorites fifty percent off!
Navajo Feed and Pawn.

Approuching on the border between Oklahoma and Texas, we saw signs for the Gene Autry Museum. You had to pull off the main highway and drive about twelve miles to get there and, unfortunately, when we arrived, it had closed a half-hour before. Terry had seen something very disturbing on the way in, and alerted me to look for it on our way back. I won't soon forget it. It was what we presumed was a scarecrow. But it had a black bowling ball for a head, the holes being the eyes and nose. And it had a noose around its neck.

I looked at Terry and said, "Wow, are we really in the twenty-first century?"

Dallas isn't that far, once you cross the border into Texas. We were going to pay a visit to an old Navy buddy of mine, a physician who lived in the suburb of Arlington. I'd been to Dallas twice in recent years. The first time, as governor, I wanted to see Dealey Plaza. After leaving office, I came back in 2003 to participate in commemorating the fortieth anniversary of President John F. Kennedy's assassination.

I'd been a young teenager when Kennedy was killed. I remember the country being sad but, at the time, numb and surreal. Then, when I was at junior college in the 1970s, Mark Lane came to speak about the questions he had concerning the Warren Commission. I started to wonder. When I went into my wrestling career, on airplanes I started reading all the books I could about the assassination.

It caused quite a stir when I told an interviewer from *Playboy* that I did not believe the official conclusion that Lee Harvey Oswald had acted alone. That was my first year as governor and, as far as I'm aware, I was the highest ranking official who'd ever made that statement. My most basic reasoning is this: If Oswald was really who we were led to believe—a disgruntled little Marine private who got angry with capitalism and became a communist, tried to defect to Russia, came back and thought he'd make a name for himself in history by shooting the president—then why would any of the evidence need to be withheld and locked away in the National Archives for seventy-five years because of "national security"? As a Navy SEAL, I had top-secret clearance. That was higher than Oswald's, and I know a few secrets, but not enough to jeopardize national security.

When I was traveling around the country to promote my first book, the publisher said I could go to either Houston or Dallas. I said, "Give me Dallas." First I went to where Jack Ruby shot Oswald, inside police headquarters. A cop gave me the tour. The eerie part was that there was the elevator we all saw on TV—and down on the floor, almost on the exact spot where Oswald lay dying, the tile had oil on it that still looks like blood.

From there, I went to Dealey Plaza. I walked the picket fence where a second gunman most likely was firing from. I took my time. I walked out on the street, looked at the decline of the road. Then I went into the Texas School Book Depository, where Gary Mack—curator of the Sixth Floor Museum at the time—met my party. The actual supposed sniper's nest on the sixth floor is sealed off. But you can go to the next window, which would seem to be an easier shot, because you're eight feet closer to where the motorcade passed and at basically the same angle. When you look out, you see a massive Texas oak tree. I turned to Mack and said, "Clearly, forty years ago, this tree was much smaller." He said, "No, this is maintained by the federal government as a National Monument, so it's trimmed to be kept as close to authentic as can reasonably be done." Even if the tree had been several feet smaller in 1963, I didn't see how three shots could have cleared its branches and still lined up right on the presidential motorcade. Besides, Oswald had seven seconds to get three rounds off. He was using a bolt action weapon—with which he's going to miss the first shot and somehow hit with the next two?

After my book-signing was finished, we headed out to the airport. At the time, I was smoking cigars, so they found me a restricted area outside where I could light up. It was a beautiful day in Dallas. We were all laughing and making small talk. As it came time for me to put out my cigar and board the plane, the police officer who'd been our guide all day took me off to the side.

He said, "Be very careful, governor. You are a high-profile person who might say things that certain people don't want said."

Well, if Oswald was indeed the lone assassin, and was the "lone nut" that they told us he was, how could my making comments about this forty years later affect anybody? In hindsight, I wish I had canceled the flight and gone to the policeman's home that night. I wanted to ask him, "Why are you warning me about this? What do you base it on?" I had the distinct feeling from him, however, that he didn't want to be asked.

Jack Tunheim was a Minnesota federal judge who, after Oliver Stone's *JFK* film came out, was put in charge (by President Clinton) of reviewing the still-classified assassination archives for potential release. As governor, I figured I ought to have access to Tunheim.

So we had dinner together one evening at the home of another federal judge. We were joined by Kathleen Blatz, who was then chief justice of the Minnesota Supreme Court. The topic of the evening was Kennedy.

Tunheim told me, in essence, that everything had now been revealed, unless it referred to a CIA undercover operative who was still alive and whose life could be put in danger. He told me that, in following up on the intelligence side, he'd encountered some of the shadiest characters that he'd ever come across. The judge told me I had great knowledge of the case, and that I was on the right track.

Well, why does it end there? This is a homicide, and there's no statute of limitations on murder. The Warren Commission is meaningless, because it was merely an investigation supposedly done to bring everything into the light of day, and it doesn't stand up as a court case. Why is it that so many allude to more people being involved with Oswald, but prefer to let the sleeping dog lie?

On the fortieth anniversary of the assassination on November 22, 2003, I decided to go to Dallas to pay my respects. I'd left office the previous January. I was the only elected official who spoke in Dealey Plaza that day. No one else even bothered to show up. Does our government still have a collective guilty conscience when it comes to John F. Kennedy?

Teaching at Harvard in 2004, I decided to focus my next-to-last class on the Kennedy assassination. I knew that was a gutsy move to make at the Kennedy School of Government. I hadn't wanted to try it too soon because, if Harvard objected, I didn't want to go through a big fight. Anyway, I got away with it. My guest speaker was David Fetzer, a University of Minnesota Duluth professor and former Marine who's an expert on the ballistics evidence that shows it had to be more than just Oswald shooting.

I noticed there were people in my class that day whom I'd never seen before. They were too old to be students. Their sole purpose in being there was apparently to debunk any conspiracy theories. They didn't completely disrupt the class, but they would speak out of turn and insinuate that it was un-American and undermining our great country to bring up the past and question the integrity of all those great men on the Warren Commission. Never question your government, was the message. (Kind of like what former president George H. W. Bush said at President Ford's funeral; We know the Warren Commission is accurate because Gerald Ford said it was.) So where did these people come from? I suspect they were plants, sent in by somebody in the government.

If I ever became president, I would push for opening up every document in the National Archives after a limited number of years. Unless, as Judge Tunheim said, it was a case where someone's life might be in jeopardy if a particular document were made public. But the moment that person died, that document would automatically become public record. I just don't like the idea of secretive government, and we're going in that direction more and more, by leaps and bounds. I do not believe that a democracy can survive when it's hiding secrets.

Another sign noted in Terry's journal: Accept Jesus as your savior and live forever. Or you will regret it forever.

Leaving the Dallas–Forth Worth area, we passed through a small town. On the outskirts, there was a huge cross. It seemed almost the size of a skyscraper, the biggest built structure in the entire area. And it wasn't the last one we'd see.

I created a furor in 1999 when, in my interview with *Playboy*, I called organized religion "a sham and a crutch for weak-minded people." Looking back on that comment today, I might be accorded prophet status.

My belief in spirituality is probably not the norm, I'll admit. Definitely not in the United States. I don't go to church on Sundays. I believe we all worship God in our own diverse ways. And I view organized religion as strictly a business, top to bottom, like all other businesses. I am still very frustrated over the fact that the Catholic Church is not being prosecuted under the federal racketeering laws that apply to organized crime, the RICO statute, when it comes to the rampant child abuse practices that some members of the church hierarchy knowingly allowed to take place. Nobody's even brought that up. Apparently the church is untouchable. Well, I don't believe that religion *should* be untouchable. God is untouchable—He doesn't have to worry—but to me, religion is created by man.

I'll also say this: If Jesus came back today, I think he'd throw up. Didn't Jesus throw the money-changers out of the temple? By all accounts I've read, he was with the downtrodden, the underdog. Not with the people living in suburbia, for whom everything is going great. Or, as I like to call them, born-again Republicans.

I was the only governor out of all fifty who would not declare a National Prayer Day. I took a lot of heat for that, and my response was very simple: Why do people need the government to tell them to pray? Pray all you want! Pray fifty times a day if you desire, it's not my business! On the counter-side, I said, Look, if I declare National Prayer Day, then I've got to declare National No-Prayer Day for the atheists. They are American citizens too.

Instead, I declared "Indivisible Day" one Fourth of July. The proclamation went like this: "WHEREAS: The unique feature of this nation at its founding was its establishment of a secular Constitution that separated government from religion—something never done before; and WHEREAS: Our secular Constitution has enabled people of all worldviews to coexist in harmony, undivided by sectarian strife; and WHEREAS: President James Madison made clear the importance of maintaining this harmony when he said, 'The purpose of separation of church and state is to keep forever from these shores the endless strife that has soaked the soil of Europe in blood for centuries'; and WHEREAS: The diversity of our people requires mutual respect and equal protection for all our citizens, including minority groups, if we are to remain 'One nation, indivisible'; and WHEREAS: It is the unfettered diversity of ideas and worldviews that has made our nation the strongest and most productive in the world; and WHEREAS: Eternal vigilance must be maintained to guard against those who seek to stifle ideas, establish a narrow orthodoxy, and divide our nation along arbitrary lines of race, ethnicity, and religious belief or nonbelief. NOW, THEREFORE, I, JESSE VENTURA, Governor of Minnesota, do hereby proclaim that Thursday, July 4, 2002, shall be observed as: INDIVISIBLE DAY in the State of Minnesota."

For me, the lines between church and state seem to become more blurred by the day. The First Amendment protects freedom of speech, thought—*and* religion. Nowhere is it mandated that we're the Christian States of America. As Thomas Jefferson once said, "Religion is a matter which lies solely between a man and his God. . . . he owes account to none other for his faith or his worship." Who you pray to, in other words, is none of the government's business.

That's made us, I think, a stronger and more democratic nation. If you look at history, religious belief can be a powerful tool in the hands of the corrupt. Remember the Inquisition of the Middle Ages? It's abundantly clear that our Founding Fathers wanted to prevent our government from establishing a "national church." Today, though, if the Religious Right has its way, you either believe wholeheartedly in Jesus cleansing you of all sin—or you're destined to rot in hell. Be prepared to succumb to the fiery furnace while all the true believer zealots get wafted into heaven on a glorious, rapturous cloud come Armageddon. They're waiting with open arms for the Apocalypse. Woe be unto you if you happen to be a Hindu or, worst of all, a Muslim.

To me, this attitude is an absurd abdication, a retreat from trying to make a difference and fight for a better world, for the sake of future generations on the only planet human life exists upon, as far as we can know.

I'd like to see organized religion's tax-exempt status removed. Churches receive the same benefits as you and I—they get fire and police protection, and their streets plowed. That's what your local taxes pay for. How come they get off the hook? It would be one thing if they weren't political, but even local churches are political nowadays.

Back in 1981, Gary North, one of the leaders of a Christian Reconstructionist movement, made this statement: "Christians must begin to organize politically within the present party structure, and they must begin to infiltrate the existing institutional order."

Today, televangelist Pat Robertson boasts about having 150 graduates of Regent University, which he founded, in the Bush administration. And we wonder why Christianism dominates the political agenda?

"The interesting thing about you," Terry is saying as my religious rant winds down, "is that your great hero in life is a Muslim."

As we roll onto Highway 20 heading west, I'm remembering when I came to the stage on election night to give my acceptance speech. After thanking my supporters, I'd said this: "You know, it was back in '64 that a hero and an idol of mine beat Sonny Liston. He shocked the world. . . . Well, now it's 1998 and the American dream lives on in Minnesota 'cause we SHOCKED THE WORLD!"

Muhammad Ali, then Cassius Clay, had been that hero and idol of mine growing up. I was at the impressionable age of twelve or thirteen, and naturally boxers are the epitome of toughness. Along came Muhammad, who broke the mold, reciting his poetry and predicting in what round he would win. Up until then, athletes were supposed to be modest people who were blessed by the Lord for having these wonderful physical bodies. Now here was this flashy, charismatic young black man proclaiming how pretty he was. Black men in America had never been pretty!

The big fights weren't on pay-per-view then, but all heavyweight title bouts were broadcast live on the radio. My brother and I occupied the upper part of our little house in south Minneapolis, and whenever a heavyweight fight happened, my dad would come up and sit with us. All three of us would be glued to the play-by-play on the radio. When Sonny Liston knocked out Floyd Patterson in the first round, that "family experience" lasted all of about fifteen minutes.

When the Clay-Liston bout was about to happen, I'd actually been predicting that Clay would win. Even though nobody got past a few rounds with the "Big Ugly Bear," and the "Louisville Lip" wasn't given a chance. I had Clay's record album, *I Am the Greatest!* I'd memorized it.

So I was ecstatic when Liston failed to come out for the eighth round. I always remembered Clay screaming, "We shocked the world!" after the fight, and that's all I could think of when I went out for my acceptance speech. Not long after this, I was in the transition office of the Capitol when on my schedule appeared the name Harvey Mackay. He's a prominent businessman who wrote the book *Swim with the Sharks.* Harvey came walking in with a big gift-wrapped box, and I was thinking, "What the heck could this be about?" Setting the box down, he said, "You'd better open that, governor."

Inside was a pair of red Everlast boxing gloves and, written in magic marker on one of them was: "To Governor Jesse Ventura— You Shocked the World. Muhammad Ali." I was stunned. Harvey told me that Muhammad was watching TV the night I won.

Harvey then set it up for us to go visit Muhammad on his farm in Berrien Springs, Michigan. Four state troopers accompanied us— my two security guys from Minnesota, one from Indiana, where our plane landed, and another from Michigan. We spent a whole afternoon with Muhammad. It was a dream come true for me to be sitting on a couch with the Champ, creating a friendship. His wife, Lonnie, told me that he'd barely slept the night before, he was so excited I was coming. I was awestruck—Muhammad Ali, excited to see me?

As the world knows, Muhammad suffers today from Parkinson's disease. So you do most of the talking, and he answers more with his eyes. We walked out to his gym and got in the ring together. They took some photos of us boxing, as well as my putting him in a headlock. It was there that Harvey talked me into reciting "I Am the Greatest" from the record album.

"This is the legend of Cassius Clay, the most beautiful fighter in the world today, who talks a great deal and brags indeedy, of a muscular punch that's incredibly speedy. The fistic world was dull and weary, with a champ like Liston things had to be dreary. Then someone with color, someone with dash, brought fight fans a-runnin' with cash. . . ."

I hadn't heard that album for thirty years, but I did the whole thing from memory. Muhammad was standing next to me and, when I finished, I could see a tear in his eye.

Isn't it ironic that a white kid from south Minneapolis would have a black Muslim for a hero? Some people have said to me, "How can you, being a Vietnam veteran, look up to a guy like him who refused induction into military service?" My response is, "Because Muhammad is a man who gave up everything for his convictions. He was willing to sacrifice the greatest title in the world for his beliefs." You know damned well that Ali would never have seen Vietnam. He'd have done his boxing exhibitions on the military bases. But he wasn't going to play that game. I have tremendous respect for that.

Something I noticed when I walked into his home: On a shelf in his living room, in equal prominence, are the Koran and the Bible. Obviously, they both carry a deep meaning for him. I imagine he reads both. For people who don't believe that Ali truly believes, they're wrong. Like I said, he's a man of conviction. Always has been, and always will be.

Muhammad is also big into magic. While we were there that day, somebody said to him, "Muhammad, do you feel strong enough to levitate today?" He gave a nod and moved slowly along the tiled floor to the center of his kitchen. What I saw next remains one of the most astonishing moments of my life. I watched both of his feet raise two inches off the floor, stay there for a period of about thirty seconds, and then go back down.

When we left an hour later, my companions and I sat looking at each other in the car, and I said: "Now—who saw something different?" None of us could say otherwise. So, if it was a magical trick, I tip my hat because Muhammad does it exceptionally well, having fooled a governor and four state troopers.

And if it wasn't a trick, then I really believe that Muhammad Ali is "The Greatest."

CHAPTER 4

Thinking Politics in Bush Country

"I like to tell people, Laura and I are proud to be Texas—own a Texas ranch, and for us, every day is Earth Day."

—*President George W. Bush*

Traveling across West Texas on Interstate 20, after you pass by Abilene and Big Spring, before long the big oil derricks loom on the horizon. Every direction you look, the landscape is all scrubby desert and completely flat—except for the endlessly rocking motion of the black pumps. And as you close in on Midland, the dusty air is permeated by a propane smell. There's no escaping it, even inside the camper.

I turned to Terry and said, "I really don't see how people can live in this. But I imagine, like anything else, you become accustomed to it."

"They have my deepest sympathies," Terry said.

"This is about the last place on the planet I've seen that I'd want to live," I said.

I didn't remember until later that this was Bush Country. The elder George had come to Midland for the first Permian Basin oil

65

rush in the fifties. George W. grew up here, and later came back just in time for the second oil boom in the 1970s. Midland was his wife Laura's hometown, and this was where they met. It's where the younger George declared himself a candidate for Congress in 1977, when his dad was running the CIA. And Midland is where George W. has expressed a wish to someday be buried.

My first impression of him had been a positive one. After the Supreme Court awarded Bush the 2000 election, his people approached me to be part of his transition team. I sat in on three or four conference calls. I thought, this guy's going to be all right. He was very personable, a man it seemed like you could go out and drink a few beers and go fishing with.

Not too long after his inauguration, Terry and I went to Washington for the annual National Governors Convention. On a Sunday night, there's always a huge party in the White House. You're dropped off at a side entrance, and your security team goes to the basement and waits down there with the Secret Service until it's over. When it's your time to go into the ballroom, a military man in full dress uniform greets you. Your wife takes his arm, he escorts her, and you follow right behind. You stand in a line with all the other governors and their wives, waiting to meet the president and the First Lady.

I watched as the governors' names were announced and they shook hands, exchanged a greeting, and talked for a moment. Well, as the line progressed, President Bush glanced over and saw that Terry and I were up next. Before they could even say—"Governor and Mrs. Jesse Ventura, Minnesota"—Bush, with a big smile on his face, blurted out in front of everyone: "I have to meet the most patient woman in America."

Apparently, George was up on all the controversy I was causing. Every time I'd open my mouth, I'd be in trouble. So I thought that was a great line. He didn't care about me, he wanted to meet the woman who could put up with me!

It must have been about a year later that Bush came to visit Minnesota. I took my son, Tyrel, to meet him. The president looked Ty in the eye and said, "So can you kick the old man's butt yet?"

"Oh, no!" Ty exclaimed.

And the President said, "I can't either." Referring, I presume, to George, Senior.

From these moments, I knew that Bush had a good sense of humor. But my first inclination that he was not a man of his word came at that same governor's meeting early in 2001. Monday morning is a business session, where all fifty governors sit down with the president. He discusses domestic policy—where he sees it going, what he expects from you, and what you should expect from him. He stated at the time that he was a strong believer in giving more power to the states, which I applaud. He was going to be, he said, an old-style Federalist president. I believed him.

Yet just about every move he's made since that day has taken power *away* from the states. Cases in point: Twelve states have now passed laws to allow the medical use of marijuana. The federal government under Bush says no way, it won't let the states do this. Two states have voted for dignity in death. If I'm living in Minnesota and terminally ill, I could have the option of moving to Oregon and fulfill my wishes not to prolong the agony. Again, the Bush administration says, oh no you can't.

It's a shame that Bush has turned into what he has. That deception about returning power to the states was only the first of many, the foremost being how his administration lied to the American people in justifying our disastrous invasion of Iraq. Leaving the Midland region that day, I couldn't help thinking about our dependency on oil, whether it's from the Middle East or the West

Texas variety. We should be taking the billions being wasted in Iraq and putting all this money toward renewable energy sources that won't destroy the planet. We should be doing everything we can to draw energy from the sun, the wind, and the water.

Bill Clinton was the other president I'd had a chance to become acquainted with. Actually, my first encounter was with Hillary, and we didn't start out on a positive note. When I was running for governor, naturally the Republicans and Democrats began calling in some of their big guns to try to influence the voters. The last week of the campaign, Skip Humphrey brought Hillary to Minnesota. She was still First Lady at the time. Her first quote to the media was, "Okay, it's time for the carnival sideshow to end and let's get down to real politics." I'd just climbed out of an RV in Rochester, Minnesota, when the press came charging over, thrusting about fifty microphones in my face and saying, "Did you hear that Hillary Clinton called your campaign nothing but a carnival sideshow act?"

I have respect for Hillary, but I felt insulted. And if somebody's going to fire a round over my bow, they can expect to get one back. I deadpanned: "Well, it seems to me that, rather than being concerned about Minnesota politics, Mrs. Clinton should be more concerned about leaving Bill alone in the White House." I added something about how, when the cat's away, the mice are going to play.

Later on, meeting the President and Hillary, she had decided to let bygones be bygones. If she did remember my remarks, she didn't make an issue of it.

TERRY: The first time we went to the White House, right after Jesse was elected, I was simply overwhelmed by the sheer magnitude of where we were. I felt embarrassed, not worthy. Every time we came into a room, there was a guy who would announce your name out to everybody. I felt like walking with my purse in front of my face.

I have to hand it to the Clintons, and their ability to make a person feel at home. We went to a big formal dinner in the State Dining Room at the White House. It was awesome. The tables were decorated with china and crystal, the centerpieces filled with all kinds of flowers and surrounded by silver candlesticks and votive candles. They sat me down next to Dan Glickman, the secretary of agriculture, because I liked farming, and I thought that was very clever of them. He was really nice, and so was everybody at the table, because I was such a beginner. When the waiters came around with potatoes that were fried in the form of a statue, I knew I was in big trouble. "How do they get potatoes to do this?" I asked. Nobody else seemed to know either, which was comforting.

Jesse was seated about six tables away. After the violinists came by our table playing "God Bless America," finally I said to my group, "Is it all right if I leave my chair?" Oh sure, they said. I made a beeline for Jesse, who of course was holding court at his table. I just grabbed him and said, "Isn't this great?! Oh my God, do you believe this?" He's going, "Honey, go sit down now, you're okay."

It's unique that, when you eat in the White House, you don't sit with your spouse. You get randomly placed, and that's done intentionally because they want different people to meet. The food was excellent, as you might imagine. When the meal is over, the president gets up and gives a talk, and then you all adjourn to the East Wing, down the hall, where the entertainment will be. Generally, there's some type of dancing. One time with Clinton, it was Kenny G. This first night we were there, though, was more the Glenn Miller ballroom-type music. Which isn't my cup of tea, but I can live with it.

When Terry and I walked into the room, the President and Hillary were dancing. No one else was out there. It was like no one wanted to even enter their space. I turned to Terry and said, "What will you give me to walk up to them and cut in?" She grabbed my arm, gritted her teeth, and whispered, "Don't you dare!"

So I grabbed her and said, "Fine, if I can't cut in, then come on!"

I figured, by God, I'll break the ice! I'm the independent, anyway. I won't get chastised by any upper echelon of the party. I took Terry out onto the floor and we started dancing right next to Bill and Hillary. When the music ended, naturally they turned to us and we engaged in a great conversation, talking intimately for a couple of minutes. I told them about my very first proclamation as governor, which had been to declare February fifteenth "Rolling Stones Day" in Minnesota. They thought that was great.

Looking back on it, I still wish I would have walked up and tapped the president on the shoulder, just to see what he would have done. I think they would have found my cutting in very humorous. Terry now says she should have let me do it.

TERRY: Then they had a big thing where all the First Ladies went out to Mount Vernon for a luncheon. At the end, everybody got to meet Hillary and have their picture taken with her. I'm talking to one of the First Ladies behind me in the line when, all of a sudden, before my name is even mentioned, Hillary says, "Terry!" She knew my first name? She grabbed my hand, looked me in the eye, and said, "I have been so worried about you." I said, "You've gotta be kidding." I went mute. She went on and on about having seen my picture and how concerned she was for how I was holding up. "Uh huh, uh huh," was all I could say. I was like a total country bumpkin.

The second time I went to the White House, I brought along my chief of staff, because I thought it would be a good perk for him. When we went to be greeted by Bill and Hillary this time, as soon as I shook her hand, Hillary said, "And how are Terry and the horses doing?" They'd met only once, a year earlier.

I said, "Mrs. Clinton, how do you know that Terry has horses?"

She said, "Oh, I keep an eye on Terry. I don't want anything bad to happen to her."

I'm stunned, thinking: This woman as First Lady meets how many people a day, 365 days a year? And she not only remembers your first name, but the fact that you train horses? Unbelievable, this woman's memory!

At one point I leaned in and asked her, "Madame First Lady, are you sure you want to run for the Senate? Are you positive you want to do this?"

She just laughed and said, "Yeah!"

Toward the middle of my term, I spent a night in the Lincoln Bedroom at the White House. It came about because I had teased President Clinton—were we never going to play golf together? And he'd said sometime we would. He found out that I was in Washington for a couple of days, testifying before Congress on the issue of international trade. Then his security called my security with a surprise invitation. The message was: President Clinton was returning from a trip that night, why doesn't Governor Ventura spend the night at the White House and we'll get up early in the morning and play golf? I thought, this is terrific!

I got to the White House around 8 p.m. The president wouldn't arrive back until about 11 p.m. So, I received the full tour from a lady there: the whole White House, all except for the president's bedroom, which I can understand. That was off-limits in my governor's residence, too. But I got to see parts of the White House that ordinarily nobody did. The public tours never include the private quarters on the second or third floor.

Eventually I was put way upstairs in a TV room. I was sitting in there with two of the president's relatives, cousins or something, when we heard the "helo" land on the pad outside. I had butterflies in my stomach. You feel overwhelmed, is the best way to say it. Especially in my case, when I look at myself and where I come from. The product of a street laborer and a nurse, growing up in a little house in south Minneapolis where both of my parents worked, a latchkey kid. You pinch yourself and say, I'm really *here?*

When President Clinton walked into the room, he tore off his suit jacket, threw it onto a chair, loosened up his tie, looked at me and said, "Governor, can I get you a beer, water, anything?" I said, "No sir, I'm fine." He got a beer for himself, came over, plopped into a chair, and gave a big exhale. It shows you that, at the end of a long day, presidents are human, too.

Earlier that day, I had given a keynote speech at Georgetown University, which is where Clinton went to college. I knew C-SPAN had been there with the cameras. So here I am sitting with the president, when he flips the channel to C-SPAN—and it's my speech! I'm thinking to myself, "Oh my God, I hope I didn't say something derogatory about the president or Hillary today." Because my speeches were always ad-lib. Whatever struck me, I was going to talk about it, and I never knew where I'd end up. So this was kind of a strange situation, sitting there having the president watch me giving a speech, almost as a critic. Well, he made a few comments now and then but, when it was over, I hadn't said anything bad. What a relief!

Then the fun part came. The relatives went to bed, and it ended up just the president and me. I had always wanted to smoke a cigar with him, on the balcony of the White House. But the White House is a smoke-free building. And the Secret Service won't allow the president to go out on the balcony and have a cigar, because anybody from a nearby building with a high-powered rifle would have a pretty clear shot at him. And if you had an infrared scope, you could do it at night. So I never did have a cigar with him, but we ended up sitting together and talking in his library.

This was toward the end of President Clinton's second term, and he was working overtime to try to get a peace accord between the Palestinians and the Israelis. This was really the legacy he wanted to leave behind. He started talking about this and he said, "You know, governor, it's so frustrating. Because it all comes down to one mound of dirt."

I said, "A mound of dirt?"

He said, "Yeah, there's a hill over there,"—or maybe he said "mountain," I can't remember the name of it—"and all the Israelis believe that their sacred religious artifacts are buried there. All the Palestinians and Muslims also believe their sacred relics are buried there." The president explained to me that both sides have agreed no one will ever touch the spot. No excavations or anything like that. But neither religion will allow the other one to be in control of it.

I sat there thinking: There's the rub. Until the religions change their positions, they're going to be fighting forever. We all know what it takes to get religions to take a different viewpoint. Good luck! You might have to wait for a thousand years or more.

So, after hearing the problem, I sat back in the chair and I said, "Mr. President, I have a solution."

His eyes flashed. He looked over at me and said, earnestly, "What would you do?"

I said, "Here's what I'd do. Why don't you call in an air strike, and blow that hill off the face of the earth? We can say the computers malfunctioned. We can apologize twenty times like we did when we hit the Chinese Embassy in Sudan by mistake, or supposedly by mistake. Just keep apologizing up and down for the next year. Eventually, they'll forgive us, won't they, for this miscalculation of our computers? We blow it up, it's gone! They won't have anything to fight over!"

I used the analogy of two children fighting over the same toy. How do you stop it? Take away the toy, then neither of 'em gets it. Standard Child-Rearing 101.

Well, you should have seen the look I got. I could only assume that this hadn't come up in the negotiations. Or with any of his advisers. A stunned expression is putting it mildly. President Clinton didn't say anything, but if I could put words in his mouth, they were: "You've gotta be shitting me." As best I could determine, he wasn't quite ready to consider my solution. He might even have been thinking, "And this guy could end up with his finger near the nuclear button?"

Unlike Bush, who goes to bed around 9 p.m. every night, Clinton was a night owl. He never went to sleep until three or four in the morning. But we finally said our good nights, and I walked alone down to the Lincoln Bedroom. It's on the second floor, almost directly opposite the President's bedroom.

This is where the feeling of being here really got to me. I stood in the bedroom looking around. Under glass off to one side is Lincoln's entire handwritten Gettysburg Address. Signed by him. Lincoln's penmanship is some of the most beautiful I've ever seen. I sat on the edge of the bed and thought, my God, he wrote this almost 150 years ago! Then I lay down, and began thinking of everything I could possibly remember about different presidents who had occupied the White House.

I have a disease that some people get, a ringing in the ears, so I have to sleep with another sound in the bedroom. If it's dead silent, it's difficult for me to sleep. Usually I sleep with the TV on very low, so it gives me background noise. It was about four in the morning now, and I started channel surfing. Suddenly, right there in Lincoln's bed, I began laughing so hard that the iron bedposts were shaking!

What had come on the TV while I was trying to fall asleep? Woodward and Bernstein's *All the President's Men*, the movie with Robert Redford and Dustin Hoffman. Here I am in the very same White House where Nixon had probably walked up and down the halls, swearing like hell, trying to figure—"How do I get out of *this* one?" And there's Deep Throat at four in the morning down there in the bowels of the parking lot, telling Woodward, "Follow the money."

It's a funny dichotomy. You start imagining the history of this amazing place, and it makes you feel small, insignificant. On the flip side, you realize that these were only men, too. Mortals, human beings; no different in many ways than you or I.

President Clinton and I ended up not playing golf. Something happened that he had to deal with, and some business came up that I couldn't cancel. But when I got up the next morning and checked out what the golf game would have been like, I'm just as glad it never happened. There were seven Suburbans lined up outside the White House, and each one was loaded with personnel and automatic weapons. I thought, how do you relax and play golf, when behind every sand trap is going to be a fellow holding an H&K MP5?

Driving across Texas, listening to our favorite CDs and a couple of books-on-tape. . . . Terry wants to know, "What is it with you and

Louis L'Amour?" He wrote dozens of what used to be called "dime novel Westerns," and I was a big fan.

"When I deployed overseas the first time," I recall, "we all got into reading his books. When you wrote home to your parents, you didn't ask for money—only more Louis L'Amour. You could literally leave one on your bed next to a hundred-dollar bill, you'd come back and the hundred would still be sitting there but the book would be gone."

"Well, that's a little hard to fathom," Terry responds.

"Yeah, but it's true, honey," I tell her.

She's got her camera trained on me again, and I don't like it. "Turn that off, it's distracting," I continue.

"Here I am trying to do a video diary," Terry says, exasperated. "You've been in front of cameras your whole life, saying the most outrageous things! But now, whenever I try to get you talking about something, you're all of a sudden camera shy?!"

"It's just that I know it'll be aired in front of the family," I admit. "I don't like them having any ammunition on me."

"Oh, wow," she says, then pretends to be filming out the window while she hatches a secret plan on how to catch me candid again.

"Do you ever wonder," Terry goes on, "what ever happened to that other Texas politician?"

"LBJ? He's dead."

"No, no, I know that! I'm talking about Ross Perot."

Terry knows how to get me going.

In 1996, two years before I was elected governor, the Independence Party of Minnesota had affiliated with the Texas Reform Party that Henry Ross Perot had formed the year before, because we saw in him a chance to go national. By God, this Texas billionaire seemed committed, with the finances and the organization and the passion.

I viewed him as a great hope for this country, even after the debacle of the 1992 election, where at one point he actually led in the polls. Then, all of a sudden, he withdrew from the race, claiming that Republican operatives had attempted to disrupt his daughter's wedding and he wanted to spare her from further embarrassment. Perot changed his mind in October and started running again, but he'd lost two crucial months. Even so, he'd ended up receiving about 19 percent of the popular vote, making him the most successful independent candidate since Teddy Roosevelt in 1912.

My theory is that Perot never really wanted to win, he just wanted to make a statement. And when he saw the momentum building for him that summer, he got scared that he might actually pull it off. Only Perot could really answer whether he secretly preferred working in his empire, but that's what I suspect. Still, I did see this glimmer of hope for a legitimate third party—and then I watched it start to flicker out as fast as it had risen.

When different affiliates from third parties all around the country came together in 1996, three-time Colorado Governor Dick Lamm had joined the movement. He is a brilliant man, a savvy politician, a speaker of truth in many ways. Some of us had groomed Dick to get the Reform Party nomination in 1996. Perot would always hold the status of being its creator, but we felt this would show the party growing beyond him. But at the eleventh hour, the Perot forces undercut Lamm and put Perot up again as the candidate.

Right then and there, our group from Minnesota and a lot of other supporters started to question what was really going on. All of a sudden, our new national party was being labeled vindictive because we brought forth another possibility. Isn't that what politics is supposed to be? Not a dictatorship. But apparently, Perot and his Texas group didn't truly want to create a legitimate third-party movement. It was really about Ross Perot's ego.

He won 8 percent of the popular vote in '96, less than half of what he'd done in '92, but still respectable for a third party. Let me tell you what happened when I needed his help during my run for governor two years later. It was the time when I was trying to secure a bank loan for the $325,000-plus in campaign financing that was due me, but getting stymied by the powers-that-be. Remember I mentioned that a half dozen banks had turned me down, until the little Franklin Avenue Bank came through?

Before that happened, I flew to Atlanta with some of my key people to meet with Perot. The law doesn't say that the loaning bank can't be from out of state. We figured Perot must know a bank in Texas; he probably even owned a few! We sat down for a meeting, told him what was going on—that we thought we could win this election but that the money was critical—and could he help us in some way?

Perot never said no directly, but he couldn't seem to look any of us in the eye. When we left the room, I immediately turned to Dean Barkley and Doug Friedline and said, "He's not going to help us one bit." I could read it in his body language, and the tone of his voice. At that point, I knew that this Reform Party was bogus. It's all about Ross Perot, and anything that threatens him is going to get squashed. He never did endorse me for governor that year. And I never saw him again.

I couldn't make it to the third annual convention of the Reform Party in the summer of '99, because my plane got delayed due to bad weather. My back was killing me anyway, from an injury I'd suffered playing golf a few days earlier. I did address the delegates by phone hookup from my ranch, and told them that we owed Perot a great debt as the party's founder. When Perot gave his speech, he didn't even mention my name. But our candidate, Jack Gargan, got elected to party chair over the Perot wing. And the Reform Party became eligible for almost $13 million in federal funding for the 2000 presidential election.

I'd already made it clear that I would not go for the presidency that year. As the millennium dawned, I'd only been governor for one year. I'd made a four-year promise to fulfill my obligation to the state of Minnesota. I didn't believe that, all of a sudden and for your own personal political gain, you start campaigning for another job.

There was only one person, I decided, that I would break my promise for. At the time, it was John McCain.

When Senator McCain came to see me in Minnesota early in 2000, he had just begun taking on George W. Bush. He was going hot and heavy, with the very distinct possibility he would get the Republican nomination. I was supporting him, because I believed then that a veteran, like him, and a moderate—which he no longer is today—was what the country needed.

We were sitting in my office when I looked McCain in the eye and broached a possibility. "Senator," I said, "if you will quit the Republican Party, I will break my promise to Minnesota and I will run with you. You for president, me for vice president. And we will win the 2000 election."

He smiled and said, "Well, I'd love to have you on board, but I can't quit the Republican Party."

I said, "Well, if you can't do that, then I can't join you. Because I will not join either of these parties."

He repeated, "Well, I won't quit the Republicans."

I said, "Okay, so be it."

That's where it ended. We went out and met the press and smiled for the cameras. I respected McCain; he didn't have to give me a reason why. I would have loved to have seen him break free then, because the possibility was there. If he and I had run together, I think there's a strong chance we could have won as independents. I'll always remember flying into New York City that same winter. I was in a limousine heading into Manhattan in the middle of the night, with the window down, when we passed by a construction site. One of the workers recognized me, pointed, and said, "Hey—the wrong governor is runnin' for President!"

So I believe it was wide open in 2000. Neither candidate, Bush or Al Gore, really inspired anyone. But, of course, McCain knows Karl Rove and the Republicans better than I do. They sabotaged his candidacy a couple of months later, spreading false rumors that cost him the South Carolina primary.

Now that Bush's term is almost up, the right-wing Republicans have resurrected McCain. I wouldn't make my offer again today, I'll tell you that. Not to an arch conservative who still supports the Iraq War.

Not too long after my meeting with McCain, I called a press conference.

Headline: VENTURA QUITS REFORM PARTY, CITING LEADERS

Gov. Jesse Ventura of Minnesota, the Reform Party's highest-ranking elected official, said yesterday that he was resigning from the party over his growing dissatisfaction with its fractured leadership.

Speaking outside the governor's residence in St. Paul, Mr. Ventura described Party leaders as 'hopelessly dysfunctional' and said he could not support a political organization that might have Patrick J. Buchanan, a former conservative commentator, as its presidential candidate and David Duke, former leader of the Ku Klux Klan, as a party member.

—The New York Times, *February 12, 2000*

I encouraged the state party to follow suit and, about a week later, they withdrew also, and we went back to being the Independence Party of Minnesota again. I couldn't be with any party that would consider having Pat Buchanan as its presidential nominee; not a man who'd been involved with "dirty tricks" in the Nixon administration, and who wanted to expel the United Nations from New York.

All of a sudden, Donald Trump came forward as a possible alternative. He thinks a lot like me, and we had several meetings together. I've known Trump since the early WrestleManias he staged in Atlantic City, which were the fastest sell-outs he ever had. At least you could look at Trump and say, "This guy knows how to do business." So I came out in favor of his receiving the Reform Party's nomination. And Donald has said publicly that, if I ever run for president, he will fully support me, financially and any way that he can.

But in 2000, I saw the handwriting on the wall. There was a loophole that allowed Buchanan to come in and claim the Reform Party nomination. You see, the party wasn't put together in an ironclad way. You could walk into the convention and become a delegate that same day, just by signing up. That's what Buchanan did. He had the power in all the states to bring in more delegates than the other candidate, an Iowa physicist named John Hagelin. This divided the Reform Party into warring camps. It got so bad that dual conventions ended up being held at the same time in separate areas of the Long Beach Convention Center. Ultimately, the Federal Elections Commission ruled that Buchanan would receive ballot status—as well as that nearly $13 million in federal campaign funds.

Basically, Pat Buchanan hijacked the Reform Party. Nobody had ever thought ahead as to whether someone with the steamroller he had could do this. I'm sure he had plenty of help from Republican operatives. In fact, when Buchanan called the Republicans a "beltway party" and announced he was leaving in October 1999 to seek the Reform Party nomination, my belief is that it was a set-up all along by the Republicans. A way to destroy the momentum for a third party.

Buchanan had huge debts from his previous campaign when he was seeking the Republican nomination in '96. He saw an opening to be almost like a corporate raider—take that federal funding and retire his campaign debts with it. After he raided our treasury, he didn't even put on a campaign. It was reported that he was sick. Even though he was on the ballot in forty-nine states, he finished fourth in the general election with 0.4 percent of the popular vote.

Well, they wanted a third party gone and, in my opinion, Buchanan was the black knight sent to do it. Throw the last bit of dirt on the casket, at least temporarily. The Reform Party destructed, and it's a shame. In hindsight, had Perot graciously stepped aside and allowed for natural evolution, and for Dick Lamm to be the candidate in '96, there's quite the possibility that today you would have a legitimate three-party system in this country. But it came down to the fact that Perot and his cronies didn't want to relinquish the power for the common good.

Movements of third parties rise and fall, much like the tide. Right now, we're at a very low ebb. But it'll come back. The corruption of the Democrats and Republicans ensures that it will. I call them the Demo-crips and the Re-blood-licans. No different really than the Crips and the Bloods street gangs—except that these guys wear Brooks Brothers suits.

Eventually people will start seeing the light again, and some leader will step forward and raise the third-party banner.

CHAPTER 5

Crossing Borders:
A Curious Sense of Security

"For some time I have been disturbed by the way CIA has been diverted from its original assignment. It has become an operational arm and at times a policy-making arm of the Government."

—*former President Harry Truman, December 1963*

The longer we drive through Texas, the more I realize the monotony of American culture today. Whether you're in Dallas, Austin, San Antonio, or El Paso, it's the same stores, the same everything, and it's continuous. It's not just McDonald's—every sit-down place is now part of a chain. The only way to get away from it is to pull off onto a side road and go into some Podunk town. One time Terry and I finally find a little rib joint—we and two others are the only white people in there, and what a moment of fresh air!

What are we doing to our country? I wonder. Lord, I think, give me one of the so-called underdeveloped nations, where I can walk into a local man's shop with its own unique character, not a con-glomerate like Wal-Mart that offers everything under the sun.

Coming in east of El Paso, right in the residential section—which I'm sure wasn't residential when it was built—is a huge oil refin-ery. Now the city has expanded out to contain it. All the wealthy citizens live across on the New Mexico side. El Paso itself is down in a valley and, as we cross it east to west, the smog lingering beneath the mountains looks almost worse than L.A. I realize, here's another place with environmental destruction I wouldn't want to live in.

For a whole day, we are literally going down the highway with all the NASCAR people. They had a big race in Dallas and now they're going to Phoenix. One thing about NASCAR—they've got some money! You ought to see these rigs! The best looking semis I've ever seen in my life, all polished and chromed, freshly painted. State of the art.

An excerpt from Terry's journal: We were going through Flagstaff, a really big down grade to Phoenix. Husband was in a really good mood. On a sixty-degree grade, he took his foot off the gas and was going fifty-five miles an hour without any help from the engine. I was looking over the side of a gorge about fifty feet below us and said, "Hey, could you slow down a bit?" And husband said, "I'm not losin' face by slowin' down, I'm goin' out NASCAR, baby!"

We stay a couple of days with old friends in Phoenix. They haven't seen us since my governor days, and we have a lot to catch up on. They've gotten into studying Eastern religions, and I notice a copy of *The Tibetan Book of the Dead* on a coffee table. Which, of course, inspires me to tell the story of my meeting with the Dalai Lama.

We have a Tibetan population in Minnesota. I don't think they're a huge population anywhere, but we seem to have a fairly substantial number. So, when the Dalai Lama was traveling the country in the spring of 2001, he came and spoke to a joint session of our legislature. I was scheduled to visit with him privately for twenty to thirty minutes in my office.

As the meeting date approached, I thought, what am I going to ask this guy? "Mr. Dalai Lama, please tell me the meaning of life?" I mean, how many times has he heard that from people? What could I ask that I'll bet no one in the world ever has?

Then it came to me. I'm a big fan of the movie *Caddyshack*, as any golfer is. Remember the great scene with Bill Murray, where his character—Carl the Groundskeeper—is telling the kid how he used to be a caddy? And who did he get but the Dalai Lama himself? Big hitter, even wearing all his robes. At the end of the round, he figures, "The Lama's gonna stiff me." So he says, "Hey, Lama, how about a little something for the effort here?" That's when the Dalai Lama tells him, "Gunga gunga la gunga." Which means, "When you die, you'll have total consciousness." And Bill Murray says, "So I've got *that* going for me!"

I was really curious whether the Dalai Lama had ever seen *Caddyshack*. But I wouldn't just out-and-out ask him, I wanted to get a feel for him first. He sat down across from me and my family in his flowing robe. Apparently he had done his homework on me, because he wanted to know what diving under the water was like. I told him, "You need to do it. It's very hard to describe, but it's a whole other world that you can explore very easily. A world where you go right down into the food chain. That's what makes it exciting, because you're very helpless in many ways. Everything down there is a whole lot more mobile."

So after we'd talked for a while, and I realized that the Dalai Lama is a remarkable person—very honest and with a tremendous sense of humor—I thought: why not? I had warned my son and my wife that I was going to do this. As I was leading up to it, they caught on. Tyrel, already flushed with embarrassment, excused himself. My wife was left there to face the consequences, I guess.

TERRY: I knew right when he was going to do it. He knew all the important stuff was over. I watched his body language. I saw that leg start to bounce up and down. That's when Ty jumped out of his chair: "I have to use the restroom." I was experiencing what can only be described as total mortification. And I figured by the time Jesse was done, all chances of my having a life-changing event were also going to be over.

I looked at the Dalai Lama and I said, "Your holiness, can I ask you a personal question?" He said, sure.

I said, "Do you watch movies?"

He said, "Not very often."

I said, "So—you've never seen the movie *Caddyshack*?"

He said, "No."

I said, "Well, you should, because you're in it."

He gave me this kind of puzzled look. Like, gee, I don't remember being on the set. When did I do that? And where are my royalties?

I said, "Well, you're in it, though not actually in it—but there's a whole scene about you."

The Dalai Lama started to laugh. He gets asked all these mystical questions, to which he can always give you an answer. But someone had finally asked him a real question, which he didn't *know* how to answer. I suspect he found this a relief.

I was also hoping that, wherever he stayed that night, his people would run out and get the movie and he'd sit down and watch it.

We snuck the Dalai Lama out of the Capitol Building. It has secret underground passageways where you can get people out if you need to. Then I went out to meet the press, a big mass of the Minnesota reporters. By this point in my career as governor, they weren't exactly at the top of my list. I was staring quietly at them with a straight face. Of course, the first question was, "Well, what did the Dalai Lama say to you?"

What a lead-in! How could the press spoon-feed me any better? I stayed stone-faced and I said, "Well, the Dalai Lama said to me, 'Gunga gunga la gunga.' Which means that when I die, I'll have total consciousness. So I've got that going for me!"

Only one of the media picked up on the humor. That was the fellow from Public Radio, Erik Eskola. He burst out laughing. I turned around and walked back to my office. No more questions. That's the only quote I gave 'em.

The Dalai Lama did bless me and give me a silk prayer scarf that I have today in my home office, hanging right over the back of my name-chair.

"Hey, honey, we're almost at the border." Terry has dozed off. From Phoenix we've driven south and then west again, through Yuma, and now to a crossing point into Mexico just over the Arizona-California line, at Calexico. On the other side is the border town of Mexicali. I think of the old Gene Autry song, "Mexicali Rose": "I'll come back to you some sunny day . . ." I want to get here in time to cross at dawn, anticipating we can make it to Guerrero Negro by the next night. That's the separation point between Baja Norte and Baja Sur, 450 miles from the U.S.

You don't even realize there is a border until you see the looming chain-link fence, covered in canvas so you can't have a view across from one side to the other, with all these high-powered lights making it look like a night-time sporting event. We find a vacant lot next to the immigration office. I ask the U.S. border patrol officer if it is okay for us to sleep there. He says he has no problem with that and, in fact, they are getting a lot of infiltration, so they'll be there all night long.

I say to Terry, "If you were a Mexican wanting to cross the border, why would you do it here where the authorities are so well-prepared for you? Why not go two miles up where there aren't all these lights?" Yet, the officer tells me, people are caught crossing right here all the time.

I think back to when I went to China on a trade mission, and climbed the Great Wall in Beijing. Which had sparked my contemplating the "great wall" that the U.S. is planning to build between us and Mexico, as a supposed answer to illegal immigration. By the end of '08, about 670 miles are supposed to be completed along our southwestern border. Why is it we don't see that if you don't learn from history you're destined to repeat it? The Great Wall of China did not work. The most formidable barrier ever built by mankind—and it failed! In 1644, the Chinese were overrun and now the Great Wall is nothing but a tourist attraction. At least their Great Wall is an architectural wonder that people built by hand, all day long, many of them living and dying there. So I hope they end up making our "great wall" tourist friendly. I tell Terry that, when it gets built, I'm gonna find where it's on public land and I'm gonna cross it into Mexico, in protest. I don't want my country to be East Berlin.

"That's probably another of my ideas that won't sit too well with the powers-that-be," I say. Terry nodded.

We sleep on that for a while. When we wake, the sunrise fills the desert sky as we cross over into Mexico.

The first thing you realize, when you reach the other side, is that your cell phones don't work anymore. Neither does the OnStar Locator on your vehicle. That's the button you push that tells you where the next restaurant is, or can summon the police if you break down, because a satellite pinpoints your location. Of course, at the same time that they're available to help you, it means they can also monitor you. Who's to say, with the computers that exist today, that someone isn't keeping tabs on where everyone is driving? So, in a strange way, not having these things gives me a sense of breakaway freedom. I want to escape, to have anonymity.

Terry and I were no strangers to the feeling we were being observed—and I don't mean only publicly. After I was elected governor, the state sent a big crew over to our ranch house to install a hotline phone. We kept it on the floor under our bed. It connected directly to the local police and, if anything ever went wrong, all we had to do was knock the phone off the hook and they'd be over like gangbusters.

"Remember that hotline phone, Terry?" I am musing about this, thinking about how cut off from communication we are in Baja. "They put it in one day when we were gone."

"Do I *remember*! I started noticing after a while that, every time I would use the phone at our house, it sounded like someone had picked up an extension in another room. Of course, there was never anyone there. And it always happened whenever you were involved in anything controversial. Then, all of a sudden, that clicking sound was there. It got so bad even my mom could hear it. She'd say, 'Someone's listening again, I guess we'd better be careful.' It became like a family joke."

"Then there was the time you found that little electrical transmitter laying there with the two little wires hanging from it," I remind her. "Of course, you always notice when something isn't right."

Terry smiles. "I was opening up the sliding door when I saw all these bits and pieces of electrical wire. And then the transmitter out on the patio."

I'd taken Terry's find to a friend of mine who worked for the phone company. He knew instantly what it was: a bug. My friend used to install these. Not by choice. He'd be ordered to do it. He told me, "The government would come around, and you've simply got to do what they tell you."

I was shocked, but what could we do? There was nobody to make a complaint to; the media would have just said I was paranoid. Who do you go to about something like this, when you can't trust your own government—and you're *in* it! In fact, you're at the top of it!

Terry continues: "Then, after you were out of office, all of a sudden our bedroom phone line quit working when they removed the hotline. I had two different guys come over from the local phone company to try and repair it. They said, 'We have no idea who's been working on the lines. We can't figure out what they did, or why, and we can't repair this.' The weird clicks on the phone continued to happen, even after we moved to our new house. But only at times when you'd stuck your neck out and sounded off on something to the media. When you were away at Harvard—nothing."

We sit in silence for a little while. Finally I say, "Well, I guess they can't track us anymore down here, can they?"

The first inkling that certain people inside the government were out to keep an eye on me came within the first couple months of my taking office. Sometime early in 1999, a meeting was set up for me in the basement of the Capitol. The Minnesota Legislature was not in session at the time, so there were plenty of empty rooms down there in the bowels of the building.

I was a newly elected governor who, as far as I understood it, was supposed to be giving orders, not taking them. Yet it seemed I wasn't being given any choice about whether to attend this meeting. I was more or less being *ordered* to go down there. No one actually said that. No, I was told, this was a training exercise for the Central Intelligence Agency, the CIA, and they wanted to know if I would be willing to participate.

I thought to myself, doesn't the CIA's mission statement say that they are only supposed to be operational *outside* of the United States? At the same time, being a former serviceman and a patriotic citizen, when your government wants to question you, you almost feel obligated to do it. It was maybe the case, too, that it hadn't truly set in that I was the governor. You don't yet fully realize the power you have—or think you have. So, while I felt this pressure to cooperate, and the whole premise seemed outrageous, it also piqued my curiosity. Okay, I guess I'll go down there and find out what this is all about.

There were twenty-three CIA agents waiting in a conference room for me. I counted.

What stunned me when I first walked in was—these people looked like "the neighborhood." I mean, some appeared to be in their early twenties, right out of college, alongside what looked like sixty-five-year-old grandmothers. Men and women. It was very diverse. As I looked around at them, I thought, there's the lady down the block you see sweeping her front step in the morning, and wave to—"Mrs. Jones, how are you today?" Just an average middle-class neighborhood. Except they were all with the CIA.

They sat in chairs in a big half-moon circle, and I was placed in the center. They had notebooks on their laps, waiting there intently. I believe it really was some type of learning class, or why would there be so many of them together? If the CIA simply wanted to inter-rogate me, they'd have sent over a couple of well-seasoned agents and gotten the job done. Well, all twenty-three didn't ask me ques-tions; probably only eight or ten of them did. Actually, the meeting didn't last all that long. Because I don't think they considered me overly cooperative.

I opened the conversation by saying: "I have some questions for you, before you question me. First of all, what are you doing here? Supposedly, this is the FBI's jurisdiction. According to your origi-nal charter from when the CIA was created in 1947, you're not sup-posed to be working directly within the United States of America." (I knew some background on the CIA from all my reading on the Kennedy assassination.)

Well, I got the hem-haw. So, I then said, "Okay, before I answer anything, I want to go around the room, and I want you to tell me your name and what you do." I couldn't get both those answers out of more than three or four. With the rest, either they'd tell you a name but not what they do, or they would briefly describe what they do without identifying themselves, or they'd do neither. I thought that was kind of brash on their part, considering that I'm a sitting governor who's supposed to be in charge of his state. Even if you're CIA, you're still an American citizen. And I think most citizens, under most circumstances, would answer the governor's question.

I scanned their faces again and said, "Well, being that you're not being too cooperative with me, it's going to be difficult for me to cooperate with you."

But I got the gist of what they were after. All their questions centered around how we campaigned, how we achieved what we did, and did I think we truly could win when we went into it from the start? In short, how had the independent wrestler candidate pulled this off? I'd say it couldn't have been terribly productive for them. Some questions I answered and some I didn't, sometimes just out of spite: "I don't feel like answering that." Give back a little of the arrogance they'd shown me. But they were always very cordial and proper. It wasn't like anyone raised their voice to me, or tried to make me feel that somehow I was being interrogated. But it was one of the strangest experiences of my life. When I left that day, I pondered the meeting all the way back to my house, about a forty-five-minute to an hour drive, depending on traffic. I felt baffled. Somehow, I had to find out more.

I sat down in my study, and called my friend Dick Marcinko. I figured if anybody whom I knew operated around the CIA, he was probably the guy. Even though Marcinko is now out of the military and in the private sector, he's still fairly well connected in those circles. He's the author of the *Rogue Warrior* books, and he created the antiterrorist SEAL Team Six unit.

When I reached Dick at his home, and told him the scenario of what had transpired, he started laughing.

"Why do you think this is funny, Dick?" I asked.

"Well, I'm not privy to exactly why they were there," he said, "but I could give you my educated guess."

I said, "Well, that's better than I've got. Give me your thoughts."

He said, "They didn't see you coming. You were not on the radar screen. And, all of a sudden, you won a major election in the United States of America. The election caught them with their pants down, and their job is to gather intelligence and make predictions. Now, next to Bill Clinton, you're probably the most famous politician in America."

Then Dick added this: "I think they're trying to see if there are any more of you on the horizon."

Which I don't blame them for. It's like when you're on a SEAL team and you get caught up in some type of ambush that you weren't expecting. The first thing you do upon completion of that "op" is dissect what happened, so you'll never get caught like that again. Because the next time, you may be dead. So I can't begrudge them doing their jobs. But it was still very weird. I guess they needed information so that they could be fully prepared to know if it was going to happen again. Or did they need the information to eninsure it would *never* happen again? Was I that much of a threat?

It wasn't long after that meeting when I found out something else. I won't mention any names, in light of the "outing" of Valerie Plame. But I was stunned to learn that there are CIA operatives inside some state governments. They are not in executive positions—in other words, not appointed by the governor—but are permanent state employees. Governors come and go, but they keep working— in legitimate jobs, but with dual identities. In Minnesota, this person was at a deputy commissioner level, fairly high up.

Here's how I found out about this: The CIA person contacted my chief of staff, who then set up a meeting between the three of us. My chief of staff and I were informed that only we would know of the operative's identity, nobody else in state government. Later, when there was a change of status, I was also briefed by the new CIA person.

No one ever made me swear that I wouldn't talk about this and, now that I'm out of office, maybe I'm taking a chance. But I want to get it on the record. I could only speculate about other states, but I'm fairly certain the same situation exists all across the country. It would seem odd that only Minnesota would have CIA operatives, especially since Minnesota is not exactly a world port and doesn't have any really immense cities.

Are they put there to spy? To see the direction that state government is going, what's happening, and report back—to whom? And for what purpose? Do they think there are traitors in certain states?

I don't know. That part, I wasn't told. I'm left to wonder why our Constitution is being violated. It wasn't the last time that I'd run into the CIA, either.

TERRY: I didn't find out about it until after he was out of office. Jesse did try to protect me about a lot of things.

Was I afraid that something could happen to him? Are you kidding? Every day. When he was running for office, we didn't have a gate on the property at the time. I came out at six o'clock one morning, going to feed the horses and the chickens in the barn, and there was a guy sitting in his car in our driveway. I said, "Who are you?" He said, "Well, I want to talk to Jesse." I said, "Well, everybody knows that he's on the radio right now." There I was telling him, I'm here all alone, in the middle of nowhere. How stupid is that? Thankfully, the man simply drove off.

Another time Jade had come home from junior high school and was out in the barn doing chores. I had to go to the store, and I saw a car in front of the barn. I walked in, and there was some guy following Jade around. When I demanded to know who he was and what he was doing there, he said, "Oh, I'm just somebody who's gonna vote for Jesse, and I wanted to come see if he was home and talk to him." He turned out to be a perfectly nice man, but . . .

Then, after he became governor, there were always death threats and constant security. At first I would go off alone to the grocery store and one of the security people would end up telling me, "First Lady, please don't go anywhere unless you tell us." In the beginning it was kind of annoying, but, when you have security around you all the time, you end up figuring you must need it. I was terribly afraid when Tyrel refused to accept security. At the end, when they'd come and say, "Everybody get in the car, you have to go back to the mansion, there's been a threat," you think, Oh my God, somebody must be trying to kill us all the time.

The state patrol had me go and take self-defense lessons, along with my assistant and my executive protection person. They made me do gun training. I bought a purse that executive protection women carry, with the little zipper on the side. I learned how to quick-draw out of my purse. I was very accurate.

If I have to fight for myself, I can. It's not like I'm above violence. One time I was on a pay phone at a restaurant, when a drunk came up and started talking to me. Finally I said, "Hold on just a minute"—I was checking on the kids—and told him, "If you say one more filthy thing to me, I'm going to hit you with this telephone." I went back to talking, and he kept on. So I took that phone and I hit him as hard as I could, right in the forehead.

After Jesse left office and there was no protection around us anymore, it took a really long time for me to be comfortable going anywhere.

Toward the end of my term, on one of my days off, I was playing golf and having a bad round. It's competitive, me against the course, and I don't like the course to win that easily. (Which it usually does.) Anyway, I was already in a bad mood—when, all of a sudden, squad cars started pulling onto the golf course.

It turned out that some guy in a pickup truck had been in a restaurant that morning, said he'd seen me the night before and should have killed me then—but he was for sure going to get me tonight. As he left, a waitress wrote down his license plate, picked up the phone, called the local police, and said: "We just had a guy here threatening to kill the governor."

I had a public appearance that night. Right away my security had to cancel it. They will not put you out in public until the person making the threat gets apprehended. So an all-points bulletin goes out to all jurisdictions. My wife and daughter were about to go horseback riding. This also had to be canceled, and they were taken back to the residence. Meantime, they wanted me to leave the golf course.

I told them, "No! Damn it, we're on the fourteenth hole and I'm playing like crap. I'm not leaving until my game gets straightened out!"

Then I told them, "Guys, how come every time one of these fruitcakes comes out of the woodwork, I have to run and hide? This time it's changing. When we're done here, we're going to my house. I'm getting my Sig Sauer P-226 handgun. I have many boxes of Black Talon bullets sitting in my gun safe."

(The minute the announcement came that the sale of these bullets was being banned, I'd gone to my gun shop and cleaned the shelves. I would tease my security, "I've got more firepower than you." Law enforcement isn't allowed to use Black Talon, but, as a civilian, you still can.)

I said, "We're done being the hunted, boys. Starting today we're the hunters. We're gonna find this guy. And when we do, I'm gonna get him on the ground, and screw my nine-millimeter right into his ear. And I want the press to come and get a photograph of this. We're gonna send a message. That way, the next nut case who wants to try this is gonna know what the consequences are."

Oh my God, my troopers were panicked! As governor, I'm their commander in chief. They have to do what I say. I heard later from my friend Tony—who's still doing security for the new governor— "You should have seen the state public safety headquarters that day, when you said you were going after that guy. The brass were all going crazy, saying, '*Now* what do we do?'"

I proceeded to finish my round of golf. Fortunately for the troopers, I finished strong. I think I parred three of the last four holes, and felt pretty good about myself again. Thanks to the game of golf, I simmered down and came to my better senses.

And they caught the guy later that afternoon. They nailed him because this bozo even put out his intentions over the Internet. How dumb can you be? That's worse than leaving a fingerprint. Threatening a public official with violence is a felony, and he ended up serving time.

I had just gotten tired, after the incessant threats, of feeling like the hunted. My SEAL came out in me. We've got an old saying, "We don't get mad, we get even." And we make no bones about being the hunters.

"Can we quit talking about this now?"

I can tell these particular "fond memories" are making Terry a little anxious, so we begin reminiscing about the first time we went together to Mexico. It was a trade mission, my first one as governor, in the summer of 2000. "Honey, remember when we went to the famous Corona brewery, and found out that all the beer is made with Minnesota corn?" I ask her.

"Well, sure," she says, "Minnesota has the best corn, and Mexico knows it." They'd shown us pallets of corn, all with Minnesota stamps on them, which come down by train. So every time I drank a Corona, I thought, it might have the Mexican lime, but there's also a little taste of Minnesota.

One of the other highlights had been attending an authentic Mexican rodeo in Guadalajara. The *charros*, their cowboys, are unique, especially when it comes to calf roping. Our American cowboys rope the calf, then jump off the horse, run over and flip the calf and tie him up, and get all dirty in the process. The Mexican cowboy never leaves the saddle and accomplishes the same thing.

I was so pleased when they allowed my First Lady to pick any horse and ride it in the rodeo. Terry chose a beautiful Palomino. It was remarkably well trained, and she was out there spinnin' the circles with her dark hair flying. Traditionally in Mexico, women don't ride the *charros'* horses.

"I think they were pretty impressed with your horse skills," I say to Terry. "Also the fact that you would ride, and I wouldn't."

"Well, you're not a horse person," she says.

"Yup, you can out-ride me any day, babe. But put us on Harleys, and I'll beat you!"

She laughed. "That's true," she says.

I started thinking about how so many of us in the United States, myself included, have a false impression of Mexico because of the border towns—which *we* created. Mexicali, Tijuana, Nuevo Laredo, Juarez, and others largely came into existence because of our outlawing of alcohol. When Prohibition happened in the U.S. in the 1920s, a lot of drinkers simply ran across the border into Mexico. That's what also brought about all the prostitution and gambling activities in those little towns. Mexico is still dealing with this today, the result of our Prohibition.

Border areas like Mexicali are also coping with another of our exports—the multinational corporation. Since the passage of the North American Free Trade Agreement (NAFTA) in 1994, which eliminated most trade restrictions between our two countries, hundreds of factories called *maquiladoras* have sprung up. There they make goods on the cheap and ship them back across the border. Companies like Sony, Mitsubishi, Honeywell, and Daewoo now have assembly plants in Mexicali. The big food processors like Nestlé are visible, too.

President Clinton predicted this would be a boon to everyone. It certainly has been for the corporations, which have cut back their labor costs and increased their profits. Thousands of workers from Mexico's poorest southern states have arrived to work in Mexicali. They make the equivalent, I was told, of a little more than four dollars a day. But it's better than having no job at all. So, on the one hand, Mexicali is experiencing an economic boom. It's constantly growing, with close to a million people now. Many of the newly rich have moved into gated communities.

I'm a staunch capitalist, and I was a big supporter of NAFTA in the beginning. Today, I have a lot of reservations about what it's brought about. NAFTA has resulted in hundreds of thousands of job losses in the U.S., because employers moved south of the border. Half of the people working in these Mexican *maquiladoras* are women, and there is also child labor, and long hours, with no right to unionize. They're really nothing more than sweatshops, in a lot of cases.

On the outskirts of town, you see the ramshackle homes made from cinder blocks and scraps of metal. You see the waste-littered streets. Often, these people have no running water or electricity. They are the people of the *maquiladoras*. So driving through Mexicali does make you wonder—what price, in terms of quality of life, are a lot of people paying in order to enrich these companies? Would they maybe be better off sticking with agriculture, since the Mexicali Valley produces some of the biggest crops in all Mexico?

"It makes me think of my grandfather," I say to Terry as we ease out of town onto Mexico Highway 5. "He'd grown up working in the coal mines of Pennsylvania, after his parents came to this country from Slovakia. He knew it was gonna kill him, and that's why he brought my dad and his other kids out to Minnesota. Looking for a better life. So you can't blame the poorest Mexicans for coming to northern Baja, trying to find the same thing. It's just . . ."

My voice cracks for a minute. Terry fills in my sentence. "What are the real opportunities?"

CHAPTER 6

Breaking Down Barriers: China and Cuba

"History will absolve me."

—*Fidel Castro*

Passing through Mexicali, I can't help but think about another country I've had an opportunity to visit: China. Early in the twentieth century, Mexicali was actually more Chinese than Mexican, and even today the border town has probably the highest concentration of Chinese residents within Mexico.

Originally, the Chinese came as laborers working for the Colorado River Land Company that was building a massive irrigation system in the Valle de Mexicali. As often happened with immigrant labor, the high wages they were promised never came to pass. In fact, a desert peak below Mexicali is still called "El Chinero," commemorating the deaths of about 160 laborers who never made it across the San Felipe Desert. A Mexican boatman had dropped them off with assurances that Mexicali was close by; in fact, it was forty miles of burning desert away.

The laborers who survived created their own Chinatown which, during the Prohibition era, had an underground tunnel setup that led to the whorehouses and opium dens and, for the bootleggers, across to Calexico on the American side. Later on, Mexicali served as Mexican headquarters for the nationalist Chinese party of Sun Yat-Sen. Today, in Mexicali's Chinatown, you hear people talking a blend of Spanish and Cantonese and, like one of our guidebooks says, "Only in Mexicali will you find banners of the Virgin of Guadalupe hanging side by side with Chinese paper lamps."

Interestingly, the University of Minnesota has the largest population of Chinese students of any campus in the U.S. and, when I was governor, I met with a group of about twenty of them. They'd told me that 80 percent of their people are still involved in agriculture, but that China's farmland is pretty much maxed out. I thought it would be great if U.S. farmers, in Minnesota and elsewhere, could sell their surpluses to China. Here we've got grain rotting away in silos, but the potential profit from doing this could be enormous and we'd be helping their people at the same time.

I became a big supporter of bringing China into the World Trade Organization (WTO), something that was also one of President Clinton's foremost concerns. They'd moved from a strictly command economy to one where market forces were playing an increasing part, and it was definitely time to break down the remaining trade barriers. In May 2000, Clinton invited me to the White House again as part of a gathering of dignitaries to discuss China and the WTO, for what he called "the most important national security vote that will be cast this year." I was honored to be sitting in the front row, not far from former presidents Carter and Ford. Clinton called his plan "an American vote. You know, it unites Henry Kissinger"—the president paused a moment, glancing down at Kissinger—"and Jesse Ventura. And not at a wrestling match!" (I guess Bill still had a sense of humor about me, despite my suggestion a couple of months earlier about taking out that hill in the Middle East).

His administration encouraged me to take an active role, and I'm proud to have been a part of the effort that resulted in China being admitted to the WTO in December 2001. That's how I ended up spending a week in China on a trade mission early the next year. First in Beijing for several days, and then Shanghai.

It was humbling for me to be in China. There was an entire dinner in my honor in the Great Hall of the People, right near where the students were run over by the tanks at Tiananmen Square. I sure never figured a day would come in my life when the most populous country in the world would have a dinner dedicated to me in their most important building! I remember the food came in six or seven different courses, and was just remarkable. I also remember multitudes of toasts. The Chinese seem to be very big on toasting.

Whenever I traveled, I was never caught in a traffic jam because all the streets were completely blocked off when I passed through. High-level foreign visitors are treated well. What impressed me most about China was its cleanliness, and how orderly the people are. They seem have a natural humility, going about their business and sticking to themselves.

But China is definitely absorbing Western culture. I went there expecting to see everyone running around looking like Mao Tse-tung. Well, at times you will see the traditional Chinese, if you get out to rural areas, but in the cities I saw more golf shirts and jeans than you could imagine. Not only do they dress like us, but they're building freeways now with the identical green signs that we have. Underneath the Chinese language, there are smaller letters written in English.

I was amazed at how they can be—it's almost an oxymoron—so rich and so poor at the same time. I found out from my agriculture commissioner, Gene Hugeson, that the average farm size in China is one acre. I said, "Gene, we couldn't even turn one of our big tractors on an acre!" He laughed and said, "You're right, governor."

The people live very meagerly, but construction is happening at an unbelievable rate. I was informed that, in the late 1990s, 20 percent of the world's T-cranes, the big ones that build skyscrapers, were in Shanghai. In Shanghai, you could put three or four New York Cities in the downtown skyline. I've never seen anything like it. I'm still trying to figure out where all the revenue comes from, I guess maybe in large part from us—because China now holds a large part of America's debt.

I found the two cities to be completely different. Beijing was as attractive, and seemed very businesslike. Of course, that's where the Forbidden City is, the center of government. I found Shanghai much more of a fun city beneath all the commerce going on. You walk the streets after dark, and it's every bit as vibrant as New York. Young people and lights, a rollicking night life.

In a country that's supposed to be communist, that may sound kind of amazing, but I think it's by design. Even though China now has Hong Kong back, that city is still a product of the Brits. The Chinese look at Hong Kong as something of a bastard child that they want to crack on the head every now and then for misbehaving. But they can hold up Shanghai as moving into the twenty first century the Chinese way.

The food I ate in China was unbelievably good. Unfortunately, as I would also come to find out in Mexico, we're being cheated somewhat in the United States—because the native culture's foods are far better than the so-called Mexican and Chinese that we get here. For some reason, we believe everything needs to be deep-fried. Rarely is any food served that way in China. I'm trying to figure out what gets lost in translation once it crosses our border. Like their mandarin duck—oh, incredible!

You do a lot of "stick eating" over there—food cooked on sticks like shish kabobs. It seems that's a popular way of cooking food in Asia. When I served in Southeast Asia for seventeen months, there was nothing better than barbecue on a stick! Somehow I think a stick holds flavor better than metal does. But you've got to be smarter with your barbecuing, because it's easier to burn the stick and lose the food. We Americans are in too much of a hurry, that's why we go with metal.

While I was there, Minnesota's 3M company signed a contract to produce all of China's license plates. The deal had been in the offing for a while—I really had no bearing on it—but it was signed, sealed, and delivered that week. The other thing that's going great guns in China is Hormel Meats. Minnesota has a Hormel plant that's now producing all the sausage for their pizza. And the Chinese have started to go crazy over pizza.

I hate to say this, but the McDonald's in China are packed, too. Apparently they haven't seen the movie *Supersize Me*. Did you know that McDonald's brought a lawsuit to try to keep that documentary off the air in America? I haven't eaten fast food since I saw it, and I feel guilty that I ever took my kids there. Think about it: They put warning labels on cigarettes, but ordinarily you wouldn't die from smoking in less than twenty years. With McDonald's, it's been proven that if you eat there for forty-five days straight, you're dead. There should be a warning label on the wrapper telling people to beware of eating only at McDonald's. Something like, "You need to supplement your diet with foods other than what this place serves."

Anyway, I enjoyed visiting the Hormel factory. Although it's overseen by the U.S., the upper management are all Chinese. I know it sounds like a cliché, but you could literally eat off the floor. The plant is out in the suburbs, where farming is still going on. Right up the street, you'll see the family with the one-acre farm and the big-horned cow.

I came away from China fully realizing that they will be *the* economic power of the world, and a lot quicker than anyone imagines. Within the next decade, I would say. You truly feel it being there. When the Chinese people focus on something, they are gung-ho. And what a work force they have! One fifth of the human population!

I'd predicted, when I testified before Congress in favor of China entering the WTO back in 2000, that their trade with the U.S. could triple within the next twenty years. Well, it's already started to happen. U.S. exports to China have continued to increase dramatically since they became part of the WTO. In fact, from 1999 to 2004, they went up nearly ten times faster than our exports to the rest of the world. And China has become one of the fastest-growing overseas markets for the American farmer—our agricultural exports to the Chinese topped more than $5 billion in 2003.

I only wish I could say that our government is as forward-thinking about another country that we've long been alienated from. And that one is only ninety miles off our shores.

Not long after we cross the U.S.–Mexico border, I shake my head and say to Terry: "Isn't it crazy? No one even looked at our passports. But if we wanted to travel to Cuba, and got caught by our government, our passports would end up revoked! We might even get sent to jail. Remember when the Bush people stopped you from going along with me on the trade mission?"

That was a trip Terry had really wanted to make. "They've been trying to get rid of Castro, one way or another, for almost fifty years," she says. "I wonder when they'll just give it up."

I grew up in fear of Fidel Castro. I was young in 1959 when his revolution in Cuba took place, so it wasn't high on my radar screen. But I remember the propaganda. I vaguely recall hearing about the Bay of Pigs. It dominated the Walter Cronkite news at 5:30 when I'd be home from school. As a kid, the name fascinated me. Why would they name a place after pigs?

As an adult, when I started reading books trying to figure out what really happened to President Kennedy, Castro and Cuba of course loomed large. So did Oswald and his Fair Play for Cuba Committee, his attempt to get a visa to Cuba on a trip to Mexico. So Cuba has fascinated me for years, though I never dreamed I'd have a chance to actually go there, much less to spend an hour with Castro himself.

I must admit to having another fixation about Cuba. When Clinton was president and I attended my first National Governors Convention, I raised my hand and questioned him about why we continued to have an economic boycott against the Cubans. I had definite personal reasons. At the time, I was smoking cigars, and I said that I was sick and tired of having to feel like a criminal every time I wanted a Cuban cigar, because they're some of the best in the world. At some point during Clinton's presidency, Cuba had shot down an American plane that strayed over its air space. Clinton talked about that, and the allegations of human rights violations, as justifications for why the boycott had to continue. Which still didn't fly much with me.

Jeb Bush was governor of Florida and, at the end of the meeting, he sent word over to me: "Stop bringing up Cuba. It causes me too many problems when you do that." He also let it be known that he would get me all the Cuban cigars I wanted if I kept my mouth shut. At the time I was smoking Romeo Julietas. They come in these neat-looking silver tubes and I had an empty one. So, as I passed by the governor on my way out, I stuck it in the front of his coat pocket and said, "There's my brand, Jeb, except I don't think a box of cigars can buy me off." And I kept on walking.

Amazingly, two weeks later at my governor's residence, there arrived a box of Romeo Julieta Cubans! I can't recall whether Jeb Bush personally sent it, or if it just came anonymously. But I laughed—you mean Jeb really thinks I'll stay quiet about Cuba for a few cigars?

My last year in office, 2002, a Minnesota trade mission to Cuba came about after a few of the sanctions dealing with food and agricultural products had been lifted. This provided us an opening to seek deals with the Cuban government, for humanitarian purposes. President Bush did not want me to personally go. The White House sent a clear message on that.

Headline: JEB BUSH APPEALS TO VENTURA OVER CUBA TRIP

TALLAHASSEE, Florida—Citing a lack of "basic freedoms" in Cuba, Gov. Jeb Bush urged Minnesota Gov. Jesse Ventura to reconsider his plans to attend a trade exposition there next month. . . .

But a spokesman for Ventura said the Minnesota governor did not agree with Bush's "isolationist approach" and would not alter his plans.

—CNN.com, August 30, 2002

Then the feds restricted the First Lady's passport. The only way Terry could have come would have been to sneak in and meet me there. That's when my antennae went sky-high: Wait a minute, aren't we home of the brave, land of the free? We're not at war with Cuba. As members of what's supposed to be a free society, my wife and I should be able to go there without repercussions from my own country—economic boycott or not.

Here's the part that really got to me. Bush's top man for the Western Hemisphere in the State Department, Otto Reich, came out publicly with the statement that he certainly hoped my group and I were not going to Cuba to sample the sex trade. Because, according to him, Cuba has a high prostitution rate. I demanded an apology from George Bush to myself and every citizen of Minnesota, for one of his underlings making such a reckless statement. I never got a response from anyone in his administration.

After the trip, when the press asked me about it, I said: "Well, in our week in Cuba, I didn't see any of this sex trade. And if we go back again, I would enjoy for Otto Reich to come along, because obviously he knows where it's at! Clearly he's an expert, so I can only assume he's partaken of it."

Our party on the trip was very large, people from Minnesota agriculture, and others. The Cubans had a big expo-type fair, and Castro came to that. A family from Rochester, Minnesota, had brought some cattle down and Fidel ended up befriending these two cute little kids. Castro is brilliant in that he plays his publicity like a conductor of a fine symphony. He ended up bringing the kids as his personal guests to some big function, where they got to sit with him in his private box.

I found the Cuban people exceptionally friendly, and you could tell it was genuine. Not a whole lot different from other Latino countries I've visited. They're all kind of out of the same melting pot, in their own ways of tradition. Being there reaffirmed my position that the American sanctions are wrong. You realize that these are only hurting the Cuban people. I guess the hope is that then the people will rise up and throw Fidel out. Except what I saw is that the Cuban people are also exceptionally patriotic. They're stubborn. They're not going to let us win with our embargo. They're going to stick with Fidel until he dies. Yet, by the same token, I saw amongst them a great love for America. Not America's government, but the American people.

I went to the fair for several days, and spoke at numerous press conferences, and even did my weekly radio broadcast live from Havana back to Minnesota. I also spoke at the University of Havana. That's when I realized how much respect the people have for authority. I suppose it's that way in all dictatorships, but it's a funny story. We were walking onto the campus and I was accompanied by my two regular security guys from Minnesota, an interpreter, and three of Castro's personal bodyguards. That's a total of six people around me at all times. As we approached the auditorium where I was to speak, a large group of people were congregated out on the sidewalk, not necessarily waiting for us, but just there. One of Castro's bodyguards reminded me a lot of Teofilo Stevenson, the former heavyweight boxer from Cuba—same massive body, wearing the white Panama shirt. As we reached the crowd, I saw his hand simply come up waist high, and he made a half-moon circle with his fingertips.

It was like Moses parting the Red Sea. Those people instantly separated and we passed right through the center of the crowd. I turned to my own security guys and gave 'em the burn, saying, "How come *you* guys can't do that? Maybe I'll bring these guys home with me and leave you here!" They turned a bit red in the face, and more or less had to apologize that in a free country, the people don't always act that way. In fact, back home we got pies thrown at us more times than any parting of the Red Sea. Anyway, I was impressed.

It was a full house at the university. I just talked from my heart. About what I had seen in Cuba, things that had been made known to me about their advancements in education and medicine, and what they should be proud of. Also, I spoke of how the boycott should end, and our two countries should become friends rather than adversaries. The students went wild.

Maybe some people reading this book will think I'm a traitor to the United States. But I don't think I am. I always felt, in looking at this situation, that it was wrong. And I now know why. It came to me one night in Mexico. China is communist, the same as Cuba, and yet we have no problem trading with China. In fact, today we can't get over there quick enough. The difference is simple: China welcomes our corporations. Cuba threw them out. It's a basic decision of corporate America: We will punish Cuba because Castro stuck it to us by nationalizing everything after he came to power. What other reason could there be? China is far more powerful but we now welcome them into global trade with open arms—as we should—while we continue this bitter, hostile policy towards Cuba. It must be because there are still people alive in the corporate world who got hammered by Fidel's revolution.

We spent two days in a row at the big trade fair, and that's where I was introduced to Fidel. It's amazing, but the common people on the street all call him Fidel. When I met him, I called him Mr. President. He's not really an elected president, but I didn't know what else to say. You can't really call him Mr. Dictator.

I've never known a handshake like Castro's. He comes up to me, winds up, pulls back his hand all the way to his shoulder, and thrusts it out with great excitement. I'd never seen anyone shake hands so enthusiastically—and I've shaken hands with a lot of people. That's what I'll always remember. And, of course, our conversation.

Our meeting was set up in a room at the trade fair. It was on a Friday, our last day, around noon. Fidel was there waiting for me. We sat in two chairs right across from each other. He had his interpreter along, and some of his security people. My chief of staff and my security were in the room, too. The entire time we were in Cuba, my security was allowed to stay armed, except for those roughly two hours with Castro. About a half hour beforehand, they had to turn their weapons in to Castro's people. Then a half hour after Fidel was out of the room, the weapons were returned to them. I understood.

The first words out of his mouth were, "You are a man of great courage."

I was puzzled by this and said, "Well, Mr. President, how can you say that? You don't know me."

He looked back at me and said, "Because you defied your president to come here." I guess he has pretty good "intel."

And I looked right back at him and said, "Well, Mr. President, you'll find that I defy most everything."

Castro laughed. Who knows, maybe he felt this was something we had in common.

The whole conversation, on my part, was in English and was interpreted for him in Spanish by a lady. But I don't think he really needs her. Because now and then, I'd say something that was funny and he'd laugh before the interpretation happened. As good as Castro is at masking the fact, I think he understands English very well. Let's put it this way: I'm sure he does English far, far better than I do Spanish.

Our conversation consisted of a great deal of Castro—for lack of a better phrase—bragging about his country. I don't use the term bragging negatively; I don't think it's any different from what I would do. Just as I have great pride in Minnesota, he has the same for Cuba. He was extremely proud of the fact that they have the highest literacy rate of any Latin country in the hemisphere. He's also proud that they have the best medical care. I found him very engaging. He's a master of hyperbole.

I told him the same thing I'd told the students—that I felt the boycott was wrong. It did nothing positive for either of our countries, and it was time for America to get over it. His questions of me were mainly about my political future. He was interested in the fact that I was an independent and didn't belong to either of the two major parties—a kind of rogue element being the governor of a state.

Time passes very quickly when it's only an hour and you're sitting with Fidel Castro. He's so perceptive. I'll never forget that at one point I glanced at my watch and immediately Castro said, "I'm sorry, do you have to be somewhere?"

I said, "No, sir. But I'm only here a short time with you, and there are some personal questions I wanted to ask you before our hour is up. So I was just checking my watch to see how much more time I had. So—can I ask you one?"

His answer was, "Ask me anything you'd like."

Maybe that meant, "It doesn't mean I'll answer it, but I'm giving you free rein to ask." I told him about how I was only twelve years old when John F. Kennedy was killed. And how later, as an adult, I started studying the murder. I told him that I came not to believe the Warren Commission, or what my country has portrayed as being officially what happened.

I said, "Naturally, in studying this, there are a few scenarios where you come up very strongly as being a part of it; that Oswald was somehow linked to you. You were around back then, and much older than I was, and more involved. I would like to know your perception of what happened to John F. Kennedy."

For the next twenty minutes, I couldn't stop him from talking. The things I recall are impressed in my head and will remain with me forever. First of all, he said it was an "inside job," meaning that the assassination was orchestrated from within the United States. He stared at me very intently and said—which also told me that he was aware of my military background—"You know as well as I do, Oswald couldn't make the shots."

Then he went on to explain the reason he knew that. During the Cuban revolution, he was the main guy who taught and carried out sniper work. Knowing all he did about this, he knew Oswald couldn't have accomplished the job with the antiquated Mannlicher-Carcano rifle that he used.

Then Fidel described why it was an inside job. First of all, he said, he was very close to the Soviet Union at that time. "The Soviets didn't do it," he stated emphatically. In fact, the Kremlin leaders had told him about Kennedy: "You can talk to this man." Apparently the Russians were pleased that Kennedy had enough of an open mind to at least consider their side's position, on Cuba and other matters. Besides, neither country wanted another nuclear confrontation like the Cuban Missile Crisis.

Secondly, Castro said, "*I* didn't do it." Again his gaze was penetrating. He went on, "I'm not suicidal crazy. Why would I destroy my Cuba, the country I love so much? If I would have ordered Kennedy killed, and the United States found out, we wouldn't exist anymore. They would have unleashed everything they had on us, and basically blown us off the face of the earth. Why would I take that risk?"

It made sense to me. Unless you truly believe in David and Goliath. Not only that, but look who was waiting in the wings—Lyndon Baines Johnson. I didn't see his becoming president as a positive for Fidel Castro.

He also recalled for me how, at the moment Kennedy was killed, he was meeting in Havana with a French journalist named Jean Daniel, whom Kennedy had personally sent to see him. Castro felt very strongly that Kennedy was considering a change in policy towards Cuba. I could tell that he felt Cuba was worse off without Kennedy alive.

He said again, "It was completely an inside job. It was done by people within the United States of America."

I wanted to ask for specifics—it felt like he knew some—but our time was up.

I believed what Castro said to me that day. I won't go so far as to say I trusted him, after a single meeting. He's a dictator, and dictators are a strange breed. In my opinion, they tend to become victims of their own power. They can never be fully honest. I don't think they dare to be, because there is always paranoia about someone waiting in the wings to take over. Maybe after he decided to retire, and put his brother Raul in place for good, and headed for the beach—without the pressures of being a dictator—then you could truly trust him. As it is, he needs to have informants everywhere. He has no choice.

Unfortunately, I didn't have time to talk with Fidel about Che Guevara. I'd have wanted to get to know him a bit better anyway, to bring up something as politically sensitive as Che might be to him. I've read different accounts that they had fallen out somewhat, before Che was killed in 1967. I don't believe that, because if Fidel did have a problem with Che, why has he allowed Che to become such a figure in Cuba? You don't see Fidel's picture on the side

of the most massive building in downtown Havana. You see Che
Guevara's.

Che is a very interesting individual to read about. I respect him
because, as much as I oppose communism, Che believed in it
with the same fervor that I have for capitalism. I respect the fact
that he would die for his convictions. How did a man as bright
as Che develop the hatred for the United States and all that we
stood for? I've eliminated jealousy as a reason. He was a medical
doctor, a healer. It clearly had to be that he saw the results of what
we did to other countries, in the *name* of freedom and capitalism.
Which, in many ways, was not pretty if you were on the wrong
end of it.

So, a mirror of Che Guevara has a profound place in my house.
I'm not the least ashamed to say that. When I go to wash my hands,
I look at Che.

Whenever I did a trade mission, I'd try to stay up late the last night
so that I could sleep on the plane ride home. I love to get on the
plane bright and early in the morning, conk out, and only wake up
as the wheels were touching down. It's not that I fear flying, it's just
that sleeping on flights is more entertaining.

So, that last night, I turned to my Cuban bodyguards and said,
"Well, take me for a night on Havana." They didn't seem to understand quite what I meant. "Well, where would you like to go?" they
asked.

I said, "I don't know, it's your town. I'll leave it to you."

They took me to the infamous Club Havana. It's a beautiful
nightclub, maybe the biggest one in Cuba. It's not a strip club; I
would classify it more as a Las Vegas type of entertainment show.
In a way—and I'll date myself here—like the Spanish version of Ed
Sullivan. They bring out Latino comedians, a variety of different

musical acts, and have beautiful Cuban girls who dance in their feathered native costumes.

It's also a unique place, in that, in a corner, they had a vintage Knucklehead Harley Davidson motorcycle. I went over and looked at it. If you look down at where the V-twins are on the opposite side, the first two numbers are the year, stamped into the serial number of the motorcycle. All bikers know that. This was either a 1936 or 1937. It was original Marlon Brando, with the big headlight, the handlebars out to the side, vintage. I told my Cuban bodyguards that, in America, it would sell like hotcakes. I said, "Guys, if we can smuggle that out, I can guarantee you $60,000 to $70,000 U.S. without an argument." I think they were considering it.

While we were there, the MC set up a contest. First they went table to table finding out where everyone was from. Of course, there was our table from Minnesota, as well as a table from Canada; one from, I think, Israel; a table from Australia; and a table from California. What the Californians were doing there, apparently illegally, I didn't bother to ask. Anyway, every table then had to designate someone to participate. I didn't think either of my own bodyguards, or Fidel's three, or my interpreter would be too keen on that. So I volunteered. I figured, somebody has to represent Minnesota here, why not me?

We get up on stage and find out that it's a salsa dance contest. Well, I barely know what the salsa is, I just know it's Latino. But this is my last night in Havana, Cuba, what do I care if I get laughed off the stage? I went ahead and salsa'd. In the contest, I made it to the final three. All of a sudden they were talking in Spanish and holding their hands over the other two people, and my interpreter came up saying, "Oh, don't worry, that's for second and third, you've already won."

I was trying to determine, did Castro's people ensure that I won? Or did they just let me win because I was so bad and yet having fun doing it? They actually gave me prizes—a CD and a towel. How honorable the Cubans were, to pick someone from the United States as a winner at salsa dancing! That had to be a rarity in Havana. In light of what President Bush's people had done to me before I went to Cuba, I contemplated sending a communication to Mr. Bush when I got back, asking if he'd okay my passport to return and defend my title a year from now. Wouldn't that bring great honor to the United States?

The night wore on. As I said, Castro apparently has informants everywhere. One of them came up and whispered something to one of my Cuban bodyguards, who then whispered to my bodyguard, who then told me. It seems that some CIA operatives were tailing me. I thought to myself—is that for my benefit, or for theirs? Am I in some type of danger that they need to be following me around? I don't think so. I doubt that Fidel Castro would want an American governor coming to harm on his island, when I'm there on a mission of good will. So, I ruled out that somehow the CIA were hanging around to protect me, especially considering I had my own armed bodyguards, plus Fidel's three.

The Cubans had only one question: Did I want to lose them? If this made me uncomfortable, they would help me get rid of these guys and we could go on about our business.

I said, "No, we're not going to even acknowledge that they're here. Who cares? We're not doing anything wrong. There's nothing they'll be able to blackmail me with, or take back to the U.S. about any misbehavior on my part. Let's ignore them. They're not going to ruin our night."

So we ended up going to another club, and I don't know if we were followed there or not. The subject was never brought up again. It could be the Cuban security team decided a means to lose them on the way, I never inquired. What I did do was put this incident on file in the back of my mind.

When I came back to the States, a week or so later I had a two o'clock meeting penciled in on my schedule—but who I was supposed to meet with was blank. That's very unusual for a governor's public schedule. So I asked my chief of staff, "What's the deal with the two o'clock meeting?" He rolled his eyes and said, "CIA."

I expected it, because they have their jobs to do. I had been with Castro and why wouldn't they want to debrief me? And that's precisely what it was. The two agents from the CIA came into my office—one of them I'd already met, shortly after I became governor—and they very respectfully gave me the old Twenty Questions routine. They went through their litany, and I answered them as honestly as I could. Typical intelligence questions: What did Castro's health appear to be like? Was he in control of all his faculties? Did he seem bright for his age?

I said I felt that he was very much in control. His mental capacity seemed to be right-on. I even opinioned a little bit. I told them, "I know his mom lived to be a hundred, so it's in his genes, and looks to me like he just might make it. Do I think this guy is gonna die within the next couple of years? I'd have to tell you no, he looks fit as a fiddle for his age."

Their faces were expressionless. They said they were finished, and thanked me. I looked coldly at them and said, "You're done. You're all done?"

They said yes.

I said, "You're sure? There's no other question you want to ask me, there's nothing you want to tell me, anything like that?"

"No, sir, we're all done."

In that case, I wanted to send them back with something to think about. "Well," I said, "I have something that I want to tell *you*, and

I'll leave it up to your discretion who should hear this. You take it to whoever you think is appropriate. A need-to-know basis."

They feigned being very surprised and said, "Governor, we don't understand what you're talking about."

I said, "Well, here's what I'm talking about. If you or your people ever put a tail on me again, and don't tell me beforehand, and I discover it—you're gonna find the tail floating in the river."

They looked at me in seeming astonishment. They looked at each other and pretended they didn't have a clue as to what I was talking about.

I said, "That's fine. If *you* don't get it, you can take it and tell it to somebody who does. I'm sure somebody upstairs, above you, knows exactly what I'm talking about—*if* you don't. So you be the judge. Like I say, take it to where it needs to go."

I've often wondered how far it went. Did it get to George Tenet, who was director of CIA at the time? To George Bush? Dick Cheney? Or maybe it didn't even leave the room. Maybe they didn't even bother with passing along my little message, I don't know. But at least I got it off my chest, and let them know that the next time they try to fool me, they ought to do a better job.

One other unique thing happened out of my trip to Cuba. At the turn of the year that Christmas, a FedEx messenger came and delivered a calendar. In it were twelve beautiful photos of Cuba—and it was autographed by Fidel Castro. How the Cubans managed to get this to me at my home address, I have no clue, but apparently their intelligence network within the U.S. must be fairly good. Since Fidel is not allowed to use our mail system, he had to send it by private courier.

Then, shortly before I was to leave office, Castro sent an emissary to the governor's residence. He wanted to reassure me about something.

"Always remember, governor," the man said, "a friend to Cuba will always remain a friend to Cuba."

When I was there, Fidel himself had been very strong in inviting me back. He'd said, "The next time you come, you come as my guest and you bring your family and your children." I bet I'd have a pretty nice place at the beach if I went on vacation! It's just strange to me that I'm not able to do that, not legally.

I don't look forward to Castro's death, because I fear there will be a massive amount of turmoil in Cuba, and the Cuban people have suffered enough. But they have the strength to face it, I believe.

I was appalled that President Bush and our government turned down Castro's offer of sending doctors, when Hurricane Katrina hit New Orleans. I thought that was one of the most arrogant, stupid decisions that I've seen this president make. When your enemy holds out an olive branch, it takes a far better statesman to accept it than to reject it. Had I been president, those doctors would have been warmly received. And a personal letter of thank you would have gone to Castro and the Cuban government. Have we ever helped them when they've been hit by a hurricane? I don't think so.

The man is brilliant. Was Fidel doing that for political reasons, or as an act of kindness? That's the question we'll never know the answer to. But you know what? Having met Castro, I'd give it 50–50. I think it was both kindness to the people of New Orleans, because he has personally lived through something similar in Cuba, and it was also a brilliant strategic political move on his part. A way of showing "I'm a dictator with a heart."

CHAPTER 7

Transitions:
Down Mexico Highway 5

"It was mid-February and U.S. Rep. Jim Ramstad, a Minnesota Republican, was among 24 members of the House and Senate accompanying President Clinton on a state visit to Mexico. Shortly after he stepped off the plane and moved down the receiving line, the Minnesotan got a surprise that interrupted the formality of the situation.

"The congressman recalls: 'We had just gotten off Air Force One, and President Clinton introduced me to President Ernesto Zedillo as a congressman from Minnesota.' Zedillo's eyes 'got big as saucers, and he said, "You know Jesse?" Later on, Zedillo asked me six or seven times if I would arrange a trade mission to bring Ventura to Mexico. . . . The same thing happened with cab drivers—they wanted to know about Jesse.'"

—Alternative Journalism Review, *September 1999*

Somewhere on the outskirts of Mexicali, we pass a marker noting that Ernesto Zedillo, President of Mexico from 1994 until 2000, spent most of his youth here. Terry and I had been in Mexico City on official business when Zedillo was still president, after Vicente Fox had just been elected. (By law, presidents in Mexico only serve a single six-year term.) It was the transition period, so I met with both men. I looked at Zedillo as a true statesman. Fox was the first man elected in ninety-some years who wasn't part of the PRI party, and Zedillo could have made it very difficult for him. But he didn't. He helped Fox completely, even though he took a lot of heat from his party for making the transition so smooth. Zedillo showed that the country of Mexico came first, before politics.

As Terry and I reminisced about Zedillo, it brought an incident from my own transition to mind. Arne Carlson, a moderate Republican, was the outgoing governor when I came into office. Four years earlier, when I'd ended my term as mayor of Brooklyn Park, Carlson had decided to honor me at his annual State of the State Address. While mayor, I'd managed to implement policies that helped a very high crime rate in Brooklyn Park drop dramatically. Carlson had personally taken me aside at his residence for a chat.

"Remember what he said to me that night, Terry? 'We need people like you.' He was practically begging me to reconsider and run again for mayor. I said, 'Well, governor, I did my four years, and now I'm going back to the private sector.'"

"Well, in hindsight, I think that's where he would have preferred you stayed," Terry says.

"Yeah, but I figured it couldn't hurt to remind him. When I met with him the morning after I won governor, I said, 'Well, governor, you know you're responsible for this.' He said, 'What do you mean?' I said, 'Well, back in '94 you took me aside after I stepped down as mayor and said government needed me and I shouldn't be leaving.

And I took that to heart!' You'd have thought I said the worst thing in the world! His face flushed red with anger, and he totally ignored me!"

"Gee, I can't understand why," Terry says.

"It was sort of like my relationship with the Minnesota media. I always used to have to tell them—'That's a joke—joke—joke.' I can't help it if people don't appreciate my humor!"

"Well, what Governor Carlson did to you after that wasn't so funny."

It was sad, but true. It used to be that, as a matter of courtesy, governors didn't speak publicly about their successors. That unspoken rule was broken by Governor Carlson. He would never come out to support me, but was constantly going to the media with his criticisms. Since I left, I haven't said one word about the current governor. I consider that part of the dignity of having held the office.

You think about transitions when you're in a new one. The day after the election in 1998, when it had dawned on my "kitchen cabinet" and me that we were completely clueless as to what to do next, I can't remember who broke the ice first. Our entire focus had been on winning the election and, by necessity, we couldn't look beyond that. But nobody in the Independence Party had ever held a state-level job. If anybody had held one locally, it was as a councilperson in a rural suburb somewhere. And here we were: in a matter of two months we needed to be up-to-speed and running the state of Minnesota. And not embarrass ourselves in the process—because the people had entrusted me with this responsibility.

By late afternoon, we'd all been sitting there for about three hours without getting anything much accomplished. We did go and get doughnuts and coffee. We were able to figure that out! Terry's best friend, an attorney named Shirley, had run private sector companies, but even she said, "This is bigger than what I know. I have no experience at this level."

Fortunately, Shirley was very good friends with Tim Penny, a former Minnesota Congressman. Tim was a rogue moderate Democrat, cosponsor of the famous Penny-Kasich bill to balance the budget in Washington. He'd resigned from the House out of his disgust with what the political process was becoming. I'll never forget the phone call Shirley made to the Congressman that day. She found out that my election had been his son's first opportunity to vote. He'd pulled the lever for this ex-wrestler third-party maniac, or whatever else I'd been labeled, and he'd come home and told his father.

I whispered, "Shirley, tell him we always have a twelve-step program for all recovering Democrats and Republicans."

Tim was ready to help us regardless. "There's only one guy I know who has the ability to step in and organize at this level," he said. That was his former chief of staff in Washington, Steven Bosacker. Steven now held a similar position with the Board of Regents at the University of Minnesota. Tim called Steven who, that Saturday night, came out to my house. We hadn't talked long before I knew I had my chief of staff. Not only could I see that he was immensely qualified, but when we talked politics, Steven informed me that back in the eighties he had voted for John Anderson for President. A third-party candidate. So had I. He wouldn't feel that only a Democrat or Republican could get the job done.

To give you an idea of how good Steven was: We were in the transition period and all putting in long hours; twelve-hour days down in the bowels of the Capitol. One Sunday morning, something came into my head that I wanted to make sure I didn't forget. So I called Steven's office, just to put my thought onto his answering machine. After one ring, he picked up the phone. I said, "Steven, it's Sunday, what are you doing there?" He said, "Oh, I had some loose ends to tie up. I'll probably be here until two or three in the afternoon." That showed me a man who goes above and beyond the call of duty. I need *him*—the man behind the scenes. Today, Steven runs the city of Minneapolis for the current Democratic mayor.

I took heat because a great many people who'd worked on my campaign did not receive jobs at the Capitol. Even from the grass roots, the rumbles reached me that people had expected that. I countered by saying, "If we're not going to be something different, why did I run? Which means, get rid of the nepotism and the cronyism. We're going to hire the best people for the job based on their ability, not simply because they were there."

As I started putting my team together, I told the media, "I feel like Rodney Dangerfield. It's time to go 'Back to School.'" A number of people came forward who wanted to contribute, like my commissioner of finance, Pam Wheelock. She had worked for my Republican opponent, Norm Coleman, who was then Mayor of St. Paul. During transition, I borrowed Pam to help put together my first budget, and she stayed on. Mayor Coleman was extremely gracious, saying, "I won't stand in the way."

I teased Pam about coming along to Washington, in case I someday ran for President. She paused a moment and said, "Gee, I don't know if I could handle that." I said, "But Pam, you're just dealing with a different set of numbers, changing from millions to trillions." She laughed and said, "You're right, sure I'd go."

TERRY: I assumed that the attention from Minnesotans would be intense. I had no clue—and why would you?—that the entire world would be constantly knocking at your door. That really amazed me. We received articles from Germany, Australia, New Zealand, Norway, Japan, everywhere.

The swearing-in ceremony we did very traditionally, in the rotunda of the Capitol. In my speech, I talked about how I would certainly make mistakes, but would do the best job I possibly could. I spoke of what I told the kids at Champlin Park High School, where I was a volunteer assistant football coach: "I will never, ever, punish you for losing. But God help you if you quit on me."

And they never did. A few days after the election, we played a game against a rival high school. Nobody had given my team a chance. Crouched down in the middle of the huddle with New York columnist Jimmy Breslin before the kickoff, I said to the kids: "Every play tonight you play it like your last play. We don't have to fear these guys. I shocked the world on Tuesday. Nobody gave me a chance. Nobody's giving us a chance tonight. We prove 'em wrong! Let's do it!"

On their final fourth quarter drive, Champlin Park scored the winning touchdown on a fourth and fifteen from the sixteen-yard line. Pulled the game out of the hat, so to speak, not unlike their volunteer coach.

I wanted the inauguration party to be a "People's Celebration." We held it at the Target Center. All 13,000 seats were sold out, and it was carried on live TV. I went from a black suit at the swearing-in to dressing Jesse "The Body" that night. I wore a wild Jimi Hendrix T-shirt under a buckskin jacket, sunglasses, a bandana, and three earrings. When I ran into Warren Zevon backstage—he'd agreed to be one of our featured performers—he had on a sports jacket and a turtleneck. "I thought I'm supposed to be the rock-and-roll guy," he said.

"The Body's back for tonight!" I told the crowd. "Let's party, MINnehSOHdah!" I got up on stage with Warren to do a duet on "Werewolves of London." That was a huge thrill for me, because I'd been listening to his music religiously since the late seventies.

Warren didn't have to worry about my not knowing the lyrics, but he was kind enough not to mention that I could barely carry a tune.

Earlier that night, Warren had said, "I have something I've been asked to bring to you." It was a tape cassette of music from Hunter S. Thompson, of "gonzo journalism" fame. There was also a piece of advice that Warren had been entrusted to give me verbally, eye-to-eye. "In the position you are in today," Hunter said, "never—I repeat never—answer the phone after midnight."

When you think about it, that message is extremely profound. If the phone rings after midnight, it's not going to be news you want to hear. Turn the phone off so you can sleep, and deal with it in the morning.

TERRY: *It was like you were on a tightrope all the time. I was so careful. I took all my girlfriends aside and I said, "Wherever we go in public, you must remember that everything we say and do will be watched and recorded. We can't just go somewhere and be silly and clink our martini glasses. If you want to do that, come over to my house or the governor's residence—we'll kick everybody out and be as crazy as we want. But for four years, I walk the line."*

I set up what I called the "Spouses Commiseration Luncheon," for all the new people. Both men and women. I told everybody when they came to the door, there is no press here and no one is allowed to speak outside this room of anything we talk about. If you have anything you want to get off your chest, let me know.

All the First Ladies have something like this. When you're in trouble or just unsure about something, you can call any First Lady for advice—and the code is, nothing gets said about it. I always held up my end of the bargain. At my luncheons, we had such a good time together. But it only lasted a short while before we didn't know who to trust anymore. We didn't want to have anybody coming over who might not hold to the code.

The friends we stopped to see in Phoenix told us that Mexico Highway 5 was in great shape from Mexicali all the way to the beach community of San Felipe, but they couldn't vouch for what happens after that. It's two lanes, flat, and paved—in some parts even extending out to four lanes. (Keep in mind that any paved road in Baja is considered a good road. That in itself is a big change from the United States.)

We are cruising right along when I say, "Remember when I floated the idea that you should be paid at least $25,000 a year for being First Lady?"

"Agggghhhhhh!" is Terry's first response, but then she starts to laugh. "But you know, in private, when we'd go to the governors' conferences, the other first ladies were like—yes!"

"Not just them, either. I probably received a half dozen communications, from other governors in both parties, saying thanks for having the courage to say that. Well, when I saw what your job required—basically as the building manager working on behalf of the state—how come everybody else who does that kind of thing draws a salary? In fact, a Republican from Rochester in our legislature stood up and said I was exactly correct: it's in the law that anyone working at the behest of Minnesota must be paid!"

I was forced to back off on it, because all the controversy was taking away from other things. The media just destroyed me over expressing such a heresy, I guess like going against mom, apple pie, and patriotism. When I'd announced that my official car wouldn't be the customary luxury sedan, but an SUV with extra-strong shocks "for running over reporters," I didn't realize at the time how much that statement would come to mean to me.

We pull off to the side of the road so that Dexter can take a leak and we can stretch our legs. The landscape stretches endlessly in all directions. Millennia ago, this whole part of the Baja was covered by a northern extension of the Sea of Cortez. Mexicali, in fact, lies a foot below sea level. Today Baja is the longest, and narrowest, peninsula on earth. But it used to be connected to mainland Mexico, back when mammoths, bisons, and twenty-three-ton dinosaurs roamed the plains. Over millions of years, the North Pacific plate that Baja is part of kept shifting along the San Andreas Fault. That's what allowed the Sea of Cortez—also known as the Gulf of California—to form in between, and at one point it extended all the way up to Palm Springs, California. It would have kept on slowly moving northward, except it met up with the Colorado River.

Silt flowing down the Colorado—much of it being rocks and earth once held in the Grand Canyon—created a very nutrient-rich soil over the centuries, despite the fact that the Valle de Mexicali and the San Felipe Desert only get about two inches of rain a year. With irrigation, originally established by American land companies building a canal system and later aided by a Mexican dam, the desert valley today produces an abundance of fruits and vegetables. These are grown on collectively owned agricultural lands known as *ejidos*.

Over the next hour, we begin passing the *nopal* farms, where the prickly pear cactus they grow is sold at roadside stands, fresh or pickled. They call the ripe fruits *tuna*. We stop briefly again to sample a bit of fresh *tuna*, which is juicy and sweet.

Pretty soon pasture land turns strictly into desert, as we hit the southern limit of the delta's irrigation system. Quail and dove hunters come to the marshlands around Rio Hardy, and in the river the local Indians fish for carp, largemouth bass, and catfish. Terry and I love to fish the Minnesota lakes, and I am tempted to stop.

"But I'll bet there's no muskie down here," she says, wistfully. There is an old saying among fishermen in Minnesota that it takes ten thousand casts to land a trophy muskie. Terry proved that wrong on our lake, soon after we moved into our new house. She bought a book on how to catch muskies. It was late enough in the fall that we'd already pulled in the docks, getting ready for winter. Well, that's when the muskies are notorious for cruising the shorelines for food. In the summer, they're always out in deeper water.

"I remember it was a Sunday afternoon and I was watching football," I recall, "when you said, 'I'm going outside to practice my casting.' Probably an hour and a half went by, and all of a sudden you came running in, your hair all in disarray, and announced: 'I've got a muskie.' I said, 'You mean you've got him *on*?'"

"And I said, 'No! He's on the front lawn!'"

"So I came running outside and sure enough, there's a forty-five-inch muskie. That's not a small freshwater fish, that's a lunker! And you caught him all by yourself—on ten-pound test line—from reading that book!"

We took some photographs and released the fish back into the lake. Now, of course, I was under pressure. She'd caught one and I hadn't. That bothered me for a long time. After I was no longer governor, every day when I finished golfing, I'd come home, go down to the dock, and do maybe fifty casts before dinner. One day, almost a year later, I was using a floating silver-and-black Rappala lure as bait. I threw it over by a weed bed, and let it sit until I saw all the rings of the splash disappear. Then I slowly started reeling. It would wiggle a little on the surface and had just started to go underwater when—wham!! Out of the water with it came this huge muskie!

"Now I was in the same predicament you were. I'm by myself, using the same ten-pound test line. Yet with the muskie, you can't let them have any slack, because if they leap out of the water, they'll spit the bait."

"And I wasn't even home!" Terry recalls.

"So I battled this fish in and out three times. In the interim I went over and got my landing net, dropped it into the lake, and pinned it against my waist, so that I'm leaning against it in the water. I finally tired him out to a point—I don't know how much time had gone by—and he was right underneath the net. I took a chance, dropped the pole, grabbed the net, and scooped him."

"And how big was he?" Terry can't stifle a grin, I can see.

"He was forty-two inches—only three inches smaller than yours—but actually mine was thicker. Yours was more long and thin."

I pause a moment, then go on: "The amazing thing about both fish was, I never took the hook out of either one. The minute they were in the net, they spit it out. About this time you'd arrived home, and come down there with Dexter. I remember we slid the muskie back into the lake, holding him by the back tail, rocking him slowly back and forth to get the water going through his gills again. He stayed upright, and literally sat there for five minutes right at our feet."

"Then you pushed him out towards the dock, and he went under that, and stayed there."

Terry had gotten her camera, and taken some amazing photographs of him breathing under the water. It was getting dark. He finally outlasted us, and we went in. Next morning I got up early, went out to check the shoreline, looked under the dock. And he was gone.

"So do you want to stop and fish here?" Terry asks now. I say no, I'm still determined to make time toward Guerrero Negro. Why, given what we are soon to face, I don't honestly know.

Except for probably a half dozen forays across into Tijuana when I was in the Navy training near San Diego, I've only been to Mexico one other time alone. That was in 1986, not long after I quit wrestling and the day after I finished broadcasting for WrestleMania 2 at the L.A. Sports Arena. I'd been cast as a professional killer named Blain, playing alongside Arnold Schwarzenegger in the sci-fi movie *Predator*. It was to be filmed on location in Jalisco, Palenque, and the jungles around Puerto Vallarta.

Kill the alien. That was the basic premise of the film, which ended up making about $60 million in box office after it hit the theaters in the summer of '87. I was part of the commando team in pursuit, chewing tobacco and carrying a machine gun into the bush. I insisted on doing my own rappelling, and got along real well with the stuntmen. Even though the alien bumped me off halfway through the movie, it wasn't long before I uttered a famous line that Fox Studios even made T-shirts of: "I Ain't Got Time to Bleed." That also became the title of my first book.

The best thing about doing *Predator* was becoming good friends with Arnold. Who would have imagined then that we'd both end up as governors? We hit it off right from the start. We'd get up and work out together at 5:00 a.m. One day, I decided to one-up Arnold. I started at 4:45 after soaking myself with mineral water, so it looked like I was drenched in sweat by the time Arnold showed up. I heard him tell his bodyguard and double, a fellow named Sven: "Look at this! Who knows how long Jesse's been training! We must get up earlier. We can't let him out-train me." So we both started rising earlier and earlier, until our workouts started at 4:00 a.m.!

While we were shooting, Arnold was scheduled to leave the set for a few days to fly to Hyannisport, Massachusetts, and get married to Maria Shriver. I thought he might need a little "coaching." Remember to speak from the diaphragm, I told him, and say distinctly, "I do! I DO!" I'd then sit off in a corner when he was getting ready to do a take and, just as the cameras were ready to roll, I'd let out an "I DO!" And Arnold would crack up laughing. Then the director would get a little pissed off, and I'd have to keep my mouth shut.

We did talk some politics. I was very curious why he was such an ultra-Republican. He gave me what I thought was a great reason. In Austria, where he came from, the government was so socialistic that you couldn't get rewarded for your perseverance. You're trapped within a layered system where, no matter how hard you work, you're only going to make so much money. It was before Reagan when he came to America, and Arnold said he always had felt strongly that the Republican philosophy of business—of being responsible for yourself in a free society—was the way to go.

I learned a lot from Arnold about the business of filmmaking. One day on the set, he said to me, "Jesse, always remember, never read a script until the money's right." I replied that that was pretty easy for a big star like him to say, with a dozen scripts sitting on his desk. But Arnold explained that, if you read first and like the script, you're liable to do the movie for less. "And if you can't get the money right, you've wasted your time reading the script," he went on. Then he looked me dead in the eye and said, "Jesse, in our business, we don't have time to waste."

We enjoyed each other's company so much that Arnold made sure I got a part in his next project, *The Running Man*. I asked for considerably more money than I had made doing *Predator*, and the negotiations were bogged down when Arnold called me. I told him yes, I wanted to do *The Running Man* with him. "But Arnold . . . I can't read the script until the money's right!" He burst out laughing and said, "Jesse, trust me. The script is fantastic. Just get the money right." That same afternoon, the film company phoned back and said they'd meet my price. It could be that Arnold interceded on my behalf. This time, I played Captain Freedom, an egomaniac ex-wrestler who's doing color commentary for a sadistic game show in an American police state in 2017. Some of that hit a little close to home.

The evening of the 1998 election, his wife, Maria, asked her producers at *Dateline NBC* if she could interview me before the returns came in. "We're not spending our time on losers," they told her. She went ahead and called me anyway, asking for an exclusive if I happened to become governor. I told her: "Sure, Maria. If I win, you can have the first interview." But when it became a reality, NBC wanted to hand the assignment to Tom Brokaw instead. I told the network I had an agreement with Maria; I'd go on the air with her, or not at all. So they ended up splitting the time. Maria did the first interview, then they tossed me over to Brokaw. He asked, "Should we call you Governor Ventura, or Governor 'The Body?'" Seemed like a pretty lame joke to me. So I told Brokaw the times had changed: "I'm no longer Jesse 'The Body,' I'm Jesse 'The Mind' Ventura."

Arnold was in the middle of making a film, but he still showed up in Minnesota for my inauguration. He gave me a present that I still cherish—two massive bronze eagles from the National Historical Society. On the back is a plaque that says: "Jesse, you are a true leader. Your friend, Arnold."

Then, when he was running for governor in the California recall election in the summer of 2003, it was my turn to offer Arnold some free advice. *Time* magazine asked me to do a column addressed to him, and I began by saying: "Arnold, what the heck are you doing? You're getting out of Hollywood to go into politics? Well, then forget agents and studio bosses—now you're dealing with real predators."

Headline: SOME ADVICE FROM VENTURA

Jesse Ventura, the professional wrestling bully boy who parlayed his celebrity into one term as Minnesota's governor, has some advice for a fellow entertainer-turned-politician. . . .

"Don't be spin doctored and stay away from the Republican Party, who will try to make you something you're not."

—The New York Times, *August 17, 2003*

My strongest recommendation was that Arnold simply be himself. An honest man who doesn't necessarily have all the answers. I told him to "keep your distance from special-interest groups, powerful lobbyists and their dirty money. The fact is, Arnold, you don't need them. You can win this race by going straight to the people."

Talk from your heart, be willing to take some chances and "expose the status quo politicians of both parties."

I didn't receive an invitation to Arnold's inaugural. I understand why. He's a Republican, and imagine what hoo-rah it would have caused if the so-called "high priest" of the independent movement had shown up. I did send him a bottle of champagne with a congratulatory note. But we haven't talked or seen each other since he became governor.

Then, in 2004, I appeared on TV ads in California opposing his idea that the Native American gambling casinos pay 25 percent of their revenues in taxes. That's at a time when corporate taxes in California were, I believe, at 6 or 7 percent. To me, the politicians had granted Native American tribes the rights to exclusive gambling and then, when they realized how much money it generated, they wanted to dip their hands into the till and change the game. The Native Americans had agreed they would pay what any other corporation did in taxes—but Arnold wanted them to foot the bill in order to close his budget gap. That way, like all good Republicans, he could tell the people it wasn't coming out of their taxes.

His argument was that the Indian tribes can be taxed as much as we desire because we give them a monopoly. At first glance, that seems pretty valid. The other corporations are taxed at a lower rate, because they face competition. There's only one problem with this logic, which I brought up at the time. If we're going to do that to Native American gambling, then why isn't it being done to baseball? Baseball is given a monopoly, yet you don't see California's government upping the taxes on the California Angels or the Oakland A's or the San Diego Padres. I mean, the ballplayers and the owners are making millions every year, and they're granted an antitrust exemption. But, of course, baseball is the great American pastime, and untouchable.

So, I sided with the Native Americans. Here you had the Caucasians ticked off at the Indians, because the Indians are making all this money—through an agreement that the Caucasians made with them! There we go again, breaking our deals, just like we've done to Indians for the last two hundred years.

When the press asked Arnold about my reaction, he said, "Well, what do you think friends are for?" And he laughed, which I loved. He still had his sense of humor, and I think understood that he and I simply stood on different sides of this issue. In fact, that summer Arnold ended up signing revised gaming agreements with five of California's most prosperous tribes, guaranteeing the state roughly 10 to 15 percent of their profits. Then he came out *against* a ballot initiative calling for all tribes to fork over 25 percent, which went down to defeat that November.

On most every issue today, I see Arnold's political views as being very close to my own. I highly commend what he's doing for stem cell research, and he's out in front of every other state in combating global warming—both of these directly in contrast with the hardcore Republicans. On all the social issues, in fact, Arnold has turned into a liberal Democrat.

So I'm wondering, why is he still a member of the Republican Party? He could have won the election as an independent. I'm privately hoping that he might go that way yet, as the Republicans continue to shun his forward-thinking policies. Stranger things have happened. After all, we've fought in the jungle together before.

Coming out of the northern Baja desert, our first sight of the Sea of Cortez comes at San Felipe. The little beach town was first named by a Jesuit Padre who came ashore with four canoes in 1746, and stayed long enough to call the gently curving bay San Felipe de Jesus. Hardly anybody came here before a paved road to a radar station got built after World War Two, and then American fishermen started flocking down to catch *totuava*, a croaker that gets as big as 250 pounds. The smaller ones were a little too tasty, and the fish ended up an endangered species.

There's a headland that juts out at the northern end of San Felipe, and below it an estuary and a boatyard. The commercial shrimp boats tie up in an artificial harbor at the southern end. And you see plenty of retired gringos camped along the beaches in their RVs, along with dune-buggies and ATVs racing up and down the sloping sands. We pull over to have some *mariscos* for lunch—steamed clams and oysters on the half shell.

For about twenty miles beyond San Felipe, we breeze. Past the new condo developments just south of the town, an ugly trash dump right off the highway, and then heading further inland, coming upon the strange, stunning landscape of the desert: the cholla cactus and mesquite and elephant trees.

We were about to be "stunned" by something else. I are in Southeast Asia for seventeen months, and I've been a lot of other places—but this is about to become the roughest road I've ever traveled.

An excerpt from Terry's journal: The shortcut the husband tried did not work out so well. The road that was paved ended shortly after San Felipe in a little town. We hit a pretty good stretch of gravel and then it was horrible. The dust was thick and heavy, and the road was washboard with big rocks. There were washouts here and there that we tried to get through.

Oh, the washboarding! That's where the ground ends up like the hard little waves you look at in the ocean. As your tires go over those waves, it bounces your shocks and shakes you so bad inside your vehicle that at times you think the fillings will come out of your teeth. In some places, big chunks of the road simply aren't there. I mean, these are *huge* holes on a dirt track covered with flat rocks. The *vados*, places where the road gets intersected by dry culverts, come upon you treacherously fast. By the time we've inched along for probably another twenty miles, my trailer carrying the wave runners virtually starts to disintegrate.

An excerpt from Terry's journal: The first thing to go wrong was the trailer. We noticed the red wave runner was crooked and, when we stopped to look at it, we saw the board it sat on was cracking and one of the bolts that held it into a clamp on the side was gone. Earlier, I had watched the wave runner popping up and down on the trailer. I asked to stop and try to find some bungee and rope but husband said, "Nah, we'll be fine." That was a mistake!

The uprights that hold them are breaking down, so the wave runners are riding directly on the trailer. These are fiberglass craft whose hulls you don't want to wreck, because that may be a permanent condition. Here we are, in blisteringly hot sun, unable to drive more than five miles an hour. Every mile or two, we have to stop the car, go back and readjust and re-strap the wave runners. We are using the belts from our pants, our camera bags, every belt we can think of imagine to try to secure them to the trailer.

An excerpt from Terry's journal: After about five times of straightening the one wave runner, I decided to look for something to tie the board down with and could not find anything, so I took out my brown belt. I had to convince the husband to try it and, lo and behold, it held up pretty well. Then the blue wave runner, the much heavier one, was bouncing all over the place. So we drove at ten miles an hour.

"Jesse," Terry says, with a mixture of wonderment and fury, "this is crazy!"

She is right, of course. In the middle of nowhere, cut off from all communication, not carrying any food or water to speak of. You look around and see no remnants of anything human. Or any greenery either. The land holds a kind of glowing yellowish rock, reminding me of sandstone. The dirt is red, and so are the mountains in the near-distance. This is like being on Mars, I think. Or maybe the moon.

I remember an old black man from Georgia, more than a hundred years old, who'd been interviewed when Neil Armstrong walked on the moon. Willie Smith wasn't buying it. He said, in his opinion, they were out in the deserts of Arizona somewhere. After seeing this portion of the Baja, I start to side a little bit with Willie.

And I think to myself, wow, maybe my experience in the Navy SEALS ended up preparing me even to walk on Mars. The way the camper is shaking, I guess we may be on foot any minute now.

Even in our dilemma, it is eerily neat to get out of a car and hear no human sounds at all. I think, my God, we are truly alone. In a place where seeing any living creature, be it a lizard or whatever, is a unique event. After living the life I've led on a total schedule 24/7, I feel in some way purified. If there is a Supreme Being, I feel close to it.

But we sure aren't going to make it halfway down the Baja by nightfall.

On a dark desert highway, cool wind in my hair.
Warm smell of colitas, rising up through the air.
Up ahead in the distance, I saw a shimmering light.
My head grew heavy and my sight grew dim.
I had to stop for the night.

—*"Hotel California," The Eagles*

CHAPTER 8

Longing for Light Rail

There are 552,446,061,128,648,601,600,000 (five hundred fifty-two septillion, four hundred forty-six sextillion, four hundred seventy-four quintillion, sixty-one quadrillion, one hundred twenty-eight trillion, six hundred forty-eight billion, six hundred one million, six hundred thousand) possible arrangements of the numbers on a bingo card.

—*"Bingo (US)," Wikipedia*

Our map indicates that the beach camp of Puertocitos is fifty-some miles below San Felipe. We make it that far, to a cluster of little stone houses and wooden shacks built around a cove. There is also a Pemex gas station, except the pumps apparently haven't worked in some time. Instead, a fellow is standing there next to them with some big plastic bottles of high-test unleaded "PREMIO" and regular unleaded "MAGNA." These cost a pretty peso, too.

The road goes from bad to worse after Puertocitos, and Terry starts to get a bit frustrated at our slow travel. "At the next cliff," she suggests, in all seriousness, "why don't you unhook the trailer and push it over—wave runners and all."

I say, "Honey, come on, if we run into anyone along here, I would rather *give* the wave runners away. Somebody will find a use for them. Out here, they'll probably take the engine and make a rock-breaker machine out of it. The very next occupied place we see, I promise we'll drop the wave runners off—and if we never see them again, so be it."

We drive on in silence. Being shaken to shit, as the phrase goes, is putting it mildly. Finally we come to a place where the first thing that catches our eye is a group of four small wooden shacks, obviously well cared for. Out in front is a huge resurrected whale skeleton, looking like a prehistoric dinosaur. We pull in. A Mexican gentleman comes out who speaks virtually no English, and I speak virtually no Spanish. Somehow we managed to communicate through pantomiming.

Terry's journal, continued: His name was Augustino and he agreed to keep the trailer and wave runners for us. The husband gave him $50, or 500 pesos, and we took photos of him and the husband and the wave runners and the giant whalebone skeletons he had in his yard, and a photo of his white horse. He was a nice man and lived in a stretch of terrible road in a place called Five Isles. Across the road from his house was a gorgeous stretch of beach, and in the water were giant rocks and small islands.

Augustino asks me where I am going. When I tell him, he rolls his eyes, because it is still many hundreds of miles away. I explain to him that I might not be back for a month or two. He assures me that, whenever I do, the wave runners will still be there. I believe him. Not that I really have much of a choice. I unhook the trailer, he puts rocks underneath the wheels so they can't move and covers it all with a tarp underneath a shed, so that the elements won't seep in.

And you know what? When I do come back to retrieve the trailer and wave runners three weeks later, there they both be, safe and sound.

It wasn't the first time I'd run into problems over wave runners. When I became governor, I happened to own four of the personal watercrafts. The legislature had placed a separate tax on them that applied to no other boat, to hire police to keep the people who used wave runners in line. I was getting nicked $50 apiece, $200 a year, for this new surcharge that was, in my opinion, completely unconstitutional. It was the equivalent of putting a tax on all red sports cars. So I managed to have the surcharge repealed.

I was accused of getting laws passed to benefit myself or my friends. Well, my view is, what else can you govern by except personal experience? That's why I also did my best to correct what I felt was a ten-year sales tax masquerading as something called license tab fees. You already paid a sales tax when you purchased your car. But, to be able to get your license plates, you also had to pay an additional fee to the state—a percentage based upon the price you paid for the vehicle. I happened to have bought a new Porsche in 1990 and, just to drive my car, it cost me upwards of four thousand dollars in license tab fees over the course of ten years.

How can you have a licensing system based upon the street value of the car? If you're going to do something like that, then base it on the weight of the car—that's what tears up the streets! A Lamborghini doesn't, in fact it probably does less damage because it's so aerodynamically perfect. Plus, this policy didn't apply to motorcycles. You could have the most expensive Harley-Davidson or the cheapest little Honda 50, and the license tab fee stayed at a flat rate.

So, when Minnesota showed a budget surplus in 2000, I sat down with our Senate majority leader—a Democrat named Roger Moe—and Steve Sviggum, the Republican Speaker of the House. As you might expect, we all had divergent opinions on what to do with the surplus. Finally Moe came up with what I thought was a great idea. He said, "Let's divide the surplus into thirds, and each of us can do whatever we want with our third." That's what we ended up doing. The Democrats applied their third to spending, which didn't surprise me. The Republicans gave theirs back to the people in the form of mild income tax relief, which also came as no surprise.

As the independent, I decided to use my third—which came to about $175 million—to reduce the license tab fees to a flat rate: a maximum of $99 for any car more than a year old. This represented a savings of hundreds of dollars for many Minnesotans.

So my critics, in the legislature and the media, were absolutely right that I governed from a personal approach—taking on what I felt was wrong, *as a citizen*. Here's another example: a bill was introduced at one point having to do with auto glass replacement. If you had a cracked windshield, the insurance company would be the one to tell you where to go to have it replaced. One of my best friends had his own little auto glass repair business, and I called him. He told me this law was bogus, basically being done to run smaller companies like his out of business. It wouldn't help the consumer one bit, but the insurance companies could make more money. An attorney I knew verified this. I vetoed the bill. The legislature overrode my veto and passed it into law anyway. That shows you how powerful the insurance lobby is. And it shows you how I governed. I didn't go to the lobbyists, I went to people I knew who wouldn't bullshit me.

Terry's journal, continued: After we dumped the trailer, we could go about 20 miles an hour with lots of slowdowns to keep from ruining the camper. We even went off-road onto the Baja 1000 track, which at times was smoother, but then we would have to go back on the road. We spent about four hours or more trying to navigate that road, and I think it was about 125 kilometers [a little over seventy miles] long. We had some very treacherous turns on hills going through the mountains that were very scary, with and without the trailer, where I was looking down into canyons that were about a hundred-foot drop or more.

You can't make any time on the Baja 1000 track either, because it's up-and-down like a roller coaster. But at least you don't get the washboarding. Occasionally, the road consists of volcanic black gravel and, at those times it is passably decent. At a place called Alfonsina's, a supply point for the next bay, we decide to take a break and stay the night. We go maybe one-tenth of the distance I've figured on making today.

As we get Dexter settled and climb into our bunks, Terry smiles and says: "Now here's a place where your light-rail transit system would *really* come in handy!"

I laugh. "When I take over the Baja," I say, "that's the first thing I'm gonna push for!"

Headline: LARRY KING LIVE: JESSE VENTURA DISCUSSES YOUTH VIOLENCE, POLITICS, AND THE ECONOMY

KING: What's the toughest part about not being in a party and governing a state?
VENTURA: Well, you don't have any political punch out there. You don't have spin doctors and people that can try to make it

right and all of that stuff. You really kind of stand on an island, and you have to, you know, take your own punches and weather the storm as it goes along. But I like that. I've been kind of a renegade and a loner and a rebel my entire life and career. So I'm very comfortable doing that.

But the nice thing is, too, I don't have to answer to a political party either very much. You know, I don't have to get in lockstep with a party, and I don't have to hire party cronies. I can get the best person for the job regardless of their party without having to hire within a party.

—*CNN, March 14, 2001*

I like to steal a line that I heard Kinky Friedman say when he was running for governor of Texas as an independent: "A politician looks to the next election, a statesman looks to the next generation." As governor, I tried to accomplish some things that, maybe ten or fifteen years later, people would look back at and say: "Boy, what a bright decision that was. Ahead of its time."

The light-rail transit system I fought for might fall under that category. Light rail is the modern version of the streetcar or trolley, using less massive equipment and infrastructure than rapid transit systems. Back in the early fifties, the Twin Cities had probably the best mass transit in the world—a streetcar system that could take you anywhere in the metropolitan area. That is, until the automotive, gasoline, and tire industries lobbied successfully to destroy it. Like they had done in Los Angeles a few years earlier. Thanks to those same people, all the track was pulled up and gotten rid of. I was told while governor that some of the streetcars are still in operation—in New Jersey, where Minnesota ended up selling them.

I pushed for light rail because I saw it as playing an important role in the future. Especially when it came to transportation, I felt that people need options, choices. Here's how my thinking evolved. When I'd gone to work for Ted Turner as a commentator for World Championship Wrestling down in Atlanta, in the early 1990s, I used to take a taxi from the airport to CNN Center that would cost between twenty and twenty-five dollars. Along the way you're subject to an accident on the highway that causes congestion, or whatever it might be. One day, after I'd been doing this for a couple months, a fellow who'd been sitting next to me on the plane walked me over to the Atlanta rail system at the end of the airport. It only cost a dollar and a half, and took me downtown on a very relaxing ride where I could sit and read the paper—instead of flying around in the back of a speeding taxicab wondering if I'd be alive long enough to reach my destination. Reaching downtown, I changed trains quickly, went to the first stop, and had to then walk one block to my place of work. I now knew exactly when I could catch that train to get me back to the airport. It saved me roughly forty-five dollars every round-trip. In the course of a year, that becomes pretty substantial.

In Atlanta, the mass transit riders were predominantly African-Americans. I remember some young black kids recognizing me once and saying, "What are *you* doing on here?" I guess they felt that, being a celebrity, I should be riding in a limousine stuck in traffic. I responded, "Do I look stupider than you? You're on here getting where you need to go for a buck and a half—well, so am I!" They laughed, and accepted that as pretty damned logical.

After I became governor, I went to Denver to study their light-rail system. They're way ahead of the curve. They've eliminated buses from downtown. Imagine how good that is for traffic—and the environment. It's the old wagon wheel concept; all the spokes lead to the city center, and those are your trains. Let the buses connect to the trains.

The Denver officials told me, "Governor, the most difficult problem you're going to have is acquiring the land." I said, "No, we've already got it." When I was a kid growing up in south Minneapolis, the state had come in along the Hiawatha Avenue Corridor, confiscated all the homes, and made people leave. I remembered that because friends of mine had been forced to move. They were going to make a highway along there, but somehow it never happened. The corridor sat there and I remember the locals planting gardens along this wide-open piece of land. Now the state had owned the corridor for thirty years, and it was regarded as an ideal place for a portion of the light-rail system.

The idea was that the system would run for 11.5 miles, connecting the Mall of America to the Minneapolis–St. Paul airport to downtown, running through South Minneapolis and the Phillips neighborhood. That's one neighborhood over from where I grew up. I found out that 60 percent of the people who live there can't afford to own a car. By providing them a means of transportation, they'd now have the ability to get downtown or to the mall, and find at least an entry-level job.

I tried to explain this one day to the Republican House Speaker, Steve Sviggum—how these people would no longer be stuck in their neighborhood and could go seek gainful employment elsewhere. I'll never forget his response: "I don't have anybody elected down there, what do I care?"

That floored me. I looked at him and said, "Wait a minute, I thought we were elected to serve all the people of the state of Minnesota." But he just wanted to make sure the *Republican* state of Minnesota advanced. And in the inner city of Minneapolis, places like the Phillips neighborhood, Republicans don't even bother to campaign. So those people don't count.

I took abuse from talk radio show hosts who called the light-rail plan "the big boondoggle." Or "the train to nowhere," as some

Republicans preferred to say. Their notion was, we have our cars, Minnesota doesn't need mass transit. One morning I boarded a Metro Transit bus at my home in suburban Maple Grove, along with transit officials, several lawmakers, and the media. A sign on the bus said, "Ventura Express." We headed downtown during rush hour, a twenty-mile journey that took about an hour. "Bumper to bumper, stop and start," I intoned through a microphone at the front of the bus.

A couple of hours later, a House Committee voted down my request for $60 million in light-rail funding. That money was crucial to getting the federal government to kick in another $250 million. The "Ventura Express" ran again that afternoon, back to Maple Grove, "bumper to bumper, stop and start." A few days later, the Senate Transportation Committee voted to approve the funding.

But because of the split between the two houses, the legislation didn't get anywhere. In 2000, I walked into a Senate Transportation Committee to offer personal testimony. "I know this is not the way things are usually done," I told the legislators. "But I am absolutely committed to breaking the twenty-year-old LRT logjam that has produced millions of dollars in studies but not one foot of progress."

The light-rail line also would have linked up to a commuter rail I was trying to get from St. Cloud, sixty miles northwest, to Minneapolis. It would have connected two veterans homes, meaning that veterans wouldn't have to drive to the state-of-the-art facility in Minneapolis. They could just jump on a commuter rail to downtown, switch to the light rail, go right to the hospital, and probably get home that night. I couldn't sell the Speaker on that reasoning, either.

Today, it's finally moving forward. That's because the current governor, also a Republican, needed those votes along the I-94 commuter rail line from St. Cloud to Minneapolis, and so the House Speaker finally gave in and came on board. Expected to cost $7 million a year, the light rail system ended up turning a $1 million *profit* its first year! It's safe to say that, if I hadn't fought off legislators on both sides of the aisle who wanted to eliminate any funding for it, the first line would never have been laid. The sad part is, had politics not entered into it, the system would already be finished.

Call me naïve. I'd thought that, once the elections were over, it was time to go to work until the next one, when we get political again. Unfortunately, with the Democrats and Republicans, it doesn't work that way. They're political 24/7. First on their list is the party and what benefits it. Second are the special interest people, the funders who pay their bills for them. Third on the list might be what's best for the people.

We stay at a campground facing the bay called Rancho Grande, and are on our way again by 8:00 a.m. The next stretch of road, while still unpaved and bumpy, is in much better condition than what we've already weathered. Our goal now is to reach the Transpeninsular Highway One, which is about forty miles from where we spent the night.

At about the halfway point, we come upon two *topes*. A *tope* is a speed bump. We don't have them on main drag roads in the U.S., but Mexico does. Every little town you come to—even some junctions with a single house—will have multiple speed bumps to make you slow down. You can't blame them. Most towns have many children, and a lot of dust. Anyway, as we crawl over these two *topes*, there stands one of the most unique houses I'd ever seen.

It's was called Coco's Corner. Coco has bronze, super-tanned skin, white hair and a white beard, and a prosthesis on one leg, though he's not shy about wearing shorts. He's a jovial old gentleman, and

Test firing the trusty Stoner machine gun during my Navy career.

This is why I will never be president. I wore a fringe jacket and a Jimi Hendrix T-shirt to my inaugural celebration. For one fleeting moment, everyone in Minnesota became "Experienced."

Warren Zevon was a warrior from the land of the midnight sun. Here, Warren and I are selling our souls to rock and roll.

The most I have ever done to conform
to society's standards.

The Governor and the First Lady of Minnesota on inauguration day in the governor's office.

Our first brush with "Green." We had a wonderful time at the vice presidential residence with Vice President Al and Tipper Gore.

I always enjoyed the lively political discussions with President Clinton.

Governor Ventura and the Minnesota delegation to Washington, D.C.
Left to right: Gutknecht, Oberstar, Kennedy, McCollum, Ramstad,
Luther, Dayton, Sabo, and Wellstone.

The beginning of a day in the life of an independent governor.

Jesse and Barbara Walters. I render Barbara speechless!

Chris Matthews defending the "magic bullet" theory to Jesse at Harvard University.

Cokie Roberts, George Will, and Sam Donaldson do their show at the governor's office. George Will and I are in a heated discussion.

These men are the Navy Leap Frogs, a Navy sky diving team. They came in for a golf tournament promotion, but the weather at the golf course was not favorable for a jump there. So the team came to our farm and parachuted into the pasture in front of our barn. These men have all completed thousands of jumps in their careers and are great ambassadors for the UDT/SEAL teams.

Muhammad Ali, Harvey Mackay, and Jesse Ventura.

Me and the boys. Old frogmen never die! (The Creature from the Black Lagoon was a Christmas gift to me from Terry a couple of years ago. There is a Creature from the Black Lagoon at the base in Coronado with a sign around its neck asking, "So you wanna be a frogman?!")

I designed and built this bike to try to get back the feeling of freedom.

We stopped here just to take in the view and document our trip.

I wake up in the morning with nothing to do and I go to bed at night with half of it done.

speaks enough broken English to get by. You can camp at Coco's Corner for the night if you desire, in a big open spot.

His entire house, including all the fences, is lined in beer cans. Thousands of them, end to end. When you stop at Coco's for refreshment after the hard road and the beating sun, what fills his large main refrigerator is very ice-cold beer. (In the U.S., Coco would be put in prison for giving people beer who then go back onto the road and drive. But in this portion of the Baja, probably being drunk would help!)

Another unique thing about Coco's Corner: he has about seven volumes of ledger-type books. Everyone who passes through gets a page to write something on and add their signature to. If you stay long enough, Coco will do a drawing of the vehicle you arrived in. I sign in big letters, "Governor Jesse Ventura, Minnesota." Who knows, maybe years down the road when even this sector of the Baja is well inhabited, people will find those books and know who was brave enough—or foolish enough—to tackle Mexico Highway 5.

When you walk into Coco's, underneath his first *palapa* you also notice all these baseball caps hanging from the ceiling. It's part of the tradition for guys to sign and leave one behind. Turn the corner, and on the other side of the *palapa* it's all panties and bras! Also autographed, by all the women who've passed through. I can't help but flash back to the interview I gave *Playboy* when I was governor. When asked what I'd like to return as should I ever be reincarnated, I said: "I would like to come back as a thirty-eight double-D bra."

So at Coco's, I have my picture taken in front of the biggest set of panties I'd ever seen in my life, thirty-nine by thirty-nine by thirty-nine or something like that. They have to hold a cubic meter of body! (I think Terry may be hiding in the camper at this point).

When you leave, Coco always comes over to wish you good luck. It's a mixed message. You wonder, is he wishing you good luck because he knows what's up ahead and that you'll need plenty to get through it? Or is he just wishing you good luck like everyone else does? I guess it depends on which direction you're heading.

In retrospect, I wish I'd had the language skills to tell Coco about what's gone down in Minnesota legend as "the bingo saga." I think, as an elder, he would have appreciated my efforts on behalf of senior citizens.

One day not long after I was inaugurated, I walked over to the secretary of state's office. In there was a massive wall filled with volumes of books, twenty-five times the size of an *Encyclopaedia Britannica*. I mean, there had to be close to a thousand books. I inquired, "Excuse me, but what is all this?" And I was told, "Those are all the laws for the state of Minnesota."

I sat there a moment and thought: They tell us that ignorance of the law is no excuse. In other words, we as citizens are supposed to *know* all this? That seemed pretty absurd. This aroused my curiosity to begin looking into some of the crazy laws that are on the books in Minnesota. Like the fact that auto dealerships can't sell cars on Sunday. Why is it government's job to determine when a private sector business will or won't be open? When I decided to find out, I ran up against considerable opposition. It turned out that the auto dealers want that law—because it assures them a day off. Now, in the spirit of true capitalism, if the dealer across the street from you decided to stay open on Sundays, you would have to think about it, too. But no, the car salesmen went to the legislature and made it illegal!

My solution? I wanted to change the system so that every third year, the legislature couldn't make new laws. They could only come back and repeal old ones. Trim down the size of those bookshelves in the secretary of state's office a little. Then it came to my attention that, in order to do that, I'd have to revise the state constitution. So that went down the drain pretty fast. Just the bureaucracy involved in a constitutional amendment would require ten to fifteen years.

However, I'm pleased to report my success in repealing one law. It had to do with the game of bingo. You may find this hard to fathom, but Minnesota had it on the books that elderly people living together in nursing homes were only allowed to play bingo twice a week. The homes had to fill out paperwork to be held by the State Department of Gambling for three and a half years! Have you ever gone into a nursing home and watched bingo? Half of the people are sleeping! Yet the law even dictated what the prizes should be. If you won the grand bingo game, you got to go first through the chow line that night.

I called a press conference to announce the repeal of the bingo law. I did it as a joke to show how ridiculous some of these laws were, but I played it as real. Solemn-faced, I walked in and said: "I brought you all here to make an important announcement. With eleven days left in the legislative session, it's my privilege to sign into law House File 132, Senate File 1138."

I continued: "With urgent budget issues before the state, including the future of public-education funding . . . the future tobacco endowments, the size of permanent tax cuts, providing a sales-tax rebate to Minnesota citizens, and all the other programs that Minnesotans depend upon, the legislature sent me this important legislation to allow senior citizens to play bingo in nursing homes without state regulations."

I added: "Of course, in light of doing this, we are putting a lot of responsibility on our elderly. We are trusting that they won't become addicted to playing bingo every night, to the point where this could become dangerous to their health. We are hoping that organized crime doesn't get its foot in the door now on these bingo games. Because we have made them legal seven days a week, how often the elderly wish to play bingo is up to their own good judgment. And our State Gambling Commission will no longer keep track of who wins the bingo games. I put great trust in our elderly that, with this burden lifted from them, they will not abuse this great privilege.

"And it is my hope that with this burdensome issue behind them, the legislature can now address other issues that are equally important."

Terry's Baja journal, continued: We reached the graded stretch of road and we could do about 40 on that and, finally, we hit pavement and cheered! It had been so bone-jarring on the gravel that now the paved road almost put me to sleep, it was so quiet. We were covered with dust and so were all of our belongings. We had not seen a gas station for many miles, and finally came upon one in Rosarito.

Continuing south, it is late afternoon when Highway 5 intersects with the pavement of Highway 1! Something I've taken for granted most of my adult life, asphalt, suddenly becomes the most important thing in the entire world! We hoot and holler! Trouble is, the smooth road almost has me nodding off at the wheel. We have to crank open the windows to get as much air going through the camper as possible.

We also put on a CD—very loud. "I can't get no satisfaction," Mick Jagger sings, seeming to make the asphalt hum along. "When I'm drivin' in my car, and a man comes on the radio . . . and tells me how white my shirts can be. . . . I can't get no sat-is-fac-tion."

I turn to Terry, I'm sure with a wistful look. "It's still one of the proudest things in my résumé," I say. "That I actually body-guarded for the Rolling Stones. Not once, but twice." She rolls her eyes.

I was at the peak of my wrestling career then, in 1978 and again in 1981. Came the night of the second big concert, and it turned out the promoter running the show hadn't lined anybody up to introduce them. He ended up asking me, and I got to walk out under the big spotlight and say, "Ladies and gentlemen—the world's greatest rock and roll band, the Rolling Stones!" It was one of those revolving stages and, as I rotated to the rear, there they were!

I'd remained one of their biggest fans. So, when they were coming to Minneapolis for a concert only a few weeks after my inauguration, it was hardly unnatural for me to make my first proclamation as governor. It went like this:

"WHEREAS: In the world of rock n' roll, to last four decades— and surely into the new millennium—is unheard of; and WHEREAS, their music is timeless for many generations of fans; and WHEREAS, Keith Richards was born on December 18, 1943, is now 55, and is still alive; and WHEREAS, the Rolling Stones have performed in Minnesota multiple times and this concert will represent the highest-grossing concert of all time at the Target Center; and WHEREAS, the Stones have always employed the best 'Body' guards; NOW THEREFORE, I, JESSE VENTURA, Governor of Minnesota, do hereby proclaim official recognition of February 15, 1999, as ROLLING STONES DAY."

When their private jet landed at the airport that afternoon, one of the media handed Mick a copy of my proclamation. He said he found it "very amusing," but was "very thankful." When asked if he might invite the governor onstage to sing, Mick's response was: "I don't know. I hope he doesn't want to wrestle."

That night, prior to the First Lady and I being happily ensconced in our front-row seats, the whole band came over to shake hands before the show. Mick said, "No one's ever done that for us." I told him, "Well, nobody's ever been your bodyguard and such a big fan, who ended up in a position like mine!" He said, "We're very honored."

Then Keith Richards walked up to me with a bemused look on his face. "So you used to bodyguard us in '78 and '81?" he asked.

I said, "Yup."

And he said, "And now you're the governor?"

I said, "Yup."

And in that wonderful Cockney accent he has, Keith said: "Facking great!"

After I was out of office, the Stones came through on another tour, and played the Excel Center in downtown St. Paul. Having "insider status" now, where I can get the good tickets, I was in the second row with four of my friends.

I reminisce now for Terry's benefit: "At the end of the concert, I noticed Keith winking at me. And boom!—he shot me his guitar pick, right from stage. Obviously he's done it before, because boy was he accurate! That sucker flew and hit me right in the chest."

The guitar pick has the little lips and tongue on it, and on the other side, the name of the tour. I've got it in a prominent frame back home in Minnesota.

After the ordeal of Highway 5, Terry is too exhausted to keep up her journal. We gas up in Rosarito, and join some truckers for ranchero food at a little café. It even has real coffee, filtered through a cloth strainer, which we are told is the traditional Mexican style.

We breeze on to the twenty-eighth parallel, where a 140-foot-high steel monument, topped by a sculpted eagle, denotes the border between Baja Norte and Baja Sur. The time changes here, too, from Pacific to Mountain, and the town of Guerrero Negro is only a few miles away. It's big, by Baja standards, with a population of around 10,000. The name comes from a whaling ship called the *Black*

Warrior that sank in a lagoon near here back in 1858 because it was too loaded down with whale oil.

In Guerrero Negro, we spend our first night of the trip in a hotel. Baja hotels are often surrounded by walls. It's like pulling into a fort, so there's a true feeling of security. Down here, you get back to reading the basics of life from people—a hello, a smile on someone's face. They can be said in many languages, but the feelings are still the same.

Terry is reading John Steinbeck's *Log from the Sea of Cortez*, written in 1941, a true account of a voyage the great novelist made on a boat called the *Western Flyer*. As we go to sleep after a forty-eight-hour journey I expected to make in twelve hours, she reads aloud to me this passage:

"What was the shape and size and color and tone of this little expedition? We slipped into a new frame and grew to be a part of it, related in some subtle way to the reefs and beaches. . . . This trip had dimension and tone. It was a thing whose boundaries seeped through itself and beyond into some time and space that was more than all the Gulf and more than all our lives. Our fingers turned over the stones and we saw life that was like our life."

It is mysterious to feel this way, a couple of thousand miles away from Minnesota.

CHAPTER 9

Money, Sports, and Politics: A Universal Language

"Baseball commissioner Bud Selig earned as much last year as some of the league's top players. Selig received $14.5 million in the 12 months ending Oct. 31, according to Major League Baseball's tax return, which was obtained by the Sports Business Journal.*"*

—*Associated Press, April 3, 2007*

It is the weekend, and the banks aren't open in Guerrero Negro. We need some pesos, and the hotel suggests we shop around for a *casa de cambio*, a private money-changing service. There are quite a few of these on the main drag, all posting their rates in terms of how many pesos you receive for a dollar. Right now, it all seems pretty standard—about ten pesos to the buck.

We are next in line at the counter, when the man ahead of us finishes his transaction, turns around—and recognizes me. "Governor!"

he exclaims. I resist the temptation to put a finger to my lips telling him to shhhhhhh.

"How are you?" I say quietly, as he extends his hand.

"Well, we're from Minnesota!" he exclaims again, pumping my hand like he is draining all the milk from a lactating cow. "What are *you* doing down here?"

"Traveling," I say. "Just getting away from winter for a little while."

"Us, too!" The man is nothing if not enthusiastic. Finally, he releases his grip. "Listen, can I buy you a drink this evening? Little mescal, maybe?" He winks at me.

"Sorry, I'm off the drink these days," I say, which is true. Having one from a bottle with a worm floating at the bottom could intrigue me. But doesn't.

"Well, one thing I have to tell you," the man continues. "What you did when the state had those big budget surpluses—returning the extra money to the people three years in a row—that was a noble thing to do."

"Well, thanks," I say. "It just seemed more like the *right* thing to do. But don't try telling that to the Democrats or the Republicans."

Politicians have led us to believe that only certain people are qualified to do the job of governing. It's a mystique, and a misconception. As governor, I had a terrific group of commissioners, and I paid attention to them. If you're intelligent and surround yourself with good people, they'll educate you. It's not rocket science. The greatest compliment I had came six months after I took office, from Skip Humphrey. He came up to me at a gathering out in Wayzata, Minnesota, and said, "Governor, you've put together the best administration the state of Minnesota has ever seen."

Economics was always something I'd had a knack for. In high school, I got A's in business law and business administration. When

I took aptitude tests in the Navy, they first sent me to "Storekeeper-A" school, which is all about requisitioning; basically, you're trained to run the ship's business. I've never gone out and created a business, but I did create an entity—called "Jesse Ventura"—that I've lived off quite well for my entire adult life.

We'd had multiple years of prosperity in Minnesota, and there was a projected $4-billion-plus state budget surplus through the first three years of my term. So I was able to provide Minnesotans with three consecutive tax-free rebates. The formula that Pam Wheelock, my finance commissioner, and Matt Smith of the Department of Revenue came up with was to give people a rebate equal to 35 percent of the sales tax a family or individual would have paid out over the previous two years, based on their average earned income.

I'll never forget the politicians' reactions to my first State of the State address. Every time I mentioned something about "tax cuts," the Republicans on one side of the room gave me a standing ovation. When I suggested spending Minnesota's huge settlement from the tobacco companies on social programs, the Democrats on the other side did the same. I told a journalist afterward it reminded me of one of those old "tastes great, less filling" beer commercials that I used to do.

When push came to shove, the Republican-dominated House didn't want anything except an income-tax rebate, and the Democrat-controlled Senate decided to support my proposal. With less than two weeks left in the legislative session, they were still deadlocked when I called the leadership in for a closed-door meeting. Actually, I threatened to lock Roger Moe and Steve Sviggum in the state-house library with my gaseous bulldog, Franklin. "If I feed him a little bit of hamburger," I told the press, "I got a feeling we'll have a deal in about a half hour."

I don't like cutting backroom deals, but sometimes you have no choice. We ended up providing the largest tax rebate that any state had ever given (a married couple earning $50,000 a year received a check for more than a thousand dollars), based on the sales-tax calculations. The Republicans got their income-tax cuts, the Democrats got an extra $100 million for education spending, and I got the $60 million I wanted for initial funding of light-rail transit.

Everybody came out happy. For the moment.

One of the major issues that inspired me to run for governor was Minnesota's complicated property-tax system, which I'd vowed to change. In my first State of the State, I said: "Let's face it. We've lost any logic to this system. Property taxes no longer are tied to the services that are delivered. We have created a so-called progressive tax based on the value of the property. It punishes people for doing the right thing. If I keep up my property, my value and taxes go up, even though I don't need as many local services as the property that has been allowed to deteriorate and needs more inspections, fire protection, or police patrols."

To me, it also came down to taxation without representation. You may have heard about Minnesota being the "land of ten thousand lakes." A lot of people like myself live in the city, but own a little lake cabin to spend their weekends in. That's a tradition as engrained in Minnesota as surfing is in California. You don't vote in the area where you own a second home, yet the local bureaucrats could still raise your property taxes as a levy to pay for public education. Whenever they needed money for their school district, they'd dump it onto the cabin owners—who were, unfairly, footing the bill there, as well as where their own kids attended school in the fall.

So, in 2001, I came up with a plan for the state to start paying the full costs of public education out of a general fund, rather than from local property taxes—which would then become smaller, simpler, fairer, and more truly local. To help pay for this switch, I proposed adding a sales tax onto many services that weren't subject to it—but, at the same time, lowering the overall sales tax from 6.5 to 6 percent. And we'd still come in with a balanced budget. Well, this time the Republicans loved me instead of the Democrats.

Here's the thing about sales taxes today, and I imagine it's this way in many other states: They are based upon the economy of the 1960s, when we were still about 70 percent goods and 30 percent services. Today, the economy has flip-flopped, and it's almost exactly reversed. Therefore, by continuing to tax only the goods, we are losing considerable revenue.

I pointed out in my budget speech that all of these services we buy—like haircuts, car washes, piano tuning, boat docking, dating, on and on—go mostly untaxed. Some cases in point, in terms of winners and losers: If you get a haircut in Minnesota, it's not taxed. If your dog gets one, it is. Whether the hair comes off a human or a dog should be irrelevant. If you board your horse, it's not taxed. If you board your dog, it is. This clearly shows me that the dogs have bad lobbyists. If you hire a company to plant a tree, it's not taxed. If they cut a tree down, it is. I imagine landscaping people do both, don't you?

These were the kind of reforms I'd promised people during my campaign, and mine have since been described as "perhaps the boldest, most far-reaching proposals for changing the state's tax system in Minnesota history." So what happened? The 2001 regular session ended with every single piece of tax and spending legislation left hanging. The House wanted more of the property-tax relief set aside for businesses. The Senate wanted more for homeowners. It was gridlock, and I had to order a special session and threaten a government shutdown.

I told people on my weekly radio show that if that happened, "there would be no state troopers out on the roads. There would be no prison guards. So we've come up with an idea called 'Host a Convict.' We're going to look for legislators and people that would like to volunteer to take a few convicts into their homes during the shutdown."

On June 30, at 3:30 in the morning—right up against the deadline—the legislature acted. Historic property-tax reform and relief passed. Education funding came off the local property tax rolls and went into the state's general fund. My plan to broaden the sales tax didn't make it, but I wasn't giving up yet. I still had a year to go in my first term.

Running into the fellow from Minnesota at the *casa de cambio* gets Terry and me talking that night in the hotel room about taxes. I've been audited twice. Two years in a row, in fact, when I was mayor of Brooklyn Park, even though the IRS claims that never happens to people. I hadn't cheated on my taxes. The second year, they even found a mistake in my favor. But all that did was pay for two years of my accountant's bills.

"They went so far as to make me categorize how much shampoo I used," Terry remembers.

"And they wanted to know how much money I carried in my wallet on a day-by-day basis," I recall. "That's not an invasion of my privacy? If I want to carry around ten grand, as long as I've paid my fair share to the government, it's none of their business!"

"Your mother lived with us then, and they wanted to know whether there was any chance she'd hidden some money in our backyard. It was ridiculous!"

"I was going crazy, but fortunately my accountant kept me away from them."

"The second audit, they wanted to look at my horse business. But I had a business plan and was so well organized, they ended up giving me a refund."

Summing up our frustrations—and presumably those of thousands of Americans—I say: "The IRS assumes you are guilty and forces you to either try to muddle through alone against their professionals, or hire your own expert to defend yourself, if you can afford it. They freeze people's assets, and they threaten you with fines, taking your house and property, and sometimes even with jail. To me, this smacks of Gestapo-type tactics. So what's the alternative? Abolishing the income tax, and putting in place a national sales tax instead."

This would make paying taxes strictly between business and government, and you as an individual would be taken out of the mix. No more keeping seven years of tax returns stashed away in your attic. And no more being guilty until you're proven innocent, in the eyes of the IRS, which flies in the face of our legal system.

With a national sales tax, the federal government brings in the money it needs by taxing the goods and services we buy. Food and clothing, the basic necessities, would be exempt. Only our optional purchases would be collected on. We decide how much tax we'll pay by regulating our own level of consumption. You could be a multimillionaire but live in a studio apartment and drive a beat-up Volkswagen, and keep most of your money. But if you live in a penthouse and drive a Mercedes and own a yacht, you pay in accordance with your lifestyle. Wealth isn't based on what you earn, but on what you spend.

One objection I've heard raised to a national sales tax is that our free market economy would be adversely affected. But I think the opposite is true. This would make the government inherently dependent upon the economy. If we're not out there spending, they're not making any money. With the system we have now, the government doesn't feel pain. If there's a recession, the government still gets your money first. You get to keep what they allow. Start taxing what's sold on a day-to-day basis, the government gets a piece of the action—but if the economy goes sour, so do they.

Some people also worry that a national sales tax would create a big black market, because a lot of the economy would go underground to avoid paying it. Again, I don't see that happening. Right now, people making incomes off illegal businesses like gambling or drugs don't pay income tax on them. But everybody *buys* things and, when they do, they're paying taxes. The same would be true for foreign visitors, whose purchases would all be a bigger boon to our economy.

Since our gross national product is in the trillions, I think that should be enough to run our government. If you shifted the entire economy to being based upon purchasing, I've seen studies that the sales tax could be as low as twelve percent. Not thirty percent, like most people are paying in income taxes today. And the IRS could shift from monitoring *us* to keeping tabs on our government. If the Pentagon is wasting money by buying $200 toilet seats, they get harassed, instead of private citizens.

Of course, I realize that we'd need a constitutional amendment to make this kind of change. But that's how income tax happened, in 1913. Something our forefathers never envisioned—that the government would receive the fruits of your labor before you would.

After September 11, 2001, the entire country went into an economic slump. In Minnesota, our huge surplus turned into a projected $2 billion deficit through 2003. In order to balance the budget, I had to call for something I swore I never would: raising people's taxes.

I came out for increasing taxes on cigarettes, and even newspapers and magazines. I wanted to extend the sales tax to legal services and auto repairs.

The two parties, however, chose to ignore me and set out to fix the deficit their way—which was nothing but smoke and mirrors, and an effort to do it without raising any taxes. We ended up in a stalemate in 2002. I called the legislature's approach "a classic Alfred E. Neuman 'What, me worry?' scenario." Their plans reminded me of the homeowner who makes house repairs with cheap materials that last just long enough for them to sell it to someone else. Then the new owner comes along and gets stuck with all the bills when the place falls apart. I didn't want our citizens suckered into this kind of cheap trick.

The legislature set out to isolate me and go their own way. So, I gave it back to them in kind. When they came to deliver the budget bill to my office, nobody answered the door. So, the two party honchos came out to my ranch at ten o'clock that night, bringing the TV cameras along. It was a big charade, trying to make it look like they were staying up late doing their job, while I was avoiding them. One of my state troopers guarding the ranch refused to say whether I was there. (I was inside watching a Timberwolves game.) The next morning, some legislative staff put out "missing" posters with my picture that said, "Have you seen me? Last seen 2/21/02 before 4:30."

A few days later, I vetoed the legislature's budget bill that was still going to leave a deficit of about $400 million. They then overrode my veto. One of their cost-saving items cut the budget for my security detail by $175,000. How did I respond to that? I told reporters it might be a good idea to save that money by shutting down the governor's mansion, so state troopers wouldn't need to be paid to guard it. Losing 11 percent of my governor's budget, I had to keep in place what runs the office efficiently. To me, the mansion was just a showplace where the governor or his family can meet with dignitaries. I was only half-kidding when I said that, instead, "we could have them up to the Capitol and we could order Chinese and Domino's."

The mansion is also a huge money pit, because it's an old residence built back around the turn of the twentieth century. It's had more than $5 million of renovations through the years, and you'd never know it. I said, "For God's sake, for $5 million we could go build a state-of-the-art house like Jimmy Jam Harris, the record producer, did on Lake Minnetonka." The governor's residence still had lead in the pipes, and my family was drinking water from these! I actually had to go to the Department of Health and get them to fix that, after I had my physical and the doctor found the level of lead in my blood was higher than it should be.

So if the legislature wanted to engage in a power play, I was ready. At the end of April, the moving trucks backed up to the mansion and started taking away the artwork and antique furniture to be put in storage. My family and I moved out.

Headline: MINNESOTA: GOVERNOR SHUTS MANSION

Gov. Jesse Ventura shut down the governor's mansion, laid off most of the staff and declared it unavailable for all but limited official functions. The governor said lawmakers had left him no choice but to close the 20-room English Tudor-style residence when they cut his spending and reduced his security budget.

—The New York Times, *May 1, 2002*

Well, I really got hammered for that one. I didn't realize how an ancient house like that somehow endears itself to people. Of course, the media wouldn't be clear in telling the public the real reasons. They just said I was being spiteful over the budget. The fact was that the legislature's budget left me no recourse.

Before they adjourned, the legislature used up what little remained of budget reserves, made their short-term fix, and didn't raise anybody's taxes. And they restored the $375,000 for my security and for reopening the mansion. I went and played golf their last day in session, and then vetoed the bill, which I fully expected they would override, and they did.

In the years since I left office, the state of Minnesota has had to live with, and try to recover from, what the legislature did with that last budget. The public is told the story that they were left my mess. They were not. My completely balanced budget would have solved the entire deficit problem.

Messes like that one are the reason why I also pushed for Minnesota to move to a unicameral legislature. I proposed that our House and Senate be combined into a single body of 135 members, down from 201. That way, I believed government would be more accountable and responsible. The state would also save about $20 million a year. I wanted at least to get this on the ballot, so Minnesotans could vote one way or the other.

The only state to have a unicameral legislative is Nebraska, which has had one house for the past eighty-some years. Do you know that, in all that time, they have never been forced into a special session to reach a budget conclusion? That speaks volumes. In a unicameral set-up, you don't have two separate houses holding each other up! Unlike Minnesota, where the last several years of legislative sessions haven't finished on time because of a budget deadlock. (I think the legislators shouldn't be paid at all for these special sessions but, in fact, they get more per diem.)

At the federal level, yes, we need the check-and-balance of different make-ups in a House and a Senate. Otherwise, California would run the nation, in terms of representation, because they're the biggest state. But at a state level, this actually goes against the constitution of Minnesota. It's supposed to be one person, one vote. Not one person who gets two votes. That's why Alan Speer, a brilliant constitutional scholar who sat in our House of Representatives, supported me on unicameral.

Well, I couldn't even get the legislature to bring this to a floor vote. Even at a time when the entire private sector was being forced to cut back, government wasn't *about* to consider reducing itself. I called them "gutless cowards," and I meant it.

Term limits, in my view, would be a damned good idea. Maybe politicians wouldn't then be quite so beholden to the power of corporate lobbyists. The only lobbyist I ever knowingly met with as governor was one I used—to try to get a floor vote on a unicameral legislature. Otherwise, I told my staff from the beginning: lobbyists and special interests did not elect me, so why do I need to talk to them now?

Emiliano Zapata Boulevard, the main drag of Guerrero Negro, is unpaved and dusty. The next morning, I maneuver the camper slowly past the taco stands, motels, pharmacies, restaurants, and bars, to where the street ended at a bank, a grocery store, and a small, palm-lined park. There races a group of teenaged boys, booting a soccer ball around between a pair of makeshift goal posts.

Soccer, *fútbol* in Mexico, as in much of the world, is *the* sport. I'm not a big fan, except when the World Cup rolls around every four years. My passion is the Minnesota Timberwolves. I was a season ticket-holder, and tried not to miss a game. What I'm *not* a fan of in the least is the power that money has come to exert over professional sports. And, as Terry and I pause to watch these enthusiastic kids playing soccer in a little town in Mexico, I think back to some of the brouhahas I became involved in as governor.

In 1997, the year before I ran for governor, there was talk that the Minnesota Twins baseball franchise was going to have to move unless a new stadium got built. Even Mexico City was said to be in the running to get the team. Governor Carlson tried to scare people by claiming a tristate group from the Carolinas was about to buy the Twins. Reporters went down there and discovered this was a made-up hoax.

Carl Pohlad, a billionaire banker who owned the team, wanted the state to pay for a new stadium. I'd been asked, in every debate during the campaign, would I support public money for new sports arenas? I said emphatically no. In the case of baseball, unless the stadium is under a roof for half the year, there's nothing you can use it for during a Minnesota winter except maybe to send kids in to make snowmen in the middle of the field. A pro football team spends even less time in the stadium, maybe ten games a year.

I was playing a golf tournament in Tahoe, when the greatest hockey player in the world—Wayne Gretzky—came up to me. He said, "Governor, are you being pressured to build new stadiums in Minnesota?" I said I was, and Wayne said, "These owners fly off in their jets to $10,000-a-night hotel rooms in the Bahamas to have their meetings. They laugh at how they can manipulate the government and get the public, the working guy, to pay for their stadiums. Be the first one to say no." I said, "Trust me, Wayne. I will be." (I hope he hasn't changed, now that he's part owner of the Phoenix Coyotes.)

So I told Carl Pohlad that the state wasn't in the business of financing a new stadium. He kept on making noises about selling the Twins. Pohlad happened to be good buddies with Bud Selig, the former owner of the Milwaukee Brewers who then became commissioner of baseball. Selig turned the Brewers over to his daughter and, as the closest team geographically to the Twin Cities, don't you think they might reap some benefit from getting rid of the Twins? I wasn't all that surprised when, in 2001, Selig came up with a plan to eliminate two teams from the league: the Montreal Expos and the Twins. As part of his "contraction proposal," the other owners would be paying Pohlad $120 million to liquidate the team. (Several years earlier, Pohlad had given Selig a loan, in violation of baseball's conflict of interest rules.)

So, at the end of 2001, I went to Washington to testify before Congress to oppose what I saw as an extortion scheme surrounding the Twins. Selig was there, and we sat right next to each other. He was claiming that the poor baseball owners were suffering economic losses of close to $600 million. My response was, these owners were also getting huge tax write-offs. I testified: "That's why I have a hard time believing it, Mr. Selig, that they're losing that kind of money and still paying the salaries they're paying [averaging about $2.5 million a player]. It's asinine. These people did not get the wealth they have being stupid!"

From the public response I got, I think I might have been speaking for baseball fans everywhere. Especially with the budget deficit Minnesota was then facing, I still wasn't about to back public financing for a new stadium. Well, the minute the new Republican governor came in, House Speaker Sviggum—who'd also been opposing it—suddenly carried a bill to raise sales taxes in Hennepin County in order to pay for one. That's because it's all about legacy.

If the pro teams left on my watch, the rogue independent governor Jesse Ventura would have taken the blame. Now, with a Republican governor, all stadiums will get built.

The Minnesota Vikings' owner, a billionaire from San Antonio named Red McCombs who started out selling cars, was another who wanted a new stadium. Skip Humphrey, who everybody had assumed would be the next governor, canceled a gubernatorial debate that had been planned for months, to be held in front of students from all the high schools in the state—because he was being wined and dined in Red's private box at a football game. I pointed that out at the next debate, and Skip didn't know what to say. Of course, Red called in his congratulations the day after I won the election.

After the Vikings came within an overtime period of making the Super Bowl in January of '99, Red asked if we could have a meeting. I enjoyed it immensely, although I can unequivocally say that, from a business standpoint, it was the worst meeting I had in my four years as governor. That's because Red came in with no preparation, no plan whatsoever. He simply plopped down in a chair in my office and said, in his Texas accent, "I need a new stadium, governor."

Chuckling inside, playing naïve and dumb, I said, "Well, Red, build one. I'm certain there's someone out there you could buy the land from. What do you need to see me for?"

Red cleared his throat a few times and said, "Well, I can't do that without some participation of state money."

I said, "But Red, you're private enterprise. Why would you require state money?" Maybe, having only bought the team the previous summer, Red was a rookie at the fund-raising game. Or maybe he was just used to getting what he wanted, with his holdings in oil, and TV and radio stations. I then explained to Red that our Metrodome, where both the Vikings and Twins played, was younger than my son, who was twenty-one at the time. I felt very strongly that, when government or the public participate in building something, they should expect they'll get more than twenty to twenty-five years of life from it. I went on to tell him that my Roosevelt High School had been built way back in the 1920s, and kids were still being educated there.

"Red, outside the stadium the trees aren't even mature yet," I added. "They were planted when the dome was built, and they've only grown twenty feet, and these are big beautiful trees that reach as high as fifty feet."

Red then got to the gist of the matter. Which was keeping up with the Joneses. He explained to me that the average NFL owner made somewhere between $8 and $12 million a year, but he was some 50 percent lower than the average. Well, governors are expected to think on their feet and come up with quick solutions, so I did.

"Red, if that's the problem, the dome holds about 64,000 people, doesn't it?" He said, yeah.

I said, "You have ten home games, counting preseason, that are all sold out." He said, yeah.

I said, "Okay, that makes it easy. We can multiply in tens off the top of our heads. If you raise your ticket prices ten dollars a seat, and you keep selling out, that's $640,000. Do that over ten games, it's $6.4 million. Doesn't that put you right in the middle of that average the other owners are making? In the spirit of true capitalism, Red, when your product is selling out, you have the ability to raise the price until it doesn't. I don't think ten dollars a seat, or even twenty, would upset the apple cart that bad. Why a new stadium? I would think you should look at all other options first. A stadium is a huge investment, and there may be fixes we can do here to get you happy."

"Governor," Red replied, "I can't simply just put this on the backs of our most loyal fans."

I responded back, "Red, my wife couldn't care less about football. In fact, my wife frankly couldn't give a *rat's ass* about football." (I always figured it was smart to use language a wealthy Texan would understand.) "My wife pays taxes to the state of Minnesota. So do a lot of other people who think just like her. And I have to represent all of these people, and all of their interests."

That was pretty much the end of the meeting. From that point on, any time he could, Red would tell people: "Minnesota was great until we got this character Jesse Ventura as governor." For my part, I called upon the Vikings to open their finances to public scrutiny, in order to help taxpayers make an informed decision on whether they deserved public funding.

My last year in office, Red put the team on the block. Three years later, in 2005, he found a buyer who agreed to pay him about $625 million. Since he'd bought the team for about $246 million back in '98, I'd say Red made out—for lack of a better phrase—like a bandit. With or without Jesse Ventura and a new stadium.

On our way out of Guerrero Negro, we pass a brick-and-concrete complex with a sign—ESSA, which stands for Exportadora de Sal. This was headquarters for one of the world's biggest manufacturers of industrial salt. It turns out there are some 14,000 uses for salt, everything from making plastics and paper, to glass, aluminum, and fertilizer. According to our guidebook, the company's founder back in 1954 had been none other than Daniel K. Ludwig, a reclusive American billionaire who at one time was the richest man on the planet. Always looking for new commodities to transport in his lucrative shipping business, Ludwig had sailed down the Baja coastline and bought the rights to extract salt from the nearby lagoons. In 1973, he'd sold out to Japan's Mitsubishi Corporation.

"Guess it's hard to escape from billionaires out to make a few extra bucks," I tell Terry, and put the pedal to the metal into Baja's Vizcaíno Desert, among the high cardón cactuses and the thick-tangled cholla.

CHAPTER 10

The More Things Change, the More They Stay the Same

"In any moment of decision, the best thing you can do is the right thing. The worst thing you can do is nothing."

—*Theodore Roosevelt*

Above the many miles of scrub and cactus that line the desert plains, the Sierra de San Francisco mountains appear suddenly. The Vizcaíno Biosphere Reserve we're driving through stretches across more than six million acres, and is the largest protected area of its kind in all Latin America. It's the last habitat for more than one hundred peninsular pronghorn antelope, here called *berrendo*. Terry and I are keeping our eyes out for these deer-like animals, one of the fastest in the world, with the capacity to sprint at speeds of 55 miles an hour.

Some eighty miles south of Guerrero Negro, we approach the old mission town of San Ignacio. You need to turn off the main highway for a mile to reach it. Driving down an avenue of Arabian date palms and citrus trees—first planted by Jesuit missionaries about three hundred years ago, and still the primary livelihood for the oasis's thousand residents—you come to a square shaded by huge laurels. Behind it stands what's described as one of Baja's most beautiful churches. It was built over a fifty-year period in the eighteenth century of nearly four-foot-thick lava-block walls.

We take a look inside the stone church with its whitewashed façade. An effigy of Saint Ignatius of Loyola glares down at us from the altar. When the first priest came here in 1716, our guidebook says, the Jesuit order was still among the most powerful in Rome. Most of the work of founding this mission, which for a while was the biggest and most prosperous in Baja, fell to a priest who used to tell the local Indians: "Come to the faith of Jesus Christ! Oh! If only I could make all of you Christians and take you to paradise."

That sounded familiar. The missionaries founded schools and took the native children away from their parents to indoctrinate them in the Christian religion. One historian wrote of the mission system: "There was nothing voluntary about it. . . . Every mission had its whipping post, its jail cell, its set of iron shackles, its stocks." Not to mention all the Baja Indians who died from new diseases the Europeans brought with them—smallpox, typhoid, measles, even the flu. They just had no immunity. From disease or from persecution. It wasn't a matter of choice. And I couldn't help but be drawn back, once again, to my time as governor—and the increasing intolerance I saw sweeping the country. My home state was not immune from that.

The Christian right wing in America is a polarizing force when it comes to gay rights, abortion, and patriotism. To me, these aren't "issues," they are matters of individual freedom of choice. But the militant Christians, like the Baja missionaries of several centuries ago, are just about ready to burn at the stake those who disagree with their fire-and-brimstone approach. They especially don't like anything beyond their idea of the "normal"—like the percentage of our population who happen to be gay.

To me, gay rights is simple: it's about equality. We're all supposed to be equal under the Constitution, which doesn't say anything about the "Hetero States of America." (Granted, I often wonder how our forefathers could have written a document about everyone being equal under God and the law when they owned slaves.) Gay rights hit home to me personally, through the world of pro wrestling, believe it or not. I had a good friend who was gay, and he had a partner. They'd been together for as long as any married couple, probably well over twenty-five years. At one point, my friend's partner became ill and had to go into the hospital. He was in the intensive care unit, and my friend was not allowed to sit bedside—because the hospital rules stated explicitly "spouse" or "next of kin." In the eyes of the law and of society, he fit neither category. I thought, that's just plain cruel and inhumane.

I fought hard during my four years as governor to get equal rights for Minnesota state employees who happened to be gay. We were losing some of the best and the brightest to the private sector, simply because they were gay and not receiving the benefits that should be provided. Most of the major corporations in Minnesota—General Mills, IBM, and others—provide health care and other benefits for gay couples. It's a known fact that you get paid less in the public sector. The most I could pay any of my commissioners was $115,000 a year. In the same position in the private sector, you can bet they'd be making a quarter-of-a-million. Generally speaking, you entice people to work in government because the state provides a better benefit package.

As part of the settlement of a state employees strike in 2001, I finally achieved this for gay people. The benefits didn't last long beyond my time in office, though. When the contract came up for renegotiation, and there was no strike, the new governor proposed a pay freeze—and a cut in benefits for gays. And the union accepted these terms. So much for Democrats supporting gays; that was the first thing they bargained away.

As for gay marriage, a solution I endorse comes from a woman I met at Harvard when I was teaching there. She said, "Governor, solving the gay marriage question is simple. Government should not acknowledge marriage at all. Government should only acknowledge civil unions." That way, when you fill out the consent form, your sex doesn't even have to be asked. From that point on, you allow the church—a private institution—to choose whether or not to recognize gay marriage. But when two people are forming a civil union, whether you are heterosexual or homosexual doesn't matter. The government is off the hook. With all the bickering and fighting over gay marriage, that's as simple as it needs to be.

I'm proud of the fact that in 2006, *Lavender*—the top gay magazine in Minnesota—put me on the cover and said I was the best governor for gay rights in the state's history. I find it interesting that distinction would come to a heterosexual Navy frogman, someone who could see through all the smoke and mirrors and know the difference between right and wrong. Even though I'm sure that the Christian right's opinion would be that I'm completely out of line.

My views on abortion come from my mom. She was a nurse in surgery for her entire adult life, and used to tell me how terrible it was before *Roe vs. Wade*—when back-alley abortions often placed the woman's life in danger. Today, some people live under a false premise that, if the government makes something illegal, it will go away. But then the illegal activity is simply controlled by an underground or criminal element. And, in the case of abortion, you will not receive the safety and precautions necessary.

In 2000, when I was governor, the Minnesota legislature passed what its supporters called the "Woman's Right to Know" bill. It required that abortion providers give their patients information about alternatives, twenty-four hours before they had their abortion. Its opponents, including myself, preferred to call it the "Women Are Stupid" bill. Wouldn't a woman walking into an abortion clinic already know what it is, and have come to a decision? She doesn't need to read all this material on adoption, etc., in case she might change her mind. This piece of legislation seemed more like the first step toward additional restrictions on abortion services.

Running for office in 1998, I'd been asked to fill out a questionnaire for the Minnesota Family Council. I said that, without question, I opposed any ban on partial-birth abortions. But I also stated at the time that, while I wouldn't promote any legislation calling for a twenty-four-hour waiting period, I'd sign it if the legislature passed it. So it's true that I changed my position, after doing some considerable fact-checking, question-asking, and soul-searching when the bill became a reality.

First I had my staff call up a half-dozen abortion clinics in Minnesota and ask if any of them provided abortions in less than twenty-four hours. They all assured us that it already requires more than a twenty-four-hour wait after a woman walks in—it doesn't happen immediately. So then what was the point of making the law?

I consulted with a former governor of Minnesota, Elmer Anderson. He was a great inspiration to me, and a terrific educator. He made it very clear that the Republican Party of today is not the same party that he'd been proud to be a part of. When I asked Elmer his advice on the abortion question, he said, "Abortion is religion's failure to persuade. So now they must legislate."

When even the Democratic Senate passed the twenty-four-hour notification bill only a few days after the Republican House, my office was literally besieged with thousands of phone calls from both sides on the issue. I had to either sign the bill, veto it, or allow it to become law without my signature in three days.

Terry and I were on our way to Washington, where Vice President Gore had invited us to dinner at his home.

They stayed up past midnight chitchatting about "everything under the sun." Their wives went horseback riding together. They chuckled at each other's jokes, took turns poking fun at reporters and even dressed alike, in chinos and polo shirts.

Headline: Gore's New Pal, a Favorite of Independent Voters

But the broader political point Mr. Gore seemed intent on hammering home was his own growing closeness to Mr. Ventura, a former professional wrestler who won election on the Reform Party line in 1998 and remains a favorite of independent voters across the nation.

—The New York Times, *June 23, 2000*

I like Al Gore a great deal. The first time we met, the Gores had come to Minnesota after I became governor. My daughter, Jade, was in the Cavalcade of Roses horse show, and they sat in the audience. His Washington residence was the old Naval Observatory, where they have the big telescope. A highlight of our night there was when my First Lady beat Tipper in pool.

I spoke with Al about the abortion bill situation. I told him the whole scenario, how I was taking a tremendous amount of heat, being called a flip-flopper and a bunch of other names because, as a candidate, I'd said I had no particular problem with the bill.

"What do you do in a situation like this?" I asked the vice president.

"It's simple," he told me. "You throw everything else out of the equation, and you go with what you believe is right."

The gave me the courage to stick to my convictions. I went on National Public Radio in Washington and, when asked about the twenty-four-hour waiting period, I said: "It's not like driving into a McDonald's and pulling up and saying, 'I want a number-four cheeseburger.' You have to make an appointment." I went on ABC's *Good Morning America* and told Charles Gibson: "Really, what I think the question comes down to is, how involved in our personal, private lives do we want to interject government?"

I made an offer to the right wing: "I'll sign this bill if you make all optional surgical procedures have a twenty-four-hour waiting period, which would include liposuction." They were appalled.

Back in Minnesota, I announced my decision on the bill in the governor's reception room. No lawmakers, lobbyists, or members of the public were allowed. I read my statement, and took no questions from the media. Security was tight, because of all the emotion this arouses in people.

I said: "I have decided it is wrong for government to assume a role in something I have always believed was between a woman, her family, her doctor, and, if she chooses, her clergy." And I vetoed the bill.

The next year, the House Republicans decided to attach the "twenty-four-hour notification" to a Health and Human Services bill that set aside money for health care, nursing homes, and welfare for low-income citizens. They were basically making hostages out of the sick, the elderly, and the poor. More political gamesmanship, and the Senate went for it, too!

I vetoed this bill also, and sent it back asking the legislature to remove the four pages of abortion language. That was the year I had to threaten a government shutdown. They ended up giving in.

Let's talk about a few of the other "heresies," in the eyes of the religious zealots. President Bush supports a ban on abortion, but opposes stem-cell research. That clearly shows me that he has more concern for the unborn than for the living. In fact, he apparently has no problem with sending the living off to die in a stupid war. Unlike what's happening over in Iraq, stem-cell research seems like a great potential boon to humanity.

I have a strong belief that you are in charge of your body, whether male or female. It's the house you're living in for your entire existence—your temple, as the more religious might say. When that body gives out, as happened to Terry Schiavo, I also think the family has a right to "pull the plug." Where was the public outcry over what the U.S. Congress did in the Schiavo case? After all those years on life support, Congress voted to keep the woman alive, when even her husband wanted to let her go. What Congress did was actually a violation of the Constitution—which states, unequivocally, that you cannot pass a law for one person. Was that done out of arrogance? Naïvete or stupidity? Bowing down to the religious right constituency, perhaps?

Another of the religious right's scams is marching into public school science classes and trying to mandate teaching of "creation science," as opposed to evolution. Somehow, they put evolutionism and creationism in the same category—believing that one makes the other impossible. But aren't these two separate systems of knowledge? One is a scientific theory, the other is a religious doctrine. It's kind of like comparing the law of gravity to the Sermon on the Mount. Evolution doesn't pretend to disprove the Bible's version of creation, or the belief in an all-powerful being as "prime mover" of the universe. Science only deals with what's observable, definable, and measurable. It's open to all possibilities, unlike creationism, which is a closed book. So leave evolution to the science teachers, and creation to the Sunday school of the parents' choosing.

I find it one of the ironies of our times that DNA evidence is now considered indisputably scientific when it comes to convicting or releasing criminals. Yet, to many evangelicals, DNA evidence about how old the earth is or when we humans arrived here is dismissed—because the "literal truth" of the Bible says something different.

Given how many convicts awaiting capital punishment have been cleared because of DNA evidence, I no longer support the death penalty. Minnesota doesn't have this on the books, so I'm thankful that, as governor, I never had to face the decision of whether to execute someone on death row. Again, I simply don't believe that government has the inherent right to make those kinds of choices.

I don't think that patriotism should be forced upon people, either. Patriotism comes from within. I learned about it from my mom and dad, from knowing that they went and fought in World War II. I don't find it patriotic to make our youth pledge allegiance to their government. In fact, wasn't that what the Hitler Youth did? Or something maybe the Taliban do today?

So when the Minnesota legislature passed a Pledge of Allegiance bill that would have required public school students to recite the Pledge, I had my veto pen ready again. That was the way my fourth, and final, legislative session ended. Let me expand on my reasoning a little bit. Take the "under God" part of the Pledge. If there is a child in school whose parents are atheists, why should there be a reference to God that they are forced to say? Yet what kid won't do so, rather than face the pressure from their peers if they refuse?

Especially at these young ages, I call it brainwashing to make it mandatory to recite the Pledge of Allegiance. If a teacher wants to make this part of the classroom, all they need do is simply say, "You know, I'm very patriotic. And every morning when you come into class, I'm going to stand up and say a Pledge of Allegiance to my country. You're welcome to join me if you'd like."

In my opinion, this is even more apropos in a free society where we're supposed to be able to *protest* our government if we don't like what it's doing. I saw a great bumper sticker recently, on a car being driven by an elderly couple in Minnesota. I'm going to use it now whenever I talk about my opposition to the Iraq War and to George Bush. It said, "Dissent is the highest form of patriotism."

Guess who said that? Thomas Jefferson. He is a helluva lot higher on my list than Bush, when it comes to who created this country and who knows what America is *supposed* to be all about.

"All that inspired by what the priests in Baja used to do to the Baja Indians?" Terry wants to know. I admit it's pretty easy to get me standing on my soapbox, whether or not there's anybody listening, something I do wonder about. We were back on Highway 1 again. Not far below San Ignacio, three spectacular volcanic peaks called "Las Tres Virgenes" (the Three Virgins) crown the horizon at more than six thousand feet. They were capped by clouds, and rather startling as they rose ponderously above a sea of cactus. Our guidebook says the volcano last erupted 27,000 years ago, but it still holds seething, molten rock, seeming to promise a future return to power.

As Terry finishes reading that passage aloud, she adds, "Reminds me of somebody."

"Yeah, I'm still seething, but it hasn't been *that* long!"

I think back to a headline I saw on a Mexican newspaper when we stopped for gas. In the U.S., the Virginia Tech shooting spree had just occurred. "USA 33, Mexico 20," the headline read.

"That's because Mexico had twenty people killed in the drug war that day," I tell Terry. "People are being gunned down, even governments in Latin American are being bought out and overthrown because the drug cartels have more money and more firepower. It's all because of *our* war on drugs—because of the high prices they're getting are coming from us."

"I remember you telling me what your mom said right before she died," Terry says.

"She was coherent until the very end. 'You know, this war on drugs is identical to prohibition of alcohol in the twenties,' she told me. I said, 'Why is that, Mom?' And she said, 'Because when something is prohibited, the gangsters get rich. In the twenties, it was Al Capone and all those guys. Now it's the same thing with the big drug dealers.'"

It's long been another pet peeve of mine. I wish that Canada and Mexico would legalize marijuana, because that would put the United States on an island. You'd have two countries proving, like the city of Amsterdam has, that making drugs legal is not a negative formula, but the best way to deal with the problem. Making something illegal doesn't mean it goes away, it just means criminals are going to run it.

Why not treat marijuana in the same way as alcohol and tobacco? It's so widely used, and it has medical purposes that are denied by the U.S. Food and Drug Administration. Numerous doctors and private studies have clearly shown that medicinal marijuana is a painkiller that can help cancer and AIDS patients, and can also be used to treat glaucoma. The latest breakthrough is that it helps Alzheimer's patients. The hippie generation used to be warned that, if you smoke pot, pretty soon you won't be able to remember what happened two days ago. Well, turns out it does something to protect a chromosome in the Alzheimer's patient's head to allow them to *keep* their memory. Since this has now been proven, I wonder what the next excuse will be for not legalizing it. (And yes, I *have* inhaled. Very few didn't who came of age in the sixties.)

On the Internet, I read that if you factor in the price per ounce of marijuana, it's now the largest cash crop in America. It's passed corn, wheat, and soybeans. But you have to look at how things are skewed by keeping marijuana illegal. Roughly an ounce of top-grade marijuana today costs around four hundred bucks. Well, how much is an ounce of corn, wheat, or soybeans? You're lucky if it's two cents! They don't even bother to measure these in less than bushels. What would a bushel of marijuana be worth, going at $400 an ounce? That's why it brings in more revenue than all those other crops.

The fact is, growing hemp for industrial purposes would make it a very useful plant. It can be a fiber for clothing, a source of paper, even an alternative fuel. Canada is already using hemp this way. I simply don't see that cannabis grows wild on earth just so humans can eradicate it.

Of course, the work of eradicating marijuana creates jobs within law enforcement. If we made it legal, and taxed it like we do tobacco and alcohol, maybe those law enforcement people could start paying more attention to murders and terrorism. I also think it's time for people to rise up against the prescription drug industry, the biggest opponent of legalization. You have to remember that they don't want anything out there that they can't make a profit from.

Marijuana is a weed, and that means you can grow it, essentially free. This doesn't sit well with the pharmaceutical industry, and I think our Food and Drug Administration is nothing but a puppet whose strings the industry pulls.

I continue to muse about the political process and what's happened to it. "You know," I say to Terry, "it's a myth that somehow all these career politicians are something special. My election killed that mystique. It wasn't my career. I wasn't created by the system that maintains only these supposed 'leaders' can do the job. You mean a dumb old wrestler could come in and be the chief executive in charge of a $28 billion budget?"

"We can't have *that*!" Terry echoes my thought.

"By God, then people will think the gas station attendant might be able to do it! But in essence, isn't that what we're supposed to be? According to our founding fathers, we're a government of the people, where you bring to bear whatever your life experiences are. Not today."

"You're also supposed to work for the good of the state, so . . ." I interrupt, "Today you have to be created by the political parties to lead the country."

"Paul Wellstone wasn't really like that," Terry says. "But I think the saddest example of what it can all devolve into was his memorial service."

"Oh," I say, and take a deep breath. It was painful to remember the night. "For the first half hour, I actually said to myself, 'By God, they're going to do it right.' They had the opportunity to be above it all. I guess I should have expected they'd blow it."

Senator Wellstone was killed in a plane crash in northern Minnesota on October 25, 2002. This was only eleven days before his potential reelection, in a crucial race that might determine whether the Democrats would control the U.S. Senate. A lot of people have speculated that somebody might have tampered with his plane, but I don't believe there was any conspiracy. I remember the morning he crashed, and the weather was horrible. I wouldn't have flown that day, especially in a twin-engine private plane.

Wellstone and I did not get along very well, by his choosing, I think. He didn't like me, because he'd been considered "the man of the people" and I kind of took his title from him—winning as an independent with even a more grass-roots campaign than his had been. He was quite belligerent to me once, when we were both in Washington. Toward the end, he started to mellow and soften up a bit.

Of course, I must admit I had once given him "the look." Senator Wellstone had never served in the military, but as a politician he did a lot for vets, which of course I respected. One Veterans Day, we were onstage together at a function out at a VA Hospital. They announced to us that the Veteran's Band would be playing the four different songs of the services—including "Anchors Away" for the Navy and "Caissons" for the Army. When a service's song was played, they asked members of that service to stand.

My branch, the Navy, happened to be last. The Army's was first. The Senator was sitting next to Colonel Lord, a good friend of mine, a former "helo" pilot in Vietnam. As they started to play the Army's song, naturally Colonel Lord rose to attention. I glanced over, and Senator Wellstone was standing, too! So I gave him "the look"—which meant, "Excuse me, senator, at what point did you take an oath to give a few years of your life to Army service? You stand when they play the National Anthem, but this is not a photo-op. This is for the guys who actually put on a uniform."

Obviously the senator hadn't been paying a lot of attention to what was going on. I think someone from his staff came over and whispered to him, and he then quickly sat back down.

Of course, what happened to Senator Wellstone, his wife, and one of their children was a terrible tragedy. A memorial service was held in Williams Arena at the University of Minnesota and broadcast live on national TV. A number of high profile politicians attended, including President Clinton and his wife, and Vice President Gore. I told Terry as we arrived, "I'm here to honor the senator and his death and his family, but if this turns political, we're leaving."

TERRY: We went to a little get-together beforehand. It was just the Wellstone family and a few other politicians. The husband of Paul and Sheila's daughter, who was also killed in the crash, came over and hugged me and cried on my shoulder. It was so touching, so very sad.

But I knew it was going to go badly when, as we walked into the arena, some of the mourners booed me. They also booed Trent Lott, the Republican Senate minority leader. Granted, Lott and Wellstone were probably polar opposites—but the senator from Mississippi was nonetheless traveling a considerable distance to pay his respects.

After an hour and a half, the service was going on and on. It had ceased to be a memorial. It had turned into a campaign rally for a Democratic successor to Wellstone. As things deteriorated, I sat there grinding my teeth.

TERRY: When he sits too long, he starts shaking his leg, wanting to rock and move. He's just that way. I always carry gum because my mouth gets dry all the time from taking allergy medicine. So I was going to have some, and I handed a piece to him, because then he could move his jaw instead of bouncing his leg.

By that time, I probably needed a piece of gum because I was getting so pissed off. Later on, Al Franken took me to task in his book for chewing gum at a funeral. When I ran into him on an airplane, I explained what had been happening inside me. We had a respectful conversation, and we're on good terms now.

Minnesota law required that Wellstone's name be removed from the ballot, and the replacement candidate the Democrats had chosen was former Vice President Walter Mondale. I'll never forget Rick Kahn, one of Wellstone's closest friends, saying to the crowd: "I'm begging you to help us win this Senate election for Paul Wellstone." I found this extremely offensive at a funeral!

TERRY: I kept holding him back and he kept looking at me and, when that happened, I put my head on his shoulder and said, "Okay, now it's no longer a funeral, it's time to leave."

It was too much even for her. I took Terry's hand and said, "Let's go." I think Senator Lott had already left. A bunch of us evacuated pretty fast. We took a great deal of heat from the Democrats and their staunchest supporters, like Franken, for doing this. I respect Paul Wellstone, I think he accomplished some terrific things and fought for a lot of great causes. But for his fellow Democrats to stand up there at a memorial service and tell people *not* to vote their conscience? That really crossed the line. I felt used, violated, and duped.

I had the option to pick a replacement senator to serve out the remainder of Wellstone's term through January 2003. And I went so far as to declare that I'd accept resumés for the position from everyone except Democrats. Privately, I was planning to appoint whoever won Wellstone's seat on election day. They'd get to Washington ahead of all the other rookies, which would give them seniority. When the winner turned out to be Norm Coleman, the Republican mayor of St. Paul, whom I'd defeated for governor, this would still have been fine with me.

The reason I changed my mind was because, when a debate was held between Coleman and Mondale shortly before the election, they wouldn't allow Jim Moore of the Independence Party to participate. Moore was the candidate from the *governor's* party, which was obviously as much a major party as the other two. So I said to myself, "That's how they want to play? Well, then watch and see what I'm going to do."

Headline: MINNESOTA GOVERNOR APPOINTS SENATOR

As if the 107th Congress had not been sufficiently unpredictable, Gov. Jesse Ventura confounded its final days today with his appointment of an independent interim senator who refused to say whether he would vote with Republicans or Democrats. . . .

"I know where the Capitol is," Mr. Barkley said. "So I know where to tell the cabdriver to take me."

Asked what he would do in the Senate, he said, "As much mischief as I can."

—The New York Times, *November 5, 2002*

On the day before the 2002 elections, I appointed my state planning commissioner, Dean Barkley of Minnesota's Independence Party to complete the remaining two months of Wellstone's Senate term. The Democrats and Republicans hollered that I'd finally appointed a crony. But I had good reasons. Dean had run for Congress in the past, so it wasn't a case of my sending someone to Washington who had no experience. He's the man who got me excited about third-party politics in the first place. Now I had appointed an independent U.S. Senator!

Dean came to me and said, "What do you want me to do?" Normally I would have replied, "Be the independent, don't play their game." Had he been going into the Senate for six years, I would never have given him any other advice. But in this instance, for a brief moment in time, Dean would be the swing vote in a Senate that was deadlocked 50–50. Whichever party could sway Dean to their side would prevail. So I wanted him to go to Washington and prove how an independent could bring home the bacon for Minnesota.

So I said, "Play the game, Dean. Get the pork. We need some things done for the people of the state. So get everything you can in exchange for your vote." That's just what he did, on a health care reimbursement that had been languishing for several years, and some other things.

Health care is something you think about driving in Baja. I only drive by day, because the two-lane highway is so narrow. There are no shoulders on parts of it, and often you've got semis coming right at you. Lots of times the curves aren't well marked and, should you go airborne, the landings would tend to be very quick and very fast. It's actually a death-defying experience.

An eerie feeling comes from seeing all of the religious monuments along the side of the road, sometimes as many as three or four to a mile. "Terry, do you think all of these mark places where drivers have had a fatal accident?" I wonder aloud. "You start looking at them all and think, God, I'd be safer driving the triangle in Baghdad! How can there be any population left?!"

Later, we come to learn that, while some of the monuments do indicate a person died there, the majority are simply how the Mexican people honor their dead. Toward dusk, many times they are lit with candles. Yet neither Terry nor I have ever once *seen* anyone lighting them. We know that families must tend these little sacred spaces—but how? When?

I tell Terry that my goal is to continue driving the Baja until we finally see a burning monument with someone standing beside it.

It's at Santa Rosalía where the winding Highway 1 finishes its nearly 130-mile journey from the Pacific coast over to the Sea of Cortez side. In San Ignacio, due to the missions, the architecture has a strong Spanish flavor. But when you start down the narrow streets of Santa Rosalía, you're surprised to see all these French colonial–style houses with the wood frames and the long verandas. There's even a French bakery. And a church that was designed by the French architect Eiffel himself—the same man the Eiffel Tower is named after! Turns out the church, made from prefab iron panels, was originally shown off by Eiffel as a model for inexpensive, ready-made mission churches. It was shipped in sections to Santa Rosalía, from a warehouse in Belgium, and reassembled here toward the end of the nineteenth century.

All this French influence comes from the fact that a French mining company bought the mineral rights to this area in 1885 after huge copper deposits were discovered nearby. They ended up bringing in a copper-smelting foundry by ship, building an eighteen-mile-long railway, and more than 375 miles of mine tunnels. Not to mention a labor force of Yaquí Amerindians and a couple thousand Chinese and Japanese who were told they'd be able to plant rice. (They nearly all left when they found out that rice wouldn't grow in central Baja.)

Anyway, the French smelting went on into the mid-1950s, when the company sold all the facilities to the Mexican government. Driving through Santa Rosalía today, you still see the old mining locomotives all repainted and looking like monuments, amid the rusting smokestacks and abandoned warehouses.

It's like much else you encounter in Baja—always the unexpected. Our next port of call will prove no disappointment along those lines.

CHAPTER 11

In the Eye of the Hurricane

"The trouble with history is that the people who really know what happened aren't talking, and the people who don't, you can't shut 'em up."

—*Tom Waits*

We've been looking forward to seeing Mulegé. It is said to be a charming small town right on the Sea of Cortez, filled with palm, mango and banana trees, a mountain range on the horizon, and the desert on both sides. We'll find scuba centers, and kayaks, windsurfers, and mountain bikes to rent. I was really starting to miss my wave runners.

Reading Steinbeck's *Log from the Sea of Cortez* as we approach, Terry comes to a passage describing how his crew had bypassed Mulegé because they'd heard that "there may be malaria there" and "the port charges are mischievous and ruinous." Maybe we should take that as an omen.

Mulegé is built around a wide arroyo formed by a river that feeds into the Sea of Cortez. So it has an abundance of water, which makes it an ideal place to grow figs, dates, and other crops. As we are about to learn, though, all that water can be a curse as well as a blessing.

Driving through Mulegé almost makes us physically sick. A couple of months earlier, Hurricane John devastated the little town. About a thousand homes, among a population of only 3,000, have been wiped out. An incredible deluge—twenty-five inches of rain inside of twenty-four hours—poured down from the mountains into the valley. The river rose fifteen feet and flooded pretty much everything and swept it out to sea. Not only did the storm flood the roads but it picked up jeeps as if they were toy cars. It collapsed sturdy brick walls, and left houses in pieces. Now most of the people are living in a tent city while they set out to rebuild. Because the sewer systems are damaged, there is still a threat of diseases like cholera, hepatitis, and dengue.

We find out all this at a gas station from an American who brought down a truckload of supplies to help the people. "But I thought hurricanes like this didn't usually hit the Baja," I say. The man shakes his head. "Used to be true," he tells me. "But this year, there were three of them, although not as bad as the one that hit Mulegé. The weather's changing. You can't depend on anything anymore."

Mulegé is the Baja's version, on a small scale, of New Orleans after Katrina. It's a known scientific fact that ocean heat is the main ingredient for forming hurricanes. A new study recently came out showing that hurricanes and typhoons have gotten stronger and longer lasting over the past thirty years, by a factor of about 50 percent! This can be traced directly to a rise in the sea surface temperatures. And that, of course, is all about global warming.

Terry and I had put off seeing Al Gore's movie, *An Inconvenient Truth*, for a while. To be truthful, like a lot of Americans, I was living in some denial about the consequences of global warming. I didn't want to know how bad it might really be. When we finally watched the film, it was every bit as grim a scenario as we'd imagined. The earth's climate is close to a tipping point, about to become warmer than it's been in a million years. Temperatures are going up steadily, the glaciers and polar icecaps are melting, the sea levels are rising. And our kids are looking at a very scary future.

Al Gore doesn't think it's too late. The United States, with all the fossil fuel we burn in our cars, offices, and homes, sends more carbon dioxide into the atmosphere than any other country. Gore says we need to impose an immediate "carbon freeze" on our emissions and, by 2050, reduce these emissions by 90 percent. That obviously means moving to many forms of alternative energy. We also need a carbon tax, and could put aside a portion of revenues from it to help low-income people meet the challenge. We can't build any more coal-fired power plants, and we need to ban incandescent light bulbs and switch over to fluorescent.

After seeing Gore's film, and then the human tragedy of Mulegé, I've become a staunch advocate of doing my part to help slow down global warming. For one thing, I would highly recommend that all new homes, no matter where they are, have included in the mortgage a type of solar-power system that at least works as an auxiliary.

And here's something I would come to find out from a solar expert in Mexico: When we aren't watching our televisions, if we would simply unplug them, there would be no energy shortage in the U.S. We have about 220 million television sets. All of them use stand-by power. But have you ever had a manufacturer tell you that, even if you're using the remote to turn them off, they're still using units of power and draining energy?

When I started unplugging all three of my TV sets, I watched my power usage drop by an amp and a half. I was amazed. Before you push the "on" button, all that's required is a few seconds to walk over and plug in the TV. By the time you've gone back to your chair, it will have warmed up enough to have your picture. Think of how much energy this small gesture could be saving! (Plus, you could have some fun with it. Remember the movie *Network*? Before shutting your TV down for the night, switch over to Fox News and shout out, "I'm mad as hell and I'm not gonna take it anymore!") The fact is, if all the televisions in America were unplugged for eight hours a day, the energy savings would be more than 3,800 gigawatt-hours.

The Bush administration would rather keep its head buried in the sand and keep subsidizing its friends in the oil, gas, and coal industries. They'll stop at nothing to downplay the impacts of global warming. When a study came out saying that polar bears are endangered because the sea ice they depend on is disappearing, the White House insisted this has nothing to do with a changing climate. The U.S. negotiators managed to get rid of language in a recent United Nations report that called for cuts in greenhouse gas emissions. This administration's policy on global warming is: Don't talk about it.

The environment isn't the only area that the federal government is suppressing or manipulating information about. It's happening with prescription drugs and public safety. Nearly two thousand scientists trying to do their jobs researching air quality and other health issues said in a survey they face "an epidemic of interference." What ever happened to the public's right to know?

Mum's the word, I guess. Ignore problems and they'll go away, and we can go on with business as usual. Of course, when the government spreads lies to justify invading a country—in order to get more oil and gas to pump into the atmosphere—what else can you expect? I know where the buck stops: at the door to the White House. I just wonder how far the deceit might go.

Seeing what happened to a place like Mulegé brings Terry and me back, in memory, to another tragedy. The one that occurred when I was governor: September 11, 2001, the day the Twin Towers came down in New York.

I remember it was a warm, clear day at the State Capitol. Within an hour of the attacks, I ordered the opening of Minnesota's Emergency Operations Center in downtown St. Paul. It's been used in the past as a command center, generally for severe weather events. At 10:30 that morning, I arrived with my commissioner of public safety, Charlie Weaver, to brief the media. I told them I'd put the National Guard on alert, and secured some public buildings in the Twin Cities.

I said, "The tragic events of this day are staggering to the sense of security, peace, and calm that we in Minnesota and the United States are used to in our daily lives. This is a time of great shock, great sorrow, and great concern, but this is a time we must be confident that we can meet the very difficult challenges put forth by these senseless and tragic acts."

It was the primary election day, and I wasn't about to call it off. We weren't going to panic. Now, more than ever, I felt, was the time to show the power of democracy.

Sometime within the first six hours, I also called the CIA guy who's based in the region. As governor, I was commander in chief of the Minnesota National Guard. I needed to know if the CIA had any "intel" as to whether Minnesota was a target. Could we be hit? What should we be doing? He told me, "We know nothing more than you do right now." Months later, when I ran into him, he said, "You were the only governor that bothered to call me that day."

We were the first state to hold an official memorial, after 9/11, that next Sunday morning. I give credit to Senator Coleman, who thought of it first. He called me and said, "Let's have a memorial at the Xcel Energy Building in St. Paul." I said, "No, let's do it outside, on the front lawn of the Capitol, because a building won't hold enough people." I ordered my staff to begin organizing what we called "Minnesota Remembers: A Memorial from the Heartland."

It was heart-rending. The crowd exceeded all expectations, even with a drizzling rain falling. Over forty thousand people showed up, every kind of person you could imagine. We had Native Americans there, medicine men pounding drums, right alongside honor guards who represented the policemen and firefighters and military. It showed that, at heart, we were all one. It still chokes me up to think about it.

The ceremony went on for more than two hours and I was the last one to speak. I remember I had on a leather National Guard bomber jacket. I looked out upon hundreds of flags fluttering in the breeze, and dozens of people embracing each other. I told them, "I stand here today humbled but comforted by your presence. That's what family is for, to share with each other the hurt, the sorrow, and the sadness.

"We will overcome this tragic moment," I continued. "We must and we will move forward. We will move forward in fairness. We will live together with tolerance. We will extend our hands to the people of the world in solidarity and unity. We will pit honor against dishonor. We will promote good against evil. And finally, we will together restore our sense of freedom by conquering this enemy! We will do all of this and we will not fail!"

We also passed out three-by-five condolence cards, and asked people at the memorial service to write whatever they wished on them. Terry and I would then personally deliver these to the citizens of New York. We brought the cards with us when Governor Pataki took us down to Ground Zero.

This was almost three weeks after it happened. The smoke was still billowing from the wreckage. Governor Pataki told me, "You'll see steel I-beams three or four blocks away, mostly from when the planes actually hit." He went on, saying that everything from the Hudson to the East River was covered with several inches of dust for the first few days. Everything. The ground, all the plants and trees, all the buildings. It was as if you were walking on the moon.

When we got our first look at the devastation, Terry was overcome. I walked over and put my arm around her. They found the bodies of several firefighters in the debris that day. Every time that happened, all the clean-up work would come to a halt and everybody there would stand in silence while the firefighters carried out the body on a stretcher under an American flag.

TERRY: The first thing I noticed was that the streets of New York were deserted. There were sometimes two or three people at a time; it wasn't like before. The closer we got to Ground Zero, it was weird, there was almost like a thing in the air—you started feeling very afraid and very sad, at the same time. When I saw the devastation, I could not comprehend: Why would anyone want to inflict this kind of damage on someone else? What kind of hatred could the hijackers possibly have, to give their own lives to kill other people like that? And innocent people . . .

Later in the year, Terry went back to Ground Zero on her own. She worked there for ten days, for the Salvation Army. We kept this very quiet, the Minnesota media never learned of it. The people she was working for didn't know who she was. She was Terry from Minnesota.

One day, she was working the chow line, when who came through but somebody she knew—Governor Christie Todd Whitman from New Jersey. She recognized Terry and said, "What are you doing here?" Terry went, "Shhhhhh." Christie moved on.

TERRY: I worked at the coroner's site, mostly in food and also seeing people who had come to receive their benefits. At the four corners, there were little tents set up, and they were still bringing out bodies. The workers could come in and get masks and socks and gloves, eye drops, nose plugs, goggles, hand cream. And teas and coffee and granola bars and aspirin, and bandaids and mercurochrome. Anything they might need out there that they couldn't just run and get.

I remember this one guy came in—I was all alone at the time— and I said, "Would you like some coffee or soup?" He said, "Yeah, maybe some soup." Basically, his job was driving a little truck that had pieces of people that they'd found. The people in there identifying body parts—they'd work twelve or fourteen hour days. Sometimes they'd come up to me and just start spilling their guts. They'd get overwhelmed by it all. It was just so terribly, terribly sad.

We set up a huge toy shop. Kids could come in with their parents and get free toys and gifts for their families. It was all donated. They had buses bringing people in. The lines were tremendously long. As we would run out of toys, some mothers started stealing from other mother's baskets.

But the Salvation Army taught me a huge lesson. When people would come to receive their benefits, they needed two pieces of identification, including a bill from their apartment. This one guy had nothing and he kept yelling at me, "I'd better get some money or I'm going to the press, I'm gonna say the Salvation Army is cheating everybody!" I got really furious. I said, "Just a minute. I have to go talk to my supervisor, because I don't know how to answer your question."

I told my supervisor, "This guy is clearly a scam artist, somebody needs to go out there and have him removed." She looked at me and said, "Terry, think about this man. He lives in such an awful state of mind in his life that he's coming here trying to take money away from real victims. If anybody needs help, it's this man." Then she went on,

"Give him fifty dollars, some free bus tokens, tell him God bless, and send him on his way. I'll bet you anything he'll go away happy. It's not worth causing a big scene."

So that's what I did. And that's the true meaning of what the Salvation Army stands for, which is really what religion is supposed to be about.

I never wanted to believe anything different than what we were told about what happened that terrible day. I didn't really have any doubts at the time. Except for one: Having been in the military, the first question that arose in me, the very day of 9/11, was: Where were our jets? How could our air defense have failed so miserably?

What happened to Payne Stewart, the golfer who died in a plane crash, makes an interesting analogy. He took off in a private plane from a private airport in Florida and, within a half hour, the tower lost communication with the plane. Within another half hour, they had a fighter jet up on the wing. The jet's pilot was able to ascertain that everyone in the cockpit appeared to be dead, because they were slumped over. It was later found to have been a mechanical malfunction that apparently killed everyone on board, and the plane was flying on automatic pilot. So the fighter jet just stayed with the plane all the way until it reached South Dakota and ran out of fuel. Of course, if it was going down in a metropolitan area, they would have blown it out of the skies. Since it went down in a wheat field, they let that happen instead.

Yet on 9/11, when you had four airplanes being hijacked roughly a half hour apart from each other, nobody from our military was up there. Maybe you could buy that the first plane snuck by the radar—but the ones after that? As governor I had been inside air traffic control, and you've got a dozen people there looking at these dials, watching every plane in their sector. They know what direction they're supposed to be going in. And here were four hijacked planes turned directly opposite of their normal flight path. Yet no bells went off, no emergency sirens, no fighter jets scrambled until very late, and then without any coordinates for intercept.

There were brass at the Pentagon, according to MSNBC reporters, who were forewarned not to fly on 9/11, along with other prominent figures. The Pentagon had actually prepared for such an attack, since it was revealed as a target for a plane back in 1995. By 1999, they had cameras and radar on the roof to detect something like that, according to the Pentagon's security director. They had an exercise for first responders in Arlington, Virginia, based on a plane crashing into the building. The breakdown in standard operating procedure on 9/11 was unprecedented, uninvestigated, and unaccountable.

Here's what *The Washington Post* reported on August 3, 2006, which is about as close as we've come to knowing *something* is being covered up: "For more than two years after the attacks, officials with NORAD and the FAA provided inaccurate information about the response to the hijackings in testimony and media appearances. . . . Some staff members and commissioners of the Sept. 11 panel concluded that the Pentagon's initial account of how it reacted to the 2001 terrorist attacks may have been part of a deliberate effort to mislead the commission and the public. . . . Suspicion of wrongdoing ran so deep that the ten-member commission, in a secret meeting at the end of its tenure in summer 2004, debated referring the matter to the Justice Department for criminal investigation." The compromise they reached instead was for the 9/11 Commission to send unresolved questions on to the inspector generals of both FAA and NORAD, and let them investigate the discrepancies. In 2005 they released their reports—and created a whole new set of excuses and yet another timeline of response events.

I need to mention my reaction when I saw Michael Moore's movie, *Fahrenheit 9/11*. Looking at President Bush's face reading the *Pet Goat* storybook to the school kids that morning in Florida, he either froze—or he knew something. The question is, what did Bush's chief of staff, Andrew Card, tell him when he leaned over to whisper in his ear? Maybe that Cheney was in control of the situation, so not to worry? I couldn't get over the fact that, after he was told about the planes hitting the Twin Towers, he would just sit there for seven minutes. In a nuclear age, seven minutes is an eternity.

I've had some Republicans say to me, "Well, what would you have done?" I told them, "Simple. If my chief of staff had walked up to me and said, 'Sir, the United States is under attack,' I would have turned to the children very calmly and said, 'Children, you know my job is very, very important. And you know that emergencies sometimes happen that a president must attend to. There's an emergency I have to take care of right now. You don't have to worry about it, we'll get it under control. And I promise you that on another day, I will come back here and read to you. Okay?' Then out the door I go."

My doubts about the official story have grown steadily over the last couple of years. My son kept telling me about things he was finding on the Internet about 9/11, so I started doing some reading. Often I'd question myself—what am I, a conspiracy nut? as some people get labeled. But I couldn't shake off the pattern I saw emerging. I wondered, why did President Bush put up roadblocks for two years to any type of investigation? If you have nothing to hide, you shouldn't care whether or not a commission looks into what happened. Naturally, some things need to remain secret from our potential enemies. But why stonewall like Bush did? It seemed our government wasn't reacting like an innocent victim, but like they were guilty of, or about, something.

When it comes to the question of "what did they know and when did they know it," as the old Watergate phrase goes, my B.S. detector antenna goes sky-high. Consider these known facts about the summer of 2001:

- July 26: Attorney General John Ashcroft stopped flying commercial airlines because of a threat assessment.
- August 6: President Bush received a presidential daily briefing that was titled: "Bin Laden Plans to Attack Inside United States," which made clear a plan was imminent that might include the hijacking of commercial planes. The briefing made specific mention of the World Trade Center. Bush later claimed it "said nothing about an attack on America." Bush went golfing that day and then left Washington for a month's vacation.
- August 27: A supervisor at the FBI stated just before the attacks that he was trying to keep a hijacker from "flying a plane into the WTC"—by seeking a warrant to search the computer of Zacharias Moussaoui, the "twentieth hijacker." He was taken to task by FBI headquarters for notifying the CIA. The CIA generated their own memo to offices in Paris and London about Moussaoui in response to the FBI's query, and said they thought he might be a "possible suicide hijacker." This was pre-9/11!
- September 10: According to *Newsweek*, a number of the top brass from the Pentagon suddenly canceled their travel plans for the next morning because of security concerns. San Francisco Mayor Willie Brown was warned not to fly that day by his security staff.

Many people have raised questions about just how the World Trade Center buildings collapsed. Could it have been not the impact of the planes, but a controlled demolition from inside? I don't claim expertise about this, but I did work four years as part of the Navy's underwater demolition teams, where we were trained to blow things to hell and high water. I walked the site shortly after the buildings came down, and something about the official story doesn't add up.

We are told that a molten, highly intense fuel mixture from airplanes caused fires that brought down these two huge steel-structured buildings. It's said that the force of gravity drives the top of those buildings down into the lower floors like a huge hammer. But why didn't the construction debris look like a large stack of "pancakes," rather than the concrete being pulverized and flying through the air for blocks as it did? Two witnesses, a worker at the Port Authority and a fireman, later said they'd witnessed explosions inside and heard the popping sound of what they believed was demolition—but their statements to the 9/11 Commission seem to have been stricken from the official record.

Strangely enough, they supposedly never could find the black boxes from the aircraft—which are generally thought to be indestructible. Some reports later from firemen said actually they were found, but all forensic data taken by the FBI for investigation is still locked up by a 9/11 Commission ruling until January 2, 2009, when Bush can reverse the release and leave office.

The large Saudi Arabian family of Osama bin Laden has long had close ties to the Bush family—and quite a few of them were taken under the FBI's wing and spirited out of Washington on a private charter when the airports reopened three days after the attacks. The 9/11 Commission concluded that, after the Saudi government requested this out of fear for their safety, the FBI had "conducted a satisfactory screening of Saudi nationals who left the United States." The commission ignores the fact that some of them had known ties to terrorist activity that should at least have caused them to be detained for questioning.

Stranger still was an overlooked story that appeared briefly on MSNBC.com, which indicated some of the hijackers might have trained at U.S. Army bases. Well, our military's School of the Americas once helped train the Central American death squads, so our providing lethal skills to terrorists—excuse me, I mean "freedom fighters"—shouldn't come as a huge surprise. It's widely known that bin Laden himself once received CIA training, in the 1980s. He had worked for a family construction company in Afghanistan carrying out CIA and Department of Defense contract work, building caves for the mujahideen rebels who were fighting the Soviet Union. I guess he must've got to know those types of hideouts pretty well.

I've got some other problems with *The 9/11 Commission Report*. It makes no mention that a secret Pentagon project called Able Danger had identified four of the hijackers a whole year before the attacks. Two unit whistleblowers confirmed that. The authorizing orders said Able Danger's purpose was to "manipulate, degrade and destroy al-Qaeda." First the commission said its members weren't informed about this, then it later acknowledged that they were. The commission also failed to mention Condoleezza Rice being warned about al-Qaeda's plotting by then–CIA Director George Tenet during the summer of 2001.

So is this another whitewash like the Warren Commission? The 9/11 Commission politely informs us that "conspiracy theories play a peculiar role in American discourse. Whenever there is a particularly surprising, traumatic, and influential moment in our history, people are left with unsettling questions." As an example, they go on to cite "conspiracy theorists [who] propagate outrageous notions that Kennedy was assassinated by the CIA, or some shadowy secret society of the rich and powerful." Outrageous notions? I find it outrageous that these commissions allow themselves to become part of the cover-up.

I want to believe that bin Laden and al-Qaeda were responsible for the 9/11 attacks, but now I have doubts. If they were responsible, I am beginning to think it was not without some knowledge of those impending attacks on our side. There are historical precedents for this occurring. Some evidence exists that FDR and Churchill were privy to the Japanese attack on Pearl Harbor, but needed a catalyst to bring America into World War Two. In recent years, we've learned two startling and very alarming things from declassified information. In 1962, Operation Northwoods was a plan drawn up by the Joint Chiefs of Staff. The idea was to stage terror attacks—including the use of hijacked airplanes—and, if necessary, kill American citizens and then blame it on Castro's Cuba to justify our invading the island.

Then there was the famous Gulf of Tonkin incident in 1964. We were told that American ships were attacked by the North Vietnamese. Now we know that the incident was manufactured by the CIA and Pentagon in order to gain support for escalating the Vietnam War. If the United States government was prepared to stage such a gargantuan event in leading our nation to war then, why would they refrain from doing so again today? Might we look at this as a trend, going into these wars under false pretenses?

A think tank called the Project for the New American Century, composed mainly of right-wing ideologues, wrote a report pre-9/11 titled *Building America's Defenses*. It promoted a vast expansion of the military budget, along with intervention plans to make us an empire. The document contains this line: "The process of transformation, even if it brings revolutionary change, is likely to be a long one, absent some catastrophic and catalyzing event—like a new Pearl Harbor."

Is that what 9/11 was? *The 9/11 Commission Report* states that "the Bush administration had repeatedly tied the Iraq War to September 11th. . . . The panel finds no al-Qaeda–Iraq tie." Bush then did some backpedaling, saying: "This administration never said that the 9/11 attacks were orchestrated between Saddam [Hussein] and al-Qaeda. We did say there were numerous contacts. . . ." That reference was to alleged meetings between bin Laden and Iraqi intelligence in Sudan back in the mid-nineties, information obtained during torture of an unreliable source, according to the book *Hubris: The Inside Story of Spin, Scandal, and the Selling of the Iraq War*, by Michael Isikoff and David Corn.

It also turns out that another link exists between Saddam Hussein and Osama bin Laden. They used the same banker, BCCI, the Bank of Credit and Commerce International. This was the same dirty offshore bank that the CIA, under President Reagan, used to help finance bin Laden, run guns to Hussein, and move money around in the Iran-Contra operation. And, when George W. Bush got in some trouble over his oil investments in 1987, one of the bank's biggest Saudi investors assisted in bailing him out. BCCI collapsed in 1991, after stealing what's been estimated as somewhere between 9.5 billion and 15 billion dollars.

What I've raised here are just a few of the questions being asked by experts and citizens all over the U.S. Maybe no one will ever know what really happened that day. One thing I feel really strongly about is that you should never listen to just one side of a story, whether that be the official side or the conspiracy side. Especially when it has affected our whole way of life and our reputation as a fair and free country around the world. Look, listen, read, explore, discuss, and do everything you can to find the truth, and then make your decisions based upon all the evidence you have. Question everything.

CHAPTER 12

At Conception Bay

"Judge me by my policies. Judge me by my commissioners, and judge me by the work that we're trying to do—not a feeding frenzy of media so that you can get ratings and make money."

—*Jesse Ventura,* The News Hour with Jim Lehrer,
February 14, 2000

Not too far below Mulegé, traveling a meandering stretch of Highway 1, one of the most breathtakingly beautiful spots that I've ever witnessed appears suddenly from around a bend. It's called the Bahía de Concepción. Conception Bay. It's vast, with a series of small islands in the middle. Looking across it, you see a mountain range—the southern end of the Sierra de Guadalupe—and, until you spy the opening, at first you can't tell whether this is a lake or the ocean.

It is a calm day, no wind. Far below us, probably 200 feet or more, the tranquil, turquoise waters are so clear that we can see all the way to the bottom. A couple is snorkeling down there, and even their shadows are visible. "Terry," I say, in a near-whisper, "this is almost too much to handle. I don't think I can concentrate on the road."

I used to say that I would someday retire to the surfing beaches of Hawaii, but this spot is more captivating than anything I can imagine; a "desert Polynesia," as the tourist brochures say. I decide to make the first turnoff we can, and find a place to park the camper.

Terry recognizes a frigate bird passing overhead. In the near distance, we think we catch the spouting of a whale. There don't seem to be many facilities for visitors, but at the base of one rise, a dirt road lead off toward the bay. I edge the camper onto it, and momentarily we emerge at a cove. We are alone. Alone on a glistening, white sand beach. Pelicans dove for fish. Fiddler crabs race along the shoreline.

"This feels pretty close to heaven to me," Terry says.

"Conception Bay." I turn the words over in my mouth. "The name sure fits, doesn't it? I'll bet this is *the* honeymoon spot of the Baja."

Terry smiles, and curles up in my arms.

We spend the night here, awakening soon after sunrise to walk the beach with Dexter. Out near one of the islands, another couple is already paddling around in a kayak. There is barely even the ripple of a wave.

"Let's just not even think about getting anywhere today," Terry says, and I nod in agreement.

Back at the camper, she returns to reading Steinbeck's *Log from the Sea of Cortez*. Long ago, his expedition had pulled into Conception Bay to collect marine life and, when Terry comes to a certain passage, she motions to me. "Listen to this," she said quietly.

"Behind the beach there was a little level land, sandy and dry and covered with cactus and thick brush. And behind that, the rising dry hills. Now again the wild doves were calling among the hills with their song of homesickness. The quality of longing in this sound, the memory response it sets up, is curious and strong. And it has also the quality of a dying day. One wishes to walk toward the sound—to walk on and on toward it, forgetting everything else.

Undoubtedly there are sound symbols in the unconscious just as there are visual symbols—sounds that trigger off a response, a little spasm of fear, or a quick lustfulness, or, as with the doves, a nostalgic sadness."

In a timeless place like Conception Bay, words like those call up a lot of food for thought. I've never spoken publicly about why I didn't run for a second term as governor. Ultimately, it had to do with my family, especially Terry's health. There were other factors, too. Times of painful realizations. The first of these happened not long after September 11.

Headline: 28,000 State Workers Strike in Minnesota, Drawing Fire

> *Nearly 28,000 Minnesota state employees walked off the job today in a demand for higher pay, drawing criticism from many Minnesotans, who said the strikers were acting selfishly at a time of national crisis.*
>
> —The New York Times, *October 2, 2001*

I'd offered them a slight pay raise and an extension of benefits— these things get negotiated every two years—and still they walked out. I had to assign National Guard troops to fill in for them at more than a hundred state hospitals, nursing homes, and veterans homes. The strike hurt me deeply. We didn't know if more terrorist attacks might be looming. In my view, the United States was at war. Going out on strike was their patriotic response? For a dollar-an-hour pay increase, at a moment like this, after the biggest attack on American soil in our history? I felt their concern for their pocketbooks potentially disrupted my ability to govern.

When I'd taken office almost three years before, Steven Bosacker, my chief of staff, scheduled me to pay visits to each of the twenty-five departments in the state. That's all I did for my first two weeks. When I'd walk in, I had state workers come up to me and say, "I've been working here thirty years and this is the first time a governor has ever set foot in this building." So I thought I really had a rapport with these employees. For them to strike now felt like a stab in the back.

I know how strongly the Democrats control the unions and, although I have no proof, in my heart I blame them for the strike. One time when I went to broadcast my weekly radio show, I was greeted by a hundred workers, and I'll never forget the signs some of them held up: "Jesse 'the Scab' Ventura." I found this personally degrading and offensive.

The strike got settled and everyone went back to work by the middle of October. But that day of the picket signs was when I'd turned to Terry and said, "Honey, I don't think I want to be their boss anymore."

The Minnesota unions had also torn me apart for leaving the state and making the twenty-four-hour trip to Ground Zero while the strike was still on. The Minnesota media were furious, too, because they weren't allowed to come along when Terry and I went to the Twin Towers site. That wasn't my call, it was Governor Pataki's. He felt it was too dangerous. With a lot of heavy equipment and workers risking their lives, you needed to minimize the presence of cameras. But by that point, my relationship with the media had already sunk below the horizon.

I had a radio show every Friday called *Lunch with the Governor*. I did that so I could speak directly to the people of Minnesota, without the press always as the intermediary. It was more than my having an adverse relationship with them. Never once was I criticized over policy. It was always personal—what Jesse said, how Jesse reacted. Which, in terms of the popularity game, might have been "powerful stuff"—but it was meaningless in terms of what I was trying to accomplish in the big picture.

Let me tell you about a double standard, in terms of how I was treated. Soon after I took office, I wrote my autobiography. It became a bestseller. I was immediately assailed by the Minnesota press for supposedly using my victory to make money. A huge effort was made to convince the public that I was nothing but a profiteer. Then, a few months later, Senator John McCain came through Minnesota on his book tour—and the same media hailed him.

I understand that career politicians write books prior to running for president. Books are used to help catapult yourself into the White House. I had no intention of going for anything like that at the time. I've always stuck to the belief that before you look for another job, you finish the one you were voted in to do. Well, as I write this Barack Obama is being hailed as the Democratic Party's new champion for 2008. He's written a new book, but do you see any public outcry about it? Yet I was chastised by the media for writing a book about my beliefs and what I felt and how I got to where I was—much the same as Obama's book, I'm sure. My question is, why was I held to such a different standard?

The reality is, the media jump at personality more than they do substance. They don't judge you for what you are attempting to accomplish, they simply want to dissect your personality. And I have a volatile personality. So I'm easy pickings for them.

TERRY: Why did the Minnesota media come to hate Jesse so much? Minnesota has a tendency, if one of their own goes beyond a certain scope, to rip him to shreds. They did it to Prince, and to a football player who got involved with drugs. If you don't walk around really humble and hang your head, once you reach a certain stature, you will get creamed. That was one aspect of it.

The second aspect was, I think, that most of the media already take a side. They are either for the Democrats or the Republicans, and there is no room for anybody else. They want to keep their connections good, because that's how they make their living. If they start getting behind an independent like Jesse, who they already know is not going to make a life out of politics, this puts their careers in jeopardy.

Besides, people are more interested in reading sensationalistic "bad stuff" than "good stuff." So the more they can dredge up, even if it's innuendo or outright lies, well, that's just more people picking up the paper.

Terry always told me, don't watch the news and don't read the papers. Stay focused on what you're doing, and don't give a damn. I could do it for a month or even a month and a half, and it worked. But eventually I couldn't stop myself; I was like a drug addict. In hindsight, if I were to become governor again, I would follow her advice explicitly to the T—for the entire four years.

Headline: VENTURA SERVES UP A WEEK OF THE JACKAL

On Tuesday the governor, an independent (big time) . . . decreed that reporters covering him would have to wear a jackal press badge.

On the front is a full-figure picture of the governor (in a finger-pointing, Jesse-Wants-You pose) and beneath that is the reporter's name and organization, and the words "Official Jackal." On the back is a warning that the governor can revoke the credential "for any reason."

The governor's office says the new badges are meant to enhance security and accountability.

Many news organizations object, and their reporters refuse to wear the badges. They say what started out as good-natured fun has become demeaning and unprofessional.

—The New York Times, *February 25, 2001*

I used to get *so* worked up. One particular journalist with the Minneapolis paper came out with a story about my once having supposedly jumped up onto a topless bar in Montana before being physically removed from the building. The source was an elderly Montana couple who were convinced they'd seen me do this. Well, I've only been to Montana three times in my life—twice on a train with my mom traveling to and from the World's Fair in Seattle when I was a kid, and another time when Terry and I were leaving the Portland wrestling territory and heading home to Minnesota. Yet this story got printed without any fact-checking, and I had to respond to it and deny it.

Another time, I remember reading a comment: "What else can you expect when you have a governor who admits that he never reads?" I never said that. If you counted every book on Kennedy I read on an airplane when I was wrestling, those alone would add up to an encyclopedia.

TERRY: That's one of the things I really liked about him, because I am a reader, and here was a man who read! In his wrestling days, the first thing he would say in the morning was: "Who's got a newspaper?"

It's little things like that that you think won't get to you but, when you're in a position like I was, all those little things become a big thing.

TERRY: See, we weren't seasoned. We didn't have the backup, and we didn't have professionals around us. Everybody that worked for him, they were all like us: We can change the world. You can't go into politics with that attitude. You are a fool if you do. You have to go into politics saying, "This is going to be the hardest job I've ever had in my life. I'm going to have to fight to stay alive, fight to get every single inch of ground"—and then hope to heck there's somebody behind you holding onto it when you're gone.

Just remembering makes me want to go and lie down for a while.

Even more important than placing term limits on politicians, I believe they should have term limits on Capitol reporters. Some of those guys have been down there in the statehouse basement for twenty-five years; they hardly ever see the sun! It would be a good policy, on the part of newspapers, to do a rotation. Move these people to another beat when they become too comfortable and entrenched. In the end, they don't take an objective point of view. They start feeding into their stories what they want to see happen. They get overrun, I think, with the feeling of power—just like career politicians do.

The *St. Paul Pioneer Press* had an editorial writer named Steve Dornfeld. Probably 90 percent or more of his editorials were negative toward me. Weeks after I left office, Dornfeld left the newspaper and became communications director for the Metropolitan Council, which is overseen by a new Republican governor. To me, that's a clear example of how aligned our media are with the two parties. The media are very comfortable with a two-party system, and don't want to see it changed.

I actually did my best to help out the media when it came to an infringement on its First Amendment rights. I'd just gotten out of office when the infamous Janet Jackson incident took place at the

Super Bowl, where Justin Timberlake ripped off her top in front of the TV cameras. I happened to catch in the paper one day that the Federal Communications Commission (FCC) had fined CBS half a million dollars for that. I also learned that Fox had drawn a million dollar fine for running some sort of "indecent" program. My curiosity was piqued. When the networks write out these checks to the government, where does the money go?

I called the FCC headquarters in New York, explained who I was, and asked my question. I was then transferred six times. No one could answer me. I thought, this is ridiculous, it should be public information. How come these people either can't tell me, or won't? Finally, I was told that someone would be calling me back. The next day, a fellow did. First he got defensive, thinking I was accusing the FCC of a "take the money and run." I assured him this wasn't the case, I simply wanted to know.

Then he dropped the bombshell: that $1.5 million in fines went into the government's general fund. This might not cause the hair on the average lay person's neck to stand up, but it should. The general fund is the trillion dollar elephant—what the entire federal government runs off of, where all your tax dollars go. When you pay taxes, you also elect public officials. But this is taxation without representation. The FCC consists of *appointed* officials; therefore it's their definition of what is obscene. If you, as the public, disagree with them, you have no means to remove them. This is the government's ability to levy fines anytime they want, because the FCC holds these stations hostage. If they pull a station's license, they're out of business. So I find this a clear case of dictatorship, in the world of communications and free speech. You're guilty if the FCC deems you so.

Some people will say, yes, but we don't need little Johnny hearing any bad words over the radio. My answer is, trust me, there's nothing little Johnny hasn't heard already on the street. And you can always turn the dial. If what Howard Stern says offends you, don't listen. If enough people refuse to listen to Howard's raunchiness, he's gone—because he has to bring in advertising dollars.

We just don't need the government controlling that dial, telling us what we can and can't listen to. We are free thinking individuals who ought to be able to make our own choices, and if we worry about what our children are hearing, that's called parenting. Rest assured that, when the government starts raising your kids, before long you're going to see the kids turning in their parents to the government.

In June 2002, when I went to China with the largest trade delegation ever organized at the state level (roughly a hundred government and business leaders accompanied me), not one TV network in Minnesota covered it. They all claimed "expenses." That's the first time I ever heard the media say something was too expensive. I was out there trying to help bring Minnesota into the future by forging a relationship with the country that's going to be *the* economic power of the world. This affected everyone in the state in some way, or it would someday.

So what was the front-page headline in the Minneapolis *Star Tribune* on the day that I returned from China? "People's House or Party Pad?" it said. Their story was quoting former members of my staff who claimed that my son, Tyrel, and his friends had been abusing the governor's mansion—supposedly draining state-purchased booze, strewing beer cans and broken glass around, and damaging the furniture.

I think the timing of that story was set up to overshadow what I'd accomplished in China. It was a case of slander and libel against a twenty-two-year-old kid. I knew the main source of the lies. His name was Dan Creed. He'd been executive director of the Governor's mansion and, in the spring of that year, I'd dismissed him and a few others for leaking stories to the media when I was threatening to close down the mansion as a cost-saving measure. Behind my back, I found out later, he was meeting with the Democrats and Republicans, who were orchestrating what he should do and how. He wanted the funding of the residence changed from the governor's office to the general fund, meaning people like him would become state employees rather than being employed at the governor's pleasure. In simple terms, he—not the governor—would then run the governor's residence and could not be fired. Creed was working on one of those so-called "tell-all books," which came out the same day that my official portrait was unveiled in the Capitol that November so that he could draw more press attention.

The Minnesota media simply ran with Creed's accusations against my son. They did no investigating. A lot of times, Tyrel would go out and meet some friends at a nightclub—he was old enough to have a drink—and bring them back to the residence. But these weren't "underaged drinking parties." And I don't know how Dan Creed could possibly have known what was going on at midnight, since he went home every day at five! There wasn't a single state trooper—and one was inside the governor's residence twenty-four hours a day, seven days a week—who ever said one thing about my son misbehaving in that house. In fact, half the time he wasn't even there because, for virtually my entire term as governor, Tyrel was working for Sean Penn as his personal assistant out in Hollywood or on a film location.

Yet the media went so far as to have investigative teams interviewing Ty's friends, trying to dig up any dirt they could, wanting to know if he did drugs or hung out with somebody who'd been busted for them. They came up with nothing. It was a choreographed attempt at character assassination. Today I view those media people as equivalent to pedophiles, because they attacked my children on multiple occasions. They even later listed my son's name in a big article about all the children who got in trouble when their parents were in office. Yet no charges were ever brought against him, so how is he guilty of this?

Tyrel will not live in Minnesota anymore. Ty feels that he'd always be looking over his shoulder, for fear he might do something that the media would then go after his father about. He's the only kid who went to Hollywood to become anonymous, instead of famous, to be able to live and work in peace. If something drove one of your children from living in a state, wouldn't any parent hate whoever was responsible?

Not only did the media go after my children, they went after my dog. At the time I had an English bulldog named Franklin. There was an instance when Terry and I were staying on for the weekend at the governor's residence, instead of going back to our house. And, of course, the dog can't stay home alone. So a state trooper who was going off-duty told me, "It's not out of my way; I'll be happy to bring the dog down to the mansion." The Minnesota media then came out with a story that my dog was being chauffeured around by state troopers. It was ludicrous.

I won't put myself in front of them again. I will talk to any other media in America, but not the ones from Minnesota. When I go on tour for this book, it won't happen in my home state. I'm not going to put them in a position to make money off me anymore. When I give a quote, they're going to have to give credit to someone else that I said it to. It's the only way I can strike back at them.

I'd made my definitive decision not to seek reelection before I went on the trade mission to China that summer of 2002. But I wasn't going to go over there as a lame duck—then why would the Chinese bother to listen to me? So the timing of my announcement, right after I returned, happened to coincide with the Minnesota media breaking the story about my son's alleged "abuse" of the governor's mansion.

I went on *Midday with Gary Eichten* on Minnesota Public Radio, a show where I was a frequent guest, and made this statement on June 18: "I will always protect my family first. You have to have your heart and soul into these types of jobs. I feel that it is time to go back to the private sector."

Beyond that, I felt it was nobody else's business, and I didn't want the media twisting it. But the foremost reason was Terry. She means more to me than holding any office does. And her health was deteriorating. It had been going on for my entire term. She'd contracted Epstein-Barr mono just as I was elected.

TERRY: I'd broken my ankle during the last phases of the campaign. I was cleaning barns and giving riding lessons with my leg in a cast. Then at the end, when I went along on that big trip, I kept feeling worse and worse. It seemed like a cold that never went away, and by March of his first year in office, I was really sick. I went in to see the doctor many times and said, "I have swollen glands, I'm so tired I can hardly move, what's wrong with me?" He always said, "You're stressed." Finally, when a state trooper physically had to help me in and out of the car and into the doctor's, I sat there and said, "If you don't do a blood test and assure me that I'm not dying, I'm not leaving your office." He did, came back, and said, "You have mono." I said, "Whaaaat? Why didn't you tell me that two months ago?" By then, I'd had the disease for a while and was still maintaining a grueling schedule every single day. The doctor told me if I didn't stop doing anything for the next month, I'd end up in the hospital and in a bad way. So for all of March, I sat in the house and did nothing.

About a year went by, and I still felt like I constantly had the flu. I never seemed able to get enough sleep. I'd sleep in the car on the way to events, and again when I got back. I'd take naps. I was on huge doses of vitamins. I tried everything. It was just a horrible feeling like you're constantly walking through deep water. And no one could tell me what was wrong with me. I thought I might have cancer. My white blood cell count was so high and I was anemic. The doctors even sent me to the AIDS Clinic at the University of Minnesota, to see if it might somehow be that. It wasn't, of course, but they had no clue either what it might be.

Terry first became ill just at the time we were thrust into a life that I've described like this: You're standing next to a treadmill that's already on seven. You jump on, and you're at a full dead sprint—for the next four years. So Terry's disease began at the very moment of all the tension and pace of living in this limelight.

I didn't know what it was like. I sat her down one day and said, "This is alien to me. Please tell me what this does." She said, "It's like when I'm shopping, all of a sudden I feel it coming on and my purse now weighs fifty pounds. I don't even know if I can carry it to the car. I feel like I'm going to collapse."

Her Epstein-Barr mono had gone untreated long enough that it turned into chronic fatigue syndrome. Except doctors didn't then know what it was. They didn't believe it was real, and it wasn't being diagnosed until a few years ago.

TERRY: The terrible thing about chronic fatigue, too, is that it wipes out your short-term memory. Our whole marriage, whenever we went anywhere, I always remembered everyone's names and faces. Jesse was never good at that, and I was like an encyclopedia. Now all of a sudden I would meet someone and an hour later, have no idea who they were.

When the two of us reached the decision that he wasn't going to run again, I just disappeared from public view.

His last year in office, Jesse then had to be hospitalized, and things seemed like they were going from bad to worse.

Three times in my life, I've had to be hospitalized because of a blood clot on my lungs. The last time it happened was on the return trip from my trade mission to China, after taking that thirteen-hour plane ride. Today, I've learned some people who fly a lot are susceptible to this. Now I get up every hour and walk around the plane, so my blood isn't allowed to pool down in my feet.

After getting home from China, I noticed I had some pain whenever I took a deep breath, so I went to the hospital and they discovered the clot with an MRI. After I was admitted, I didn't want this getting out to the media, because it's frankly none of their business. The hospital was tremendous. They kept me in an isolated ward and, the day I left, the reporters were all out front where my limousine was, while they snuck me out the back door. The state troopers put me in an unmarked squad car, and I left the media sitting there. I never did speak to them about it.

I then went to the Mayo Clinic and they found out that something in my immune system is messed up that causes my blood to clot when it shouldn't. I'll need to take Coumadin, a blood thinner, for life now.

TERRY: Finally, almost a year after Jesse was out of office, I went to a great clinic that works with cancer patients. That's still what I was afraid I had. A group of doctors were treating the patients holistically, metabolically, not just with all these heavy drugs. My girlfriend had gone there when doctors kept telling her the same thing—"you're just stressed"—and it turned out she had Crohn's disease. Now she's a whole new person because she's been treated for it. All this time, I'd been treating myself the wrong way for the chronic fatigue syndrome that I really had. I remember a doctor at the clinic saying, "I can't believe no one has told you this before." I sat there thinking, "Oh my God, I'm not going to die."

The only thing you can do when it comes over you is rest. All I wanted was for Terry to regain her health. I knew that if I became governor for another four years, God knows where it would have put her.

Terry had the highest approval rating that any First Lady in Minnesota has ever achieved—76 percent. Even when I would make these huge *faux pas*, stick my foot right in the shit bucket with something I said, it didn't affect her popularity. The people adored her, because she was so honest in everything she did. She handled everything with grace and beauty.

TERRY: But—and it's a big but—I never had to stand up for anything that was unpopular. I always felt that my job as First Lady was to create a feeling of positiveness towards whatever he was trying to do. And if I did my job correctly, the people wouldn't remember me for anything other than—"Oh, I think she was pretty nice." He was struggling so hard with everything of that, for me to start opening my yap and being controversial could have really destroyed it all.

And there are many good things I remember. I know a lot of the First Ladies say this, but I loved visiting schools and reading to the kids. I would always ask teachers about their biggest concerns and then I'd go back to Jesse and say, "This is what I'm learning." One of the commissions I set up was to help him with education. I would often meet with special-ed teachers, because I knew about these very effective public education programs through the experience with our daughter, Jade.

Jade had had a series of seizures soon after she was born, and for a while we'd been afraid we'd lose her. But she made a miraculous recovery, and was seizure-free until the age of two. I remember I was wrestling in Pittsburgh that night. I was sound asleep when, about two in the morning, I suddenly came wide awake and looked at the telephone. Within ten or fifteen seconds, the phone rang. It was Terry rushing out the door, headed to the hospital because Jade was in the middle of a grand mal seizure.

Not long before this, Jade had been inoculated with the DPT vaccine against diphtheria, pertussis, and tetanus. The government makes these shots mandatory for kids at age two, in order for them to later go to school. It's my understanding that any child susceptible to seizures should not have to get a DPT shot. I went to a convention in Chicago, concerning kids who'd been normal before the shots and were now drooling in wheelchairs. A state patrolman friend of mine attempted to sue the government over this tragedy, but it got nowhere, because no doctor will go on the witness stand and explicitly state that the shots cause this.

After Jade's grand mal seizure, she had to go on a number of heavy drugs for several years, which set her back tremendously. I feel very fortunate, because today Jade is only mildly handicapped. That isn't true for those couple-dozen children I saw in Chicago. Yes, these shots are important and have eliminated terrible diseases. But what are these other kids, collateral damage?

I talked to President Clinton about this right before he left office. He described a recent breakthrough in genetics, making it possible to determine whether a child has a certain gene that the DPT shot would affect. Then that child would be exempt from getting it. So far, though, nothing has changed.

I strongly considered resigning early to allow my lieutenant governor, Mae Schunk, to become governor. Mae had been an award-winning elementary school teacher, and this was her first foray into politics. She was gray-haired, grandmotherly, and the sweetest lady you'd ever want to meet. When we'd been campaigning together in the RV, talking "what-ifs," like who might play at the inauguration, somebody had suggested bringing in Barenaked Ladies. Mae heard that and spun around and scolded me: "You can't have that at an inauguration!" She had no idea this was the name of a band.

So, with a month to go in office, the legislature not in session, and nothing much going on, I thought, why not make some more history? I'd already done that by appointing an independent, Dean Barkley, to fill Paul Wellstone's seat in the U.S. Senate. Now this was an opportunity for another independent, Mae Schunk, to become the first female governor of Minnesota. She'd only serve for thirty days, but the Democrats and Republicans would never be able to claim that distinction. And you'd see Mae's portrait hanging in the statehouse alongside all the other governors!

I also thought this would be another way to endear myself to the Minnesota media. At that point, to borrow a phrase from Rhett Butler in *Gone with the wind*, "Frankly, my dear, I don't give a damn!"

In the end, I decided against it, because I didn't want it on my record that I'd resigned from office. Also, although I never broached the idea to Mae, I have tremendous respect for her and I don't think she would have liked it.

We still correspond on e-mail and send each other birthday cards. When somebody once mentioned to Mae that my spoken English was pretty atrocious, she got a little ruffled. "You understood what he said, didn't you?" she said. They said, "Yeah." She said, "Well then, his English isn't that bad, is it?" I really enjoyed that, coming from an educator of thirty-six years!

As indescribable as it is in many ways when you come into office, it's just as strange when you leave. Especially at the level of being a governor. As president, you're always going to have the Secret Service for the rest of your life, because you're privy to national security secrets. But that's not true at a state level. Suddenly, you're all alone. When you jump off that treadmill, it's back at zero. It's just as hard to adjust as when you hopped on at a full sprint.

During my four years, one of the big issues that mostly the Republicans kept bringing up to the media—and trying to destroy me with—was the amount of protection I had to have. The simple fact was, I had celebrity status. My security guys would call places where I was to appear and say, "We need 'rock star security' when Governor Ventura comes." It was crazy. I was under scrutiny unlike any other governor. Everything I did was covered and watched. Yet it was portrayed to the public that I was out cavorting around, spending all this money for "rock star security" and wasting the taxpayer's dollars. Well, the law says a governor is to be protected 24/7, and in reality my security budget was no higher than the current governor's.

Still, it was a bizarre feeling to leave it all behind. The first week of January 2003, I sat in the audience as Governor Pawlenty was sworn in, and at that point I was officially done.

TERRY: When the ceremony ended, he was supposed to go shake hands with the governor, but there was a huge line. And I said, "You know what, we're just distracting everybody, let's just go."

But when we went outside, all the media left the new governor and made a complete circle around my vehicle. I looked at them and said, "I'm not the governor now—he is! He's in there! Go bother him!" I actually felt embarrassed for him.

It's Minnesota tradition that your same security men and drivers give you one last ride home, with full sirens and lights. In my case, in a Lincoln Navigator, back to my ranch. That day, you say your good-byes. It was pretty gut-wrenching between me and Ron and Tony, my two main security guys. These two gentlemen were with me every step of the way for four years, in Cuba, in China, everywhere. They probably spent as much time with me as the First Lady did, because for eight hours of the day, they'd be with me and she wasn't. Of course now they were moving on, to protect the new governor.

It was so strange the next morning, when they removed the trailer, and all security was gone from the house. For lack of a better way to say it, you're naked. There's an emptiness you feel. Because, all of a sudden, you're not the focus of the state of Minnesota anymore. I don't care what anybody says, it's very addictive to be the most powerful person in a state. There's no doubt in my mind why people do it.

> TERRY: I remember when I first walked into the Capitol, looking at all the inscriptions and the paintings, how proud I was of our country and all the hope I had for the four years to come. That was equal to how very sad I was, the last day I was ever there in an official position. I thought, my husband could have done so much more if people would have truly considered what's good for the state. But I still think he did a great job, did everything he possibly could do, considering that he was not just fighting the Democrats and the Republicans, but all the media of Minnesota.

So I became kind of a recluse. Part of me wanted that. Another part of me missed being at the center of attention—even of criticism—even though I detested the media "jackals."

I started falling into a bit of a depression. What happened next, when I got hired by MSNBC, didn't make the situation any easier.

CHAPTER 13

Reflections on TV and Teaching

"One of the first things I noticed in MSNBC's newsroom: No one listens. The visual is everything. On every producer's desk, TV sets were usually tuned to MSNBC . . . but virtually no one paid attention to the substance of what we were transmitting. I fantasized about interrupting one of my debates to announce that U.S. troops had invaded France—just to see if any of the overworked, deadlined producers would notice."

—Cable News Confidential, *by Jeff Cohen*

Our second day at Conception Bay, we drive to a place called Ecomundo to rent a kayak. It is only twenty-five bucks for the whole day. Since the bay is protected on three sides by land, the winds are minimal and this is one of Baja's ideal places for kayaking.

We head out across the blue-green waters of the marine reserve, the light flap-flap of our paddles the only sound for miles. The water is still so crystal-clear that sometimes we can see schools of fish passing by underneath us—long, skinny sierras, little lisas, even an occasional lone barracuda. "Should've brought at least one fishing rod," Terry mentions at one point. Paddling on past more inlets and coves and cone-shaped islands, we say little. There is no need for words.

Only a single permanent settlement has been built along the seashore, though we do see quite a few motor homes like ours, as well as pitched tents and some *palapa* huts. For the most part, though, we must feel a lot like the Indians who used to trace this same path in their canoes. It feels great to be this far from "civilization."

I look at Terry as the day begins to wane and say, "You know, honey, being here isn't making my decision any easier."

"What decision is that?" she asked.

"The future. What I'm going to do now."

"You never can just let it all go, can you," she says, a statement rather than a question.

She's right. I can't. Not entirely. It doesn't seem to be in my makeup. At least not yet.

Headline: JESSE VENTURA REACHES DEAL FOR TALK SHOW AT MSNBC

Cable news in the new millennium has often been described as an arena where brass-knuckle politics are presented with the showmanship of professional wrestling.

Embracing the times, MSNBC announced yesterday that it had completed a deal to hire Jesse Ventura, the former professional wrestler and recently departed Minnesota governor, as a network talk show host.

The terms were not disclosed, but executives at the network said his annual salary would be in the neighborhood of $2 million.

—The New York Times, *February 7, 2003*

Coming out of office, I'd been a hot commodity. My agents had talks with CNN, Fox, and MSNBC about my coming on board to host a cable network talk show. Finally, MSNBC won out and I signed a lucrative three-year contract. I made the announcement on *The Tonight Show*. Originally, the show was supposed to be an hour a night, four nights a week.

I had never gone to a Super Bowl and, the weekend after we made the deal, MSNBC's president, Erik Sorenson, took me to the game. It was in San Diego that year, and Tampa Bay beat Oakland, 48–21. Afterward, we were driving by limo up to L.A. in the middle of the night to do the preliminaries for setting up my show. I don't remember how the subject came up, but all of a sudden Erik said something very intriguing. Later on, it kept coming back to me. Right after he hired me, Erik said, he'd received phone calls from two very high-ranking people in Washington. They wanted to know why MSNBC was giving me a national forum. They were obviously not happy about it. I said, "Come on, Erik, tell me who called you." But he said he couldn't reveal any names.

My guess is that one might have been Karl Rove, the other perhaps a big mucky-muck among the Democrats. Thinking back on it, I figured that the Republicans and Democrats might be dumb, but they're not stupid. They'd seen that, in Minnesota, where I'd had a statewide radio talk show, I won the governorship and I only had to raise $300,000. If I had a nationwide TV show, I could spend three years expounding my positions, set myself up to make a run for the presidency as an independent, and not have to spend money to do it. Up until you officially file to become a candidate in the summer of an election year, the FCC can't kick you off the air—but you can do all the "campaigning" you want.

With my show, things got off on the wrong foot because of miscommunication. They started to do the tapings in L.A., but

I had an agreement that it would be shot in Minneapolis. I didn't want to move to L.A. I also felt that most of these types of programs give you only the West or East Coast's views. Nothing comes from the heartland. And I personally think that the Midwest is the backbone of the country when it comes to common sense.

Very early on, I had to tell MSNBC that they didn't hire me to be a teleprompter reader. Unfortunately, that is basically what all these news-talk hosts are. All the stories come down from upstairs, even though the hosts pretend that it's them. People need to understand that Bill O'Reilly, Sean Hannity, Keith Olbermann, and the rest are not these individual rogues setting their own agendas. Those guys will deny it and say they have artistic freedom. And they may put their little spin on whatever the subject is, but did you ever notice it's pretty much the same stories talked about on every show? You're just getting four different "opinions" on the same topic that day.

I know this from personal experience. MSNBC tried to pablum-feed me the subjects they wanted talked about, and I began to fight them on a daily basis. Erik Sorenson might have been the channel's president, but he was beholden to a leadership cadre that included the president of NBC News—and the man above them both, who used to run the Plastics Division for the network's owner, the General Electric Corporation.

I didn't want to discuss the stories they were telling me I had to do. This was after telling me I would have complete artistic control. Now I was supposed to spend my on-air time analyzing the Laci Peterson killing. I said, "Look, there were 15,000 murders in America last year and, as tragic as Laci's was, she and her unborn baby were only two of them. California may have a big interest in it, but I can assure you that Minnesota doesn't, other than for *National Enquirer*–journalism."

I wanted to do meat-and-potatoes, things that affected people in the big picture. Such as why all our state governments continue to want bicameral legislatures, when a unicameral system would be likely to work much better. Or the situation that was happening in California at the time, where a sitting governor (Gray Davis) was allowed to be recalled by petition, making a signature more powerful than a vote.

The station also had its corporate playlist, a roster of guests that a show's host is supposed to choose from. Well, I didn't always want to talk to those people. My attitude was that I'll create my own playlist. The powers-that-be didn't like that, either.

The first thing that happened was delaying tactics. Four months after MSNBC hired me, my show wasn't even close to making a debut. I remember, that June, seeing an article in *The New York Times* quoting Sorenson. He was still saying, "It is going to be different than all the other shows you've seen before. You haven't seen this format before because we're literally still inventing it." He went on to talk about how there had been some unforeseen complications in the planning stage. Since I was six-foot-four and weighed in at 250, the producers were struggling to find a set that could properly accommodate me without appearing like a dollhouse. Supposedly they were having trouble finding me the right chair. Also, since I'd decided to broadcast the program from Minneapolis, this had forced them to start amassing a crew from scratch. Something would be in place by the fall, Sorenson said.

They sent a special guy down from New Jersey to design the entire show. Then Sorenson flew in, but didn't even watch it, as far as I know. When he met with us afterward, he said, "I can't put this on the air." I could see the handwriting on the wall. Eventually, I agreed that they would scale everything back and I'd go on once a week, Saturdays, at five o'clock in the afternoon. MSNBC made the announcement in the middle of August. The story in *The New York Times* said this "appeared to be a concession," that I was "perhaps not ready to be the prime-time star that MSNBC had hoped." Sorenson did say, truthfully, that I had little interest in topics like the Laci Peterson case or the Kobe Bryant case, but that "the cable audience has certain expectations."

So I did five weekend shows, at about the worst time slot you could possibly have to draw much of any audience—and I had the second-highest-rated news-talk show on MSNBC. I trailed only Chris Matthews. In fact, they had me guest-star once on Matthews's *Hardball*. They advertised that eight times during the week, but never once also said I had a show on Saturday. The network simply refused to promote it.

I'd brought the show to Minnesota, and probably fifty Minnesotans had been hired in various positions—but, no surprise I guess, the Minnesota media ripped me. They called it second-rate, with second-rate guests. One week, I had Gray Davis on live, the governor of California who was getting ousted from his job. Would that be considered second-rate?

The guy the network had selected to create the show was sending back "dailies" of what we'd be doing that week. If we were so far off the mark, at what point wouldn't they have said, hey, you're going in the wrong direction? But MSNBC waited until five shows were complete. Then, early in December 2003, my producers and I were brought into a room and told, "We can't keep putting this on." End of meeting. Out the door.

They maintained it was too expensive to do the show in Minnesota. It was easier to just keep me on the payroll, along with my assistant, and pull the plug on it. This, despite the fact that my contract was for huge money, well into the seven figures, like a professional sports contract. Dee Woodward, who'd also been my assistant during my four years as governor, was likewise to be paid for three years of doing nothing. Dee told me laughingly, "Gee, governor, when this is done, I'll be retiring." I said, "Good for you, Dee, you got a three-year early retirement."

My contract with MSNBC stated that they had exclusive rights to me. That's standard in the business. When they hire a personality, they don't want them to have the ability to then go and join their competition. Now that they'd canceled my show, the contract still had almost three years to run. Unless I chose to break it, I could do books, radio, speaking engagements, movies—but I could appear on no other news or cable show.

In that sense, I guess you could say that MSNBC bought my silence. An outdoor show wanted to pay me to go fishing, but I couldn't do it because it was on cable. I admit that it would have gotten political—because whenever you go fishing, you talk. I couldn't even do Bill Maher's show, because that's also on cable. I'd been a regular guest before on *Real Time*, because Maher and I think a lot alike and he'd often bring me on as an ally. I was still under contract to MSNBC during the 2004 election campaign, but they didn't even haul me out to offer an opinion. Not once.

I could have violated the contract and probably lost my pay. Did I sell out? You're damned right. If I didn't, for this kind of money, you would say I was crazy. The point was, I could do it honorably. It was a contractual agreement that both sides honored. Besides, why would I want to go on the Fox Network as a guest—just to get into a fight with O'Reilly—when you don't even get a paycheck?

TERRY: It was my fault, too. I wanted to make sure Jesse did not break his contract. We have a lot of people that we take care of who would be in a bad way if we could no longer help them financially. We do it out of love, not duty. We need to have a steady income. It sounds ridiculous to think that, with that kind of income, I would still worry about our finances but, whether you have a little money or a lot of money, the worries are the same. You spend it accordingly. Houses still need repair, cars break down, health insurance costs continue to rise, as do home, auto, and retirement insurance. Utilities cost more every year. And Jesse and I are not getting any younger. I knew he could still get his message out even if he was not on TV, or radio, or in the newspaper every day. Jesse talks about the current events of our nation to everyone he meets. He has made the effort to serve and improve our government at every level he could, since the day he went off and joined the Navy. I felt justified in keeping the contract with MSNBC.

I don't know how much of a factor the Iraq War was in MSNBC'S getting rid of me. Maybe they'd hired me thinking that, as a Navy SEAL and Vietnam vet, I was probably a right-winger who would automatically be for the war. I wasn't. I opposed it from the beginning. Remember Ashleigh Banfield, the blond with glasses who had her own show on MSNBC? She disappeared quickly, after she gave a speech at the University of Kansas and said the media were being inherently dishonest in their reporting of Iraq. Gone. Nobody was being allowed on the air who was questioning our invading Iraq. Phil Donahue got the ax, too. He was considered way too liberal by MSNBC.

I remember seeing another quote from Erik Sorenson in *The New York Times.* "After September 11," he said, "the country wants more optimism and benefit of the doubt. . . . A big criticism of the mainstream press is that the beginning point is negative."

Well, I guess he tried to steer the "right" course, but Sorenson is no longer president of MSNBC. He left that job in 2004, and I don't know where he is now. But I often wonder how good his memory is, concerning those two phone calls from Washington that he told me about when we left the Super Bowl that night.

But they could only keep my big mouth shut for so long. The contract expired in 2006.

Maybe I missed my true calling: the soaps. I was doing multitudes of interviews when I first got in office, covering a wide spectrum of topics, and one reporter wanted to know my favorite TV show. I sat there thinking for a moment, because I don't watch much network television *per se*. Then, all of a sudden, it came to me: *The Young and the Restless.*

I found that I could relate to the predicament of daytime TV. Those are the hardest-working people in Hollywood. They're also some of the most talented. Yet they're the most rebuffed, abused, poked fun at, and disrespected. But just think about the difficulty of doing daytime TV. In one week, the actors need to memorize enough script pages to fill an entire film. They're the blue-collar, hard-core, working actors and actresses. And they don't get the praise they deserve, although in many cases these daytime shows are the stepping-stone, the experience-giver. Look at the people who have gone from daytime into Hollywood stardom: Demi Moore and David Hasselhoff (a *Young and the Restless* alumni), just to name two.

When it made the papers that *The Young and the Restless* was my favorite program, apparently someone connected with the show read about it. Lo and behold, what came in the mail? The most beautiful portrait of the whole cast, all autographed, accompanied by a great cover letter. I have it hanging on the wall at home in Minnesota.

Then, in the summer of 2000, the producers invited me to CBS Studios in L.A. to make a cameo guest appearance. My scene had me knocking on Victor Newman's office door. Victor seemed very surprised to see me, but invited me to have a seat. He asked what brought me out here, and I said, "It's not another campaign contribution, if that's what you're worried about, Victor."

After a minute, Victor asked, "Why did you decide not to run for president? I mean, come November it would have been far more interesting."

"Well, there's always 2004," I said, and then stood up tall for dramatic effect and leaned over Victor's desk. "Why don't you run with me? We'd be a dream ticket!"

"That's an interesting possibility, except . . ."

"What's that?"

"Who would take the top spot?" Victor went on.

"That would be a problem," I agreed. "If our two egos were to clash, I don't think the country could survive it!"

Well, I admitted to the media afterward that I'd had some butterflies beforehand, but calmed down once the taping started—and I didn't blow any of my lines! When I got back to Minnesota, I threatened to declare the show's air date, July 10, a state holiday.

When I was out in Hollywood a year or so later, I had dinner with the *Young and the Restless* producer and Eric Braeden (also known as Victor Newman). Since I had nothing to do the next day until 2:00 p.m., I asked Eric whether he'd mind if I came down and watched. They generally shoot three weeks ahead of the air date, so this way I could get a leg up on what was going to happen.

When I arrived at the studio, they'd written me into the script again. This time I played a security guard and knocked on Victor's door to tell him I'd be his security for the rest of the day. He said thank you and then, shutting the door, gave a funny look to the camera—"Is that who I thought it was?"—and went on with the scene.

I didn't get any billing. But, no matter, as a member of the Screen Actors Guild, three weeks later I received a check in the mail.

Life is truly about failures, and how you respond to them. You can't succeed without also failing. Still, you'd like to fail on your own. When I got censored and taken off the air by MSNBC, despite still being paid handsomely, from a psychological viewpoint it was a nightmare. I think I would have gone into a deep depression—if Harvard hadn't come along.

It turned out that a student, who was also in the military reserves, had petitioned the Institute of Politics at the John F. Kennedy School of Government, saying that I ought to be teaching there. He said, don't you think that what Jesse Ventura achieved in getting elected governor has a place at arguably the greatest institution of learning in the world? The Kennedy School's dean at that time was Dan Glickman, whom Terry had met when he was secretary of agriculture under Clinton. And Glickman went for the idea. Along came a letter asking if I'd like to become a visiting fellow at Harvard. They offered me as little as a week, or as much as the entire semester. I was dumbstruck. I said to Terry, "Do you believe this, honey? I never even went to college!" I mean, Harvard had produced five American presidents and forty-three Nobel Prize winners. And they wanted me?!

I'd started growing a beard when my TV show ended that same month. I'd also started letting whatever hair I had left grow back, which I thought I'd never do. Perfect timing for going back to school, I guess. I thought, Wow, I missed that part of life. Here I am now at fifty-two, and not only would I have a two-hour-long seminar class to teach for eight consecutive weeks, but as a visiting fellow, you can audit any classes you desire. Which means getting a free semester of Harvard education. I was even to be given a stipend, and they'd provide living quarters. Amazing!

Terry and I agreed that I should do the whole semester. So she stayed home, and I went off to college, in January 2004. I parallel this to only a few other times in my life. Becoming a Navy frogman. Driving off from Minneapolis to become a pro wrestler. Getting cast to do *Predator* with Schwarzenegger. And winning the governorship.

I'd been to Harvard once before, more than four years earlier. After getting elected governor, the Kennedy School had invited me to speak at a "Pizza and Politics" evening. I'd expected Harvard to be a stuffy, arrogant place. But when I got there that day and saw how bright everyone was—what could be better? I loved it.

Even though it was kind of an awkward visit, coinciding with the release of the *Playboy* interview where I made a few statements that were considered outrageous. Like my definition of gun control: "Being able to stand there at twenty-five meters and put two rounds in the same hole." Or that drug offenders and prostitutes shouldn't get packed off to prison: "The government has much more important work to do." Or the First Amendment rights of protesters: "If you buy the flag, it's yours to burn."

When Chris Matthews interviewed me for *Hardball* that day on the Harvard auditorium's stage, he said: "I was asked recently if I would do a *Playboy* interview. Do you recommend that I do that?"

I told Chris, "I'd say do that before you do the foldout." The eight hundred students in the audience seemed to appreciate that.

Now I was coming back for real. After I landed at the Boston airport, a fellow standing by the baggage carousel recognized me, despite my hair and beard. "Governor, what are you doing out here?" he asked. I said, "Well, I'm going to teach at Harvard." I'm sure there was more than a hint of pride in my voice.

He said, laughing, "Oh, the People's Republic of Cambridge! That's the closest thing to pure socialism that we have in the United States."

The taxi let me out right by the door to the Kennedy School, where there's a little plaza. I met the people I'd be working with—marvelous people—and we drove over to the apartment where I'd be living. It was the bare essentials, a little two-bedroom with a living room and kitchen. A long way from the governor's residence, but I didn't mind—except the bed was terrible! The first thing Terry did when she came to visit was get one of those inflatable air mattresses to put on top of it. (I have something of a bad back from wrestling, and jumping out of airplanes, and a few other things I did.)

But it was fun, and exciting, to be living on campus. My apartment was over by the business school, a beautiful area overlooking the Charles River. It was wintertime and I had to wear a stocking hat and a heavy overcoat. Every day I'd walk through the business school and cross a bridge over to the Kennedy School, a pretty good hike.

Even though I was all bundled up because of the cold, I was experiencing a sense of personal freedom. No one was recognizing me in that clothing and with the beard. I just blended in. All of a sudden, I could stand on crowded street corners with no security around, and with a feeling I hadn't had for a long, long time. Not since my early wrestling days had it been like this.

One morning after I first arrived, I was passing by all the red-brick buildings in the business school when I saw—the Mellon Building. I burst out laughing so hard that I fell to my knees. People were looking at me like I was nuts. But didn't they realize? Thornton Mellon, one of the great movie characters, played by Rodney Dangerfield in *Back to School*. Remember when he throws the dirt and hits the professor? It was taken right out of Harvard! It was real!

Classes didn't start right away, so I was still getting acclimated. I was taken to see the statue of John Harvard. It's all bronze, but mostly oxidized—except for the one shoe that faces forward, which is bright and looks highly polished. I asked why, and they said: "Well, because it's a myth that, on exam days, you walk by and touch John Harvard's shoe for good luck." So its look was just from all those thousands of hands hitting the shoe!

I came to find out that the statue has an interesting history. It's based upon three lies. First, the guy isn't really John Harvard. The day they did the statue, he wasn't available, so they got somebody else to pose. Second, John Harvard didn't found Harvard. What John Harvard did was contribute his family's substantial library of books. And third, the John Harvard symbol means honesty. On top of two other fabrications! How about that?

I was given a beautiful little office, in toward the courtyard of the Kennedy School. That's when I encountered my first obstacle—this massive-looking monster, this alien thing called a computer. I thought, holy smokes, I'm going to have to learn how to *use* one of these!

You see, when I was governor, if I needed anything from a computer, I had a couple of whizzes in my office. Any subject I could bring up, within an hour or so they would have an answer for me. The job was, in many ways, an oxymoron. I mean by that, you do nothing, and yet "know" everything. Let's say, hypothetically, I needed to know how many walleyed pike had been caught in Lake Milacs last year. All I'd do is mention this to my staff, and pretty soon I'd have a full-page report on my desk. Then I could walk out to the press fully briefed as an expert on that subject. You simply have to absorb it and make it *look* like you have this supreme knowledge that the average person doesn't.

Now, the first thing I had to do at Harvard was tackle a computer. Fortunately, there were people around with a very patient attitude.

And I did conquer the monster. Eventually, I sent an e-mail on my own, to a Harvard student. I let him know this was a first for Jesse Ventura, in case he wanted to save it for posterity. Of course, once people knew I had an e-mail address at Harvard, every morning I'd come in and have thirty of them waiting! I'd sit down and try to answer them all. That was a half day's work right there, because I'd never learned how to type, either.

One day, when I was in my office putting together an outline of my schedule, a kid walked in who was part of the Hasty Pudding Theatricals. It's the oldest college theater group is the country, and has put on shows for more than 160 years. Originally, the Hasty Pudding Club was a secret society, kind of like Skull and Bones at Yale, inspired by a student named Nymphus Hatch in 1795 and named for the traditional American dessert that the founding members ate at their first meeting. The club counts five presidents among its noteworthy members, including the two Adamses, the two Roosevelts, and John F. Kennedy. Its theater started in 1844, and the modern Pudding show has evolved into a spectacle that was certainly never envisioned back then. It's a no-holds-barred burlesque, with men playing both the male and female roles in a play with lots of song-and-dance lines, mimicking a Vegas-type showgirl routine. However, as I say, it's all done in drag.

You may recall I'd already achieved some renown for my feather boa costume in my wrestling days, so I didn't lack experience in such matters. They were getting ready to do the 2004 show, and I said to the student, "Wow, I sure would love to be part of that." So the student went to see the director, who was very excited about my participating. I couldn't be part of the regular cast and crew, because they put the show on for weeks and then travel around with it every year. But they picked one particular night, and wrote in my own three lines at Hasty Pudding! Then they advertised it all over campus with posters stating: "Come and see Governor Jesse Ventura as you will have never seen him before!"

I kept my beard, and I decided to be a blonde. I went with what I called the "European Look"—that is, miniskirt with unshaven legs. If I remember right, it was pink-sequined. I told them I'd have to take a pass on the finale, where all the fellas end up in a big conga line with their legs kicking, due to my back problem. Other than that, I was game for all.

Well, the show sold out that night. The place was packed! I got so into listening and laughing with the audience reaction, instead of taking the pregnant pause, that I ended up forgetting my last line. My son was there and he videotaped it all from the audience. It's gone into my archives, never to be released.

But we had a great time and, when it was over, cast and crew all got back into our "civvies" and headed over to John Harvard's Brew House—where they make microbrews right there on campus—to wash a few down. I happened to notice these three young guys sitting at a table. They were each wearing T-shirts that said, in big black letters: "HARVARD SUCKS."

Hey, I'm teaching here, and even part of the Hasty Pudding. Which means that Harvard is my school—I'm Crimson! So seeing this brought out the old frogman in me. I thought, nobody would walk into a Navy SEAL bar and walk out again standing, wearing "SEAL TEAM SUCKS" on their T-shirt. This demanded a response!

So, I walked over to the table. I was still pretty imposing—six-four, 255 pounds—and getting back in shape by training for two hours every morning at the Harvard Athletic Club and then running three miles a day. Also, by now, I'd had a few brews. I stared hard at these three fellows and said, "What's with these T-shirts, 'HARVARD SUCKS'?"

One of them replied casually, "Well, we think Harvard sucks."

I said, "Oh yeah? Where are you from?"

"Texas," another said.

I said, "Really. Well, I go to Harvard. And I hear that, in Texas, the only thing they've got are steers and queers—and I don't see no horns on you!"

That used to be our standard line in the Navy to get any Texan to fight. The three of them glared back at me, in silence.

Then I added this: "You've got two options. One is to deal with me. Two is to take the shirts off and put them on again. Inside out."

They chose the second option.

Word spread quickly across the Harvard campus that Governor Ventura had stood tall for the Crimson.

Headline: THE BODY POLITIC

Like a pro wrestling match where the featured performer walks out and whips up the crowd beforehand, Jesse Ventura's first Harvard class began early and outside the ropes. Arriving at Lowell House for his weekly seminar, Ventura—a visiting fellow at the Kennedy School's Institute of Politics this semester— waited for another class to finish. While he stood outside, students eager to hear from the former wrestling star and Minnesota governor, whose reputation for shooting from the hip is well established, gathered around. He did not disappoint.

—Boston Globe, *February 25, 2004*

I needed a title for my seminar, and I decided to call it "Body Slamming the Political Establishment: Third Party Politics." I had access to the Harvard library, Widener, which is considered second only to the Library of Congress. Acres of books! I would spend hours there, and in my office, preparing my lectures. I didn't go to Harvard to embarrass myself.

Any classes that are taken from fellowship professors are not graded. They're intended as exchanges of ideas; getting people thinking. That's what's great about it. And anyone could attend. There would be posters all over campus promoting what my subject was that week. These had pictures of me in full battle attire, holding a big, menacing-looking rifle, above a caption that read, "BIG MAN ON CAMPUS." I'm proud to say that they had to move my classes into an auditorium setting at Lowell House, to hold the numbers. It came to pass that I had the largest class attendance of any fellowship professor in Harvard history. Hundreds came every Tuesday, packed in to the rafters.

I told the students at the first session, "Look, you're going to learn at Harvard all the academic part of politics—the theory. I'm here to teach you about the reality. And reality may not be the same as theory."

The seminars lasted two hours, with the last forty-five minutes being all back-and-forth between the class and me. They don't want a fellowship professor necessarily lecturing the kids, because they get that all day long. My first class focused on how I won the gubernatorial election in 1998. I asked the class if they knew which politician had pioneered the use of the Internet. (Hint: Not Howard Dean. Me.) We talked about why only half of the voting-age people in the U.S. even bother to go to the polls. And why there's no public outcry over the Republicans and Democrats getting around the campaign-finance laws.

A fellowship professor is also allowed to bring in guest speakers. For one seminar, I had Governor Angus King come down from Maine to talk about governing from a third-party perspective. He was marvelous. He spoke of how an independent candidate can be a mediator, in a perfect position to bring the other two political sides toward a more centrist point of view. Angus also spoke about how he helped get himself elected by writing a book, telling exactly what he believed in. He got the books printed on the cheap, and would hand them out at each campaign stop.

Another time I brought in Dean Barkley, my campaign manager in Minnesota. He was very knowledgeable about how the two parties are destroying our political process. One of the interesting things that Dean pointed out was the way they've used redistricting, or gerrymandering, to eliminate competition. Out of 435 congressmen, there are about 400 "safe seats," where nobody but the incumbent has a chance; in 2002, eighty-one of the representatives even ran unopposed by another major party candidate!

I decided to do a class on terrorism, because I felt that, today, terrorism may have to be dealt with at the local level as much as at the federal. Here, I brought in my buddy Richard Marcinko, the "rogue warrior" I'd called for some insight after my meeting with the twenty-three CIA agents in the State Capitol. I introduced Dick by saying, "You're gonna hear it today from a guy who was a shooter. This is the man killing the terrorists, not the one pushing papers around authorizing it. You're about to meet the trigger man."

Dick was phenomenal. And he brought up something that terrified *me*. "I'll tell you what," he said to the class. "You give me Governor Ventura, myself, and eight more of my fellow Navy SEALs—and we could paralyze the entire country of the United States of America."

First I thought to myself, Come on, Dick, you're talking about ten guys! But he went on to describe how the two snipers in Washington, D.C.—who weren't even that good—had intimidated 24 million people, making them afraid to go to the gas station or sometimes even leave their homes. So, if you consider a coordinated effort of, say, five sniper pairs located in different parts of the U.S.—one in New England, others in Florida, the Midwest, L.A., maybe Seattle—who are well-trained and randomly starting to blow up bridges, or fire semi-automatics, I realized: He's right, this could bring the country to its knees. It was eye-opening, and chilling.

My last classes were the ones on President Kennedy's assassination, and how wrestling prepares you for politics.

People don't realize that, if you have time on your hands, you can get a Harvard education without paying any tuition. Officially classes aren't open to the public but no one ever took attendance or asked, "Should you be in this class?" You would not get a degree, but you could learn a lot until you got caught.

As a fellowship professor, I had several students serve as my liaisons and arrange everything. If there's a particular class you want to attend, they find out when and where it is, and lead you right to the door. The one that intrigued me most was over at Harvard Law School—Alan Dershowitz's course in Criminal Law.

Unannounced to Professor Dershowitz, I just walked in and sat in the back of the room. With my new beard, he didn't recognize me. I couldn't get enough of Dershowitz; he's a remarkable teacher. He's so engaging, and has a phenomenal memory for cases of law. You wonder how anybody could remember the name, the number, and the year all of these happened. But Dershowitz can.

The topic that first day was "The Crime of Rape." The question he posed was, can a husband rape a wife? As Professor Dershowitz pointed out, there is an unwritten contract in marriage, and part of it has to do with sex. Just because one partner is in the mood doesn't mean the other one is. In light of this, does it have to be consensual? Or can a rape occur?

I thought about this for a minute, and an answer popped into my head. So I raised my hand, and he called on me. I said, "Professor, in light of what our society has deemed rape, I would have to say that, yes, it is possible for a husband to rape a wife. Because our society describes rape not as a sexual act, but an act of violence. In light of that, you can't hit your wife, or that can be deemed assault. I would think sex could be looked at in the same way."

Professor Dershowitz smiled, pointed a finger at me, and said: "Very good."

I wanted to put my chest out, I was so proud. The whole class was chuckling, because the kids knew who I was. But they'd caught on that Professor Dershowitz didn't. After class when I went down to say hello, he was beaming. He said, "I didn't even know it was you—until you spoke. Hard not to recognize that voice."

He told me I was welcome to come anytime, and I did go to a few more of his classes.

Another thing that made my experience at Harvard very unique: Every week at the Kennedy School, they have speakers in the evenings. These events are open to the public, and they generally sell tickets. Jesse Jackson came through while I was there. When we had dinner together after his talk, he said, "We need to get together and cause trouble." He felt that, essentially, we were after the same result, although we might come at it in different ways. By that, I believe he meant more truthful government.

When I first arrived at Harvard, I'd been concerned because I didn't see any partying as I walked around campus. I thought, this seems a bit un-American. Then I found out that Harvard does not have fraternities or sororities, but instead has various clubs that own buildings on campus. And that's where the students go to have fun on the weekends. I was made an honorary member of the Spee Club, the same one that JFK belonged to in 1938. I went to a couple of their parties, which renewed my faith in youth, in college, in America. Because let me tell you, they were *partying*! All night long!

By working out at the Athletic Club, where only the varsity athletes are allowed, I dropped about thirty pounds. I was able to join because, when I'd visited Harvard earlier, I'd taken time to speak to the football team. So when I came back, they made me an honorary member.

Harvard did wonders for me in many ways. I'd become very cynical by the time I arrived. Being around the energy of the young people, their quick intelligence and enthusiasm, gave me a ray of hope again. It made me wonder, could this be the generation that doesn't repeat history? Mine sure wasn't. I wanted to do whatever I could to help them see a clearer way into the future.

After I left in May 2004, some students petitioned that I be named to replace Dan Glickman, who had resigned as dean of the Kennedy School. I said, "Are you crazy? Not even Harvard will do *that*!" Their reasoning, as they explained it, was that the dean is more a figurehead than a nuts-and-bolts type. "We want to bring attention to the school," one student said, "and who would be better than you to do that?"

But, like I say: As flattering as this was, I don't think Harvard would have dared consider it. I don't have the credentials; all those Ph.D.s and other pieces of paper. I come from the school of hard knocks, no matter which arena it is.

CHAPTER 14

Thinking War in a Peaceful Place

"A conscientious man would be cautious how he dealt in blood."

—*Edmund Burke*

After spending two days at Conception Bay, I know. We are going to find a winter home somewhere in the southern Baja. We continue on down Highway 1, through the old capital of Loreto and the new capital of La Paz and, further south, we branch off onto Highway 19. That's the road toward Todos Santos, an artist's colony and a great surf spot on the Pacific side. It is also said to be the inspiration for Don Henley and the Eagles' huge hit "Hotel California," and how can we resist at least spending a night there?

The Hotel California has been renovated by new owners, and it is a treat to stay in a luxurious suite and wash away the road in an adobe sauna. Terry and I shop around and, sure enough, find a lovely stone house for sale in the vicinity, overlooking the ocean. "This is it," I tell her. She admits to me later that she's been planning to make sure I'm all set up in the first two weeks, and then she's going home.

> *TERRY: With the memory still fresh of Highway 5, I want no more of this driving a horrible road out in the middle of nowhere. But once you're down here, and the house is so nice and the beach was so beautiful, and the good people. . . .*

So she stays. I know her, and I know what interests her. And I know that you'll be able to go by yourself up an arroyo with a dog, and just explore. That's what the mystique of the Baja is about, the desert and the sea.

> *TERRY: The thing that is amazing about Jesse Ventura, if you're with him on a day-to-day basis, is that he loves to watch sports and he talks a lot and it's always about politics. But when you see the way his mind works and his strong convictions of right or wrong—just the way he looks at life—he is unbelievable. What I get out of him is always different, every time I turn around. It's not always great, but it's always different.*

"Terry, you've got to read a chapter in this book, it's amazing." The book is *Miraculous Air: Journey of a Thousand Miles Through Baja California, the Other Mexico,* by C. M. Mayo. We picked it up in Todos Santos. It had a chapter on the U.S.-Mexican War of the late 1840s, Polk versus Santa Anna. The latter having been "President of Mexico on eleven different occasions, first liberal, then conservative, always mercurial, always ruthless."

I can't help chuckling as I tell Terry, "When a French cannonball blew his leg away at the knee, he'd actually had a state funeral for it! Had his leg carried by twelve hundred members of the presidential guard, 'in solemn procession through the streets to a specially built shrine. The ceremony was attended by Congress, the diplomatic corps, and the entire cabinet.'"

"That's disgusting!" Terry exclaims. We are sitting on the porch of our new *hacienda*, each with our books and otherwise looking placidly out to sea.

"They called Santa Anna *caudillo*, the strongman. Sounds kinda like he was an early version of Saddam Hussein. What I didn't realize is that American troops once had control of La Paz, Todos Santos, even Cabo San Lucas! Along with most of mainland Mexico, too."

"Really," Terry says.

"Yeah, except get this part. 'The war was unpopular and expensive, and Polk was eager to conclude a treaty.' So, he ended up having a set of secret instructions sent to Santa Anna, saying that U.S. forces would withdraw from all the territory we had taken inside Mexico, including the Baja. In exchange, Santa Anna confirmed our title to Texas and also signed away territories that are now California, Nevada, Utah, Colorado, Wyoming, and parts of Arizona and New Mexico. Not a bad deal for the Americans."

I pause a minute to reflect, then add: "I guess we've got a long history of invading sovereign nations in unpopular and expensive wars."

I was a few months out of office when the invasion of Iraq took place in March 2003. Had I still been governor, I might have been the only one who opposed it. It had to do with the fact that we were lining up our military against that country as an aggressor and an occupier. Vietnam, as dirty as that was, was still a French colony when they asked us to support them logistically. Of course, it accelerated far beyond that in the end, with the French leaving us holding the bag and our being more than willing to do so.

But, thinking back to the months prior to the Iraq War, nobody in the national news media was questioning the policy. Here we were going it alone, or with the "coalition of the willing." Actually, except for the British, most of the "willing" didn't even have armies!

New documents that came out in April 2007 prove that a unit inside the Pentagon—Douglas Feith's Office of Special Plans—intentionally cooked up the "intel" claiming there was a direct tie between Iraq and al-Qaeda in order to gather support for a preemptive strike. It's long since been established that the other big rationale for our invading, Saddam Hussein's supposed weapons of mass destruction, was utterly bogus. I don't think the CIA is as inept as we were led to believe during the run-up to the war, but was used very much as a scapegoat. I've had that verified through some channels of mine; that there are people within the CIA who are exceptionally angry at how they were hung out to dry. The more you get into it, the more you realize that it wasn't that the CIA was giving President Bush the wrong "intel," but simply that the president and his people were choosing which "intel" they wanted to use, while the rest was conveniently pushed aside and forgotten.

Colin Powell has since admitted that he was basically duped, and it was Powell who I think pushed it over the top, because he was the one whom the people wanted to believe. In hindsight, I hold Powell somewhat responsible. He spent his entire life as a military man. You may offer resistance to the commander in chief up until the point that the decision is made. Then any good soldier must go along with the president, whether they agree with him or not. That's the position Powell was in. Personally, he probably had his doubts, but when push came to shove, his years in the military prevailed. So I can understand, to a point.

But I can't forgive the rest of the chicken-hawk cowards—Bush, Cheney, Rumsfeld, and the rest—who never served, and who sent American boys to Iraq to die. All based on a pack of lies.

I've heard people say, "W" did it ultimately to impress Daddy. George, Sr., stopped short of going into Baghdad at the end of the Gulf War, and George, Jr., had always played second fiddle to his brother Jeb, and this was his big chance to show Dad he could seize the initiative and do something that even his father didn't contemplate. Is it that? I don't know. I seem always to go back to the old line from "Deep Throat" during Watergate: "Follow the money." That's generally behind at least 90 percent of all decisions made in government nowadays, I believe.

When America entered World War II, FDR said: "I don't want to see a single war millionaire created in the United States as a result of this world disaster." Harry Truman, who was then a senator from Missouri, launched an investigation into war profiteering that ended up saving the taxpayers more than $15 billion—the equivalent of more than $200 billion today. Today, a whole lot of people are cashing in on the "war on terror." Not just Halliburton and the Carlyle Group. The big weapons makers—Lockheed Martin, Boeing, Northrop Grumman, and General Dynamics—are all reporting huge profits. It's been toted up that the defense industry's top thirty-four CEOs have collectively earned a billion dollars since 9/11. I compare the situation to the current mortgage market, where buyers are getting properties for a steal.

Iraq is the most privatized war in American history. There are as many as 200,000 private contractors over there—a number greater than our 160,000 military troops! You might call it "rent-an-Army." Halliburton, Dick Cheney's old company, was ready to roll when the war began. They've since been found to have wasted millions of our dollars in overbilling and shoddy services (Halliburton runs the chow lines, too). It's amazing, but these companies have zero accountability. Only *one* of those 100,000 contractors has been accused of any violations, or been indicted for any crimes. They are operating totally outside of any public scrutiny. Yet, by some estimates, up to forty cents out of every dollar being spent on the war is going to these corporate war contractors.

Take the mercenary force called Blackwater Worldwide. Their top brass are mostly former CIA and Pentagon people. Since the "war on terror" began, Blackwater has received almost a billion dollars in government contracts, most of them no-bid deals. They've now got 2,300 personnel operating in nine countries, and 20,000 more waiting in the wings. They've got their own major weaponry and their own private "intel" division. Think about this: a top Army sergeant makes a little over $50,000 a year, including salary, housing and other benefits. Blackwater contractors, who in fact are often retired sergeants, are getting anywhere from six to nine times that much—close to a half million dollars a year—in some instances.

And these are really little more than hired gunslingers, rogue American mercenaries operating under the banner of "patriotism." In mid-September 2007, Blackwater guards were accompanying a State Department convoy in Baghdad, when they opened fire and then launched a grenade at another vehicle. It turned out to be a young Iraqi family inside, and altogether that day, Blackwater killed as many as twenty-eight civilians. They claimed they'd been attacked by gunmen and "heroically defended American lives in a war zone." That couldn't have been farther from the truth. Iraq's prime minister, Nouri al-Maliki, called their conduct "criminal." Blackwater was apparently responsible for several other fatal shootings before that.

The money being tossed around in the name of bringing democracy to the Iraqis is staggering. By the fall of 2007, it had cost $464 billion. Bush's new budget included an extra $100 billion for a year more of fighting in Iraq and Afghanistan. That was on top of $70 billion that Congress had already allocated, plus almost $142 billion for 2008. This means that the spending on the almost five-year-old Iraq War is about to surpass the cost of thirteen years in Vietnam. Prior to invading, Donald Rumsfeld said that Iraq's oil would pay for everything. So much for that big idea. Now Bush has vetoed a bill for child health insurance because of so-called "pork barrel" politics. Well, I'd rather err on insuring kids than on the fiasco we're involved in over there.

The fact is, this war is not only draining America's resources, it's likely to eventually bankrupt us. And who is paying the biggest price? When you realize that the new Bush budget also cuts $66 billion out of Medicare payments to the elderly over the next five years, and another $12 billion out of Medicaid for the poor, it's kind of a no-brainer. *The New York Times* recently noted that, for what the war is costing, we could've instituted universal health care, provided a nursery school education for every three- and four-year-old, and immunized kids around the world against numerous diseases—and still had half the money left over.

At the same time, shortly before we turned over supposed control to the Iraqis, the U.S. Federal Reserve sent over, on military aircraft, the biggest cash shipments it's ever made—more than $4 billion, amounting to *363 tons* of dollars on these huge pallets! The funds came from assets frozen from Saddam Hussein's regime, as well as oil exports. They'd been requested by the new Iraqi minister of finance, but there was so little accountability that nobody knows how much actually ended up in the hands of the insurgents.

Speaking of big bucks, there's also a new revenue-sharing plan for Iraq's oil. After the Saudis, Iraq has the second biggest oil reserves in the world, and now its National Oil Company is going to hold exclusive control over just seventeen of the eighty known oil fields. The rest, and the ones yet to be discovered, are all going to be open to foreign control. This is just in case you thought there was any rationale for our being in Iraq other than our dependency on oil.

As of my completing this book in the fall of 2007, close to 4,000 American soldiers have been killed in Iraq, and almost 30,000 more have been wounded. The majority of casualties on the other side, as in all wars, have been civilians. A scholarly paper that appeared in *Lancet* (October 2006) estimated that about 650,000 Iraqi civilians—including huge numbers of women, children, and the elderly—have died since the Americans came in. True, many of them have been caught up in a civil war, but that sure wouldn't have happened without our intervention.

The terrible truth is, even with as many people as Saddam Hussein had to eliminate to stay in power, the Iraqis are a whole lot worse off today than under his regime. Let's imagine that we had a dictator, and some outside force came into our country and took him out. And things did not get better; they deteriorated. How would we then feel about whoever did this to us? It comes back to the old cliché: the enemy known, as opposed to the one unknown. At least they knew who Saddam was.

We always say that everyone deserves their day in court and a fair trial. With a new government completely dominated by the Shiites, who were Saddam's enemies, how could he possibly receive a fair trial? I personally would have been very interested to hear his testimony. After all, we got to watch every aspect of the O. J. Simpson trial, from beginning to end. In the realm of global politics, wouldn't the Hussein trial affect us more? Yet we could watch nothing of what he had to say, except whatever was bled to us on our news media after the censors got through with it. I'm no Saddam supporter, but he really was silenced, wasn't he?

I saw George W. Bush being interviewed when he was asked if he'd watched the Saddam hanging. He said that he saw parts of it on television—presumably when Hussein was standing there, hooded, with the men holding the noose. I think Bush should have been *required* to be there. Again, according to the credos of our democracy, don't you have a right to face your accuser? Without George Bush, Saddam Hussein would never have been hanged.

While channel-surfing recently, I noticed how the History Channel is now portraying Saddam as the new Hitler. That's what's going to be set down in our history books—that George Bush and the American government saved the world from this Hitler wannabe? Sure, he did some terrible things, but this is ludicrous. Hussein gassed the Kurds, but where did he get the gas from? He got it from *us*. But no, let's not tell the truth and reveal that, at one time, Saddam was one of our biggest allies in the Middle East, and shaking hands with Donald Rumsfeld.

Revisionist history troubles me deeply. I fear textbooks being written with a "government seal of approval." Is anything being said about Henry Kissinger's having accepted the Nobel Peace Prize at the very moment he and Nixon had ordered the secret bombing of Cambodia that would kill thousands of innocent people? Or what about ex–CIA director George Tenet, the only Bush administration official who ended up resigning over the Iraq fiasco? What does Bush do then but award Tenet the Medal of Freedom, the highest award a civilian can receive. So, in the annals of history, I guess that means Tenet goes down as a hero. Or maybe he was simply the guy who chose to fall on his sword at the time, and got the medal as his reward.

Nothing appears to daunt these people. Why are we building permanent bases in Iraq? Remember when we heard there was no pull-out strategy? That's when the light went on for me—what if there never *was* one? Why have an exit strategy if you're not planning on leaving? I believe that's part of the scam. Bush simply says we've got to "stay the course," and even got a "surge" in troop strength approved by Congress. That's exactly the opposite of what his Iraq Study Group advised him to do, and that group is headed up by none other than James A. Baker, who led the legal fight to make sure the Supreme Court would award Florida—and the election—to Bush in 2000. It's contrary to what his military commanders are telling him, too. Bush isn't just revising history, he's turning it into mythology. He's still claiming that, after the U.S. couldn't find the suspected WMDs, Saddam banned the United Nations inspectors from his country. Hence, we had to go in. But Hussein never did that.

Dick Cheney went on Rush Limbaugh's radio program and continued to insist—this was in April 2007—that Iraq and al-Qaeda were in bed together. And that, if we withdraw from Iraq, that would "play right into the hands of al-Qaeda." Again, U.S. intelligence analysts have come to precisely the opposite conclusion on both those points. In fact, Osama bin Laden has stated publicly that prolonging the Iraq War is in *his* best interest.

But then, what can you expect from Cheney? No matter what he does, a big part of his legacy will be the infamous "hunting accident" on the quail-hunting trip down in south Texas. That sad Saturday when the vice president plugged his friend Harry Whittington, a seventy-eight-year-old Austin lawyer with birdshot in the face, neck, and chest—and *the guy who got shot apologized*! I must say, that's a first. Unless you are in combat, there are no accidents; there is only negligence. If you're bird hunting, the gun should be on safety at all times until the bird is coming up. However, this basic rule of thumb may not take into account a onetime secretary of defense who successfully achieved five deferments from military service. Of course, the official investigation revealed "there was no alcohol or misconduct involved in the incident." As far as anybody knew, Cheney had always been a "straight shooter" since his two arrests for drunk driving.

But forgive me, I digress. . . . Bin Laden attacks us, so we attack Iraq. In my speeches over the past few years, I liked to bring up the

Martha Stewart case as an analogy. What did Martha actually get put in prison for? It wasn't insider trading—that charge was thrown out. She went to jail for lying to the government. Okay, if we lie to the government, we go to jail. But what happens when the government lies to *us*? I pause and then say, "Oh, that's right, we go to war." And I make the point that I'm not talking only about the current war, but about how the Vietnam War escalated after Lyndon Johnson's administration concocted the Gulf of Tonkin incident.

I'm also very angry at the Democrats, who were cowards from the beginning of the Iraq ordeal. They seemed so frightened of their political standing, or of what Karl Rove and the Bush machine had created, they wouldn't just stand up and say no. Even now that the Democrats control Congress again, they will only go so far. They want a timetable for withdrawing our troops, but they don't seem ready to hold Bush's feet to the fire to get it. I, at least, give the Republicans credit for having courage, misguided though it may be. I don't think anyone who voted for this war deserves to be president, Democrat or Republican.

What frustrates and angers me more than anything is this: It's my generation. We've been led down the primrose path once already, with Vietnam. Shouldn't we, of all people, know about being deceived? How dumb can we be? Now we've gone and done the very thing we protested so vehemently against in our youth. We've become what we feared.

Maybe it's time we recalled the words of Robert F. Kennedy, when he was running for president in 1968: "I am concerned—as I believe most Americans are concerned—that the course we are following at the present time is deeply wrong. I am concerned—as I believe most Americans are concerned—that we are acting as if no other nations existed, against the judgment and desires of neutrals and our historic allies alike. I am concerned—as I believe most Americans are concerned—that our present course will not bring victory; will not bring peace; will not stop the bloodshed; and will not advance the interests of the United States or the cause of peace in the world. I am concerned that, at the end of it all, there will only be more Americans killed; more of our treasure spilled out; and because of the bitterness and hatred on every side of this war, more hundreds of thousands of [civilians] slaughtered; so they may say, as Tacitus said of Rome: 'They made a desert, and called it peace.'"

At the end of the Vietnam War, I was actively involved in the Stop-the-Draft movement. I've done a full 180-degree turn today. My change of heart started when I ran into Bill Walton at a Timberwolves game, around the time the Iraq War was getting underway. I've known Bill since the late 1970s, before his Portland Trail Blazers won the NBA title, because we used to train together at LaPrinzi's Gym when I lived in Portland during my wrestling years. Suddenly Bill Walton—the ultra-hippie, ultra-anti-war guy—looked at me and said: "We've got to get the draft back." I was floored. "Bill, you're advocating reinstating the *draft*?!" I said.

"That will stop the war," he said. It hadn't dawned on me until then. As long as we have a professional military, it's not going to touch that many Americans whose attitude is, "Well, they all volunteered, they're there because they want to be." The fact is, a professional military is now the strong arm of our president and corporate America, and the gun can be pulled out of the holster far too easily. It creates an atmosphere where the majority of the fighting men are poor people. Trying to improve in the military is their only way of getting a college education down the line. The rich kids, even a great majority of the middle class kids, are not serving.

I'm okay with a professional military during peacetime, but the moment a vote to go to war occurs, the draft should automatically be reinstated. We need to make war as difficult as we can to declare. You've got to bring the war home. I don't care what anybody says, the country isn't feeling enough pain. It should not be only the service people and their families, it should be us as a nation. The professional military is, in its own way, an anesthetic, a painkiller.

Headline: JESSE VENTURA HELPS LAUNCH ORGANIZATION 'OPERATION TRUTH'

Former Gov. Jesse Ventura, who during his time in office diligently avoided commenting on military decisions, joined the fray over the war in Iraq on Tuesday.

"Now that I'm a civilian, I'm here to speak out that I think the current use of the National Guard is wrong," Ventura said Tuesday.

Ventura is serving as an advisory board member for a new group called Operaton Truth, a nonprofit organization set up "to give voice to troops who served in Iraq."

Emphasizing that he is an independent, not a Republican or Democrat, Ventura said the National Guard was designed to protect the homeland, not fight overseas.

—Associated Press, August 25, 2004

The reality is, a "backdoor draft" already exists through the military's use of multiple deployments. More than 85,000 troops have been kept on in Iraq, beyond their agreed-upon term of service. We haven't managed to really begin rebuilding New Orleans after Hurricane Katrina. That's what the National Guard ought to be doing, instead of being forced to remain in Iraq doing a mission they were never trained for! These are not frontline combat units. Why else is the National Guard being used so extensively, other than to fight the war on the cheap? Why doesn't Bush transfer the regular soldiers from Germany, and let the Guard man the bases there? None of it makes sense.

If I ever became president, I'd push with every ounce of power I had for Congress to pass something else into law: Every elected federal official must predesignate an individual in their immediate family who has to begin military service—the moment that official casts an affirmative vote toward going to war. This could be a grandchild, a niece or nephew, but someone. It doesn't mean they necessarily go to the war zone. What it does mean is that they and their family experience some personal discomfort because of this decision. Going to war *should* bring difficulty, especially to those who are the orchestrators or the authorizers. Right now, it's far too easy for them to go on TV with their bleeding hearts and give standing ovations to our service personnel. War should not be laissez-faire. If you're not willing to send someone from your family, how can you be so willing to send someone else's?

I don't pretend to know what we should do to get out of this quagmire. A pull-out of our troops by a certain specific date? Probably. I do think the greatest challenge facing our country is renewing our credibility internationally. Other nations now view us as an imperialist power who, if you cross us, will invade you. Until George Bush became president, this was not something that ever concerned them. They could fear us for economic manipulation or sanctions, sometimes for an off-the-books military or CIA operation. But not invasion. I don't believe ruling by fear is the sign of a great nation. Most of the world now sees us as no more than an arrogant bully.

Through all this, I'm not trying to say that terrorism isn't a real threat. There are certainly elements of the Arab and Muslim world that need to be dealt with; hard-core fanatics whose entire mission in life is to destroy us and what we stand for. But I feel very strongly that, in many ways, the terrorists are winning. Not so much on the battlefield, but in that their ultimate goal is to change America.

They're very patient. Whether the change takes two years or fifty, they would deem themselves successful.

The fact is, the Bush administration hasn't uncovered a single al-Qaeda "sleeper cell" yet inside our borders. The only terrorist convicted since 9/11 is the shoe bomber—even though, in the name of prevention, thousands of Arab and Muslim immigrants have been singled out for FBI interviews and mandatory registration and detention. I saw a cartoon in the Minneapolis paper recently. It had Bush lecturing Castro about continuing sanctions against Cuba because of human rights violations, while Bush stood there next to Guantanamo. The point was well-taken: at Guantanamo, people are being held against their will, without trials, without any human rights. How can one guy accuse another of something he's doing, too?

I would rather face the terrorists than lose my civil liberties. If protecting our safety means taking away our Bill of Rights, then could I be so crass and bold as to scream "Give me liberty or give me death"? Once freedom is gone—the bedrock foundation that built our country—what's left to stand for and believe in? Maybe we've forgotten the words of James Madison: "If tyranny and oppression come to this land, it will be in the guise of fighting a foreign enemy."

To me, the most frightening part of Michael Moore's movie *Fahrenheit 9/11* was the moment he walked into the office of Congressman Conyers to confront him about the Patriot Act. "With your voting record, Congressman, how could you have possibly voted for this?" Moore cried, or something to that effect. Then Conyers grabbed him by the elbow and said, in essence, "Sit down here, young man, there's something you need to know. Michael, we don't read *any* of the bills that we vote on!" Call me naïve, but when I heard that, I almost tipped over in my chair. In other words, they're *told* how to vote? It's all pressure from their party to say yea or nay?

The Patriot Act was rushed into law in those first scary weeks after 9/11. Most people don't know that its official title was: "Uniting and Strengthening America by Providing Appropriate Tools Required to Intercept and Obstruct Terrorism Act." Hence, USA PATRIOT Act. I hesitate to mention this but, after the Reichstag fire in Germany in 1933, Hitler pushed through legislation equally quickly called "The Law To Remove the Distress of the People and State." That has a little pithier, but eerily similar, ring to it.

The Patriot Act is 342 pages long. It alters some fifteen different statutes, most of which got passed after abuses of surveillance power by the FBI and CIA came to light in the mid-seventies. It's almost as if somebody had it all ready to be unveiled, but just had to wait for the right moment—a Reichstag fire, a Pearl Harbor type event, to make it a reality.

What does the Patriot Act enable, inside all that fine print? Oh, things like a secret court that meets whenever it chooses to approve undercover surveillance on both foreigners and Americans. Violations of various parts of the Bill of Rights, like illegal search and seizure, indefinite time in jail without a trial, seizure of private property.

And when the Patriot Act came up for reauthorization in 2007, the Democratic Congress fell hook, line, and sinker for White House propaganda. Some aspects give the federal government even broader power than before. The homes, offices, and phone records of Americans can now come under surveillance without a warrant. We can be spied on overseas. The Fourth Amendment is basically gutted.

The New York Times reported, in 2007, that the Pentagon and the CIA are now using a little-known power—known as "national security letters"—in order to get access to the banking and credit records of thousands of Americans. Banks, according to a new book I read called *The Terror Conspiracy* by Jim Marrs, already have what's called "Know Your Customer" programs. These are designed to profile people and report any potentially deviant banking behavior to the feds. Like if you sold a car you didn't need and put the cash into your bank account, the bank computer might not like it—and here come the agents to your doorstep!

In the wake of the Patriot Act, there's also a national database and ID system waiting to happen. All the easier for "Big Brother" to keep track of you. Not a surprising development in a world where John Ashcroft could say he wanted the power to take away constitutional rights from U.S. citizens and even be able to place them as "enemy combatants" in internment camps.

Such camps, by the way, are already in place. Saying these kinds of things, sometimes I wonder if one of the bunks might already have my name on it. In October 2006, when the Republicans still controlled Congress, Bush signed a bill weakening two laws that have been around for well over a century. One of them was the Posse Comitatus Act, first enacted after the Civil War to maintain a line between civil and military government. The other was the Insurrection Act of 1807, which limited how far a president could go in using the military to enforce the laws. Without any hearings or public debate, without consulting a single governor, the revised laws make it a whole lot easier for Bush—or any future president—to override local control and declare martial law. Basically, the military can now be used as a domestic police force to respond to a terrorist attack, a natural disaster, an outbreak of infectious disease, or any "other condition."

Didn't our forefathers rebel against much milder forms of oppression than this?

Everyone should read the minority report *The Constitution in Crisis*, written under Congressman Conyers, when the Republicans still controlled both houses. It's out in paperback, and it's a review of all the constitutional violations that have occurred under the Bush administration. Many of these pertain to the lead-up to the Iraq War.

Did you know we started bombing Iraq long before the invasion, when the excuse was that Iraq was supposedly violating "no-fly zones?" The report details how many pounds of bombs we dropped.

George Bush violated the Constitution by going to war under false premises. He and others in his administration did everything they could to ensure that the American people were misled. What are the Democrats going to do now, nothing? For fear of being called unpatriotic?

What's gone down here is ten times worse than happened between Bill Clinton and Monica Lewinsky. Yet the Republican House successfully impeached Clinton over his personal conduct. I want to know whether, if George Bush cheated on Laura and then lied to Congress about it, that would rise to the impeachment level. Yet sending the country into war under false premises does not?

By the time he leaves office, Bush will have spent more than a *trillion dollars* on his military adventures. While more than twenty retired American generals have come out strongly opposed to what we're doing in Iraq, our veterans are receiving shameful treatment. In the course of this war, more than 20,000 soldiers have been discharged with so-called "personality disorder," meaning that they're often being denied disability and medical benefits.

Now I ask you: Who are the *real* dysfunctional personalities here? Maybe a president who thinks he's getting messages straight from God? Or a vice president so delusional he believes we can "bunker-bust" Iran's supposed nuclear sites without opening up a whole new front in this madness?

George Bush came into office with a balanced budget and a manageable national debt. In his first six-plus years, he virtually bankrupted the country, and now we're nine trillion bucks in hock. That may not be an impeachable offense, but it sure seems like a committable one. And I think you can guess where the man ought to be committed.

CHAPTER 15

Musing in Baja on Changing the System

"In a time of universal deceit, telling the truth is a revolutionary act."

—George Orwell

In a way, here in Baja, I'm now living the life that many of us dream about—being away from the rat race. My life is far more spiritual. By that, I mean waking up in the morning and sitting on my deck and watching the sunrise. That's something I never did in the United States. I was a night person my entire career as a wrestler and afterward. I'd generally not go to bed before midnight, and I luckily had jobs that allowed me to sleep until I woke up—because I've never liked using an alarm clock. But down here, when it's dark I sleep, and when it's light I'm awake.

My typical day, I get up at dawn and, once the sun comes up, I feed Dexter and do a little bit of reading. I keep up with when low tide is. Then I generally go out and run on the beach for over an hour. I'm not saying I go fast anymore, but I'm running in the sand

and burning calories. That's what's important, and I'm slimming down quite substantially. When I come back to the house, Terry and I will usually have something to eat and I'll read some more. Afternoons could be anything—ATVs, scuba diving, swimming. Or just laying in my hammock drinking imported water from Italy. Hey, can it get any better than this? The great thing is, there's no pressure. To do *anything*. At this point in my life, I'm enjoying that very much.

As you get older, you start to think about mortality. I've also really enjoyed spending time away from humanity. Maybe it sounds self-centered, but I've spent my whole life in front of crowds and now I'm at the point where I don't want to see them anymore.

Even before we left Minnesota and began the long drive south, I played a lot of golf and, for the most part, stayed to myself. I made very few public appearances, because I wanted to remain out of the limelight. To a point, I was able to, until the media got pictures of me with the crazy beard. I'd actually started with four of those Fu Manchu–type strings—kind of like Johnny Depp as Captain Jack Sparrow—but as they grow longer, they tend to get more and more narrow, so I ended up with just one. Eating soup became a problem. I had to tuck it in like a tie, inside my shirt, whenever I sat down to eat. I'm a great believer that you don't eat with etiquette, you eat to satisfy your hunger. How it gets from Point A to Point B doesn't matter, as long as it gets there. My daughter calls me "the barbarian" at the dinner table. Anyway, I shaved off the beard right before we decided to come to Baja.

I find that living here more than rejuvenates me; it saves me. Bringing Terry down here has made a world of difference in her life, too. She's healed dramatically from the illness that plagued her the whole time I was governor. She's not been under any pressure. We can relax together and simply *be*.

And it's given me a lot of opportunity to think. To reflect upon the past, consider what's going on in the present, and meditate on the future. What's happening to America grieves me. I feel somewhat like an outcast from my own nation, that I have to come down to Mexico to get my thoughts together and find out what my next move will be. Maybe I'm just quietly re-rallying my spirits in a foreign country. By the time I've gotten this book off my chest, I think I'll know what to do. And I'm hoping you, the reader, will learn some things not only about what I've gone through, but also about what's happening to our democratic process—and what we need to be doing, all of us, the American people, to get back on track.

TERRY: I remember when he gave his speech to the National Press Club in Washington, not long after the election. It was like the first time I saw him give the State of the State address. I couldn't believe that this was the same guy who would wear huge sunglasses and have purple hair and feather boas all over him, strutting around and acting like a maniac. It wasn't that I thought he wasn't a smart person. It's just that he was such a statesman—and that he had the ability to enthrall, in that media world and among other politicians. He held them in the palm of his hand. It was absolutely wonderful for me to see that. I was so amazed at him, and I had so much respect for him. I felt so lucky to be a part of this. I really did. I was so glad that he did it.

In our country, there is a certain ruling class that won't give up the power. Who they are exactly, I'm not sure. I can call them the Democrats and Republicans, but I don't know for sure if it's them or the corporate powers: is it actually the Carlyle Group that controls things? There was a ripple of fright that what happened in

Minnesota could be a trend. Maybe the fact that I inspired voters to turn out was something the two parties do not necessarily want to have happen.

Our federal electoral system is bankrupt. I see Florida as having been stolen by the Bush people in the 2000 election. I feel the same way as a friend of mine, whom I admire as being one of the best attorneys in America. That's a gentleman named Vincent Bugliosi, who prosecuted Charles Manson. Vince has tried 106 felony cases and gotten convictions on 105 and, like he says, that other guy was probably innocent. After the 2000 election debacle, Vince came out and said: "The Supreme Court should all be put in prison for what they did."

When Congress needed only one United States senator to sign on, in order to mount an investigation into what happened in Florida, nobody would do it. Why? Who got to them? I always wondered why Paul Wellstone, who many times would be the lone dissenter on a 99-to-1 vote, wouldn't have been eager to do it—rather than have this stigma hanging over our elections from then on.

My biggest beef about the 2000 election, though, was this: Half a million more Americans voted for Al Gore to be President. In any other election in America, if you get the most votes, you win. How can we continue to justify a concept that, when it comes to presidential elections, you can win the popular vote and *lose*? This shows that the electoral college is a controlled, elitist system. It was set up when the elected officials were still riding on horseback to Washington. Today, when you can communicate on the Internet with someone in Beijing, China, why still hang onto something that's completely irrelevant?

What I wanted to see happen in 2004 was the exact opposite result of 2000. I wanted Bush to win the popular election and John Kerry to have the most votes in the electoral college. Then maybe these two groups of elitists would get together and say, it's time to get rid of the electoral college. If I ever became president, that would be one of my top priorities. The Maryland Legislature has already voted to bypass the electoral college—providing enough other states do the same.

The electronic voting machines are a disaster, too. There is strong evidence that Ohio and possibly some other states went for Bush in 2004 only because somebody tampered with these machines. What astounds me is that they don't provide any paper trail. You wouldn't go to an ATM machine that didn't offer you a receipt. Whether you want to keep it or not is your choice, but you still have a right to push the button and get one. But not with these new voting machines. No receipts! How can you have an election where there is no mechanism for a recount? All you hear about today are computer viruses, but we're basing more and more of our entire election system on computers that can be hacked into—with no means of detecting it!

The results of our first two presidential elections in this century have been, to say the least, questionable. I laugh when I hear the United States accuse other countries of voter fraud. Shouldn't we clean up our backyard before we point fingers at anyone else? I mean, look what happened in Ohio, where a federal judge had ordered all the ballots preserved from the questionable 2004 election. Well, the boards of elections in fifty-six of Ohio's eighty-eight counties either lost, shredded, or dumped nearly 1.6 million ballot and election records. Gee, they fell victim to spilled coffee, a flooded storage area, little things like that.

Besides computer scams and other methods of vote stealing, I think our elections are fraudulent today simply in how the system operates. Campaign finance "reform," that so-called bipartisan McCain-Feingold bill, is a sham. The two parties simply found loopholes and started cheating the very first year. Another of the bigger factors in why I didn't run for governor again is because I find the raising of money so despicable. My parents taught me that you work for what you earn. In contemporary politics, it's come down to panhandling. You attend the right fundraisers and you glad-hand people and, in return, they write you checks.

I cringe when I hear how many millions the 2008 presidential candidates have raised in campaign contributions. As of the end of October '07, the eight Democrats have raked in more than $244 million, and the ten Republicans another $175 million! We're supposed to believe that these donors aren't buying future favors? Interestingly, the top five American arms manufacturers are now giving more to Democrats than Republicans. Their favorite happens to be Hillary Clinton, who is also being backed by Wall Street.

I saw in the paper a couple of stories juxtaposed on the same page that I found quite ironic. One was about Minneapolis starting a crackdown on panhandlers. The other was about a heavyweight politician coming to town for a fundraiser. I called a local radio station and left a message saying I found it hard to distinguish between the two.

I'm not big on socialism, but maybe it's time we limited the campaign money to one publicly funded source so that every candidate's share is equal. If that's unconstitutional, then why not remove *all* limits and go to full disclosure? At least that way, you know who is buying the influence.

All that politicians do, at least in the House of Representatives, is look to the next election two years down the road. If you're a rookie congressman, you spend your first year getting oriented to Washington. The second year, you spend campaigning to come back again. Let's say you win reelection. You then spend one year when you can finally go to work, but you've got to be back on the campaign trail after that. Three of the four years are rendered non-productive, or certainly not as productive as they could be. So why do we continue with two-year election cycles? Why not go to four-year or even six-year terms in the House, like they have in the Senate?

I tried to do something about this situation on a state level. This was based on my experience running for governor. Remember, I was the private sector guy. The other two were already coming from jobs in public life, as a mayor and a state attorney general. How come I had to leave my job and not get paid for six months while, at the same time, they held onto their jobs (and their paychecks)—which they weren't even *doing* because they were busy running for another job!

I wondered why we allowed them to do that, using our tax dollars. Imagine if you worked for somebody in a private company and told the boss, "I'm going to spend the next six months trying to get this other job, so I won't be here for you. But I still want you to pay me while I'm out job-hunting." So I tried to get a bill passed making it illegal for seated politicians to campaign Monday through Friday between 8:00 a.m. and 4:00 p.m., at times when they are supposed to be working. I couldn't even get anybody to carry the bill into the legislature.

What the public needs to understand is, if you want honest government today, there need to be wholesale mega-changes in the way it runs. You don't change it by electing different people to go into the same system. The two political parties are so out for their own power that the people are nothing but pawns in their chess game.

Headline: LARRY KING LIVE: DOES JESSE VENTURA 'STAND ALONE'?

KING: Who are political pawns?
VENTURA: Political pawns to me are the two parties, because I find, Larry, that most elected officials, especially at the state level, come in with an attitude they want to do a good job, they want to represent their constituents, and do all the right things. And then they get there, they get involved in the two-party system that we have today and they become political pawns.

Because—in fact, we had a first-time elected representative in Minnesota who quit after the two-year term. And her quote to the news media was, "I got tired of checking my conscience in at the door."

—CNN, September 20, 2000

At the time of his election, Abraham Lincoln was a member of a relatively new third party called the Republicans. He won the presidency with only 39 percent of the vote, and he wasn't even on the ballot in many states. I guess all the Republicans have forgotten that today, now that they're the status quo. But, logically, aren't we going in the wrong direction? If this country had three legitimate parties back in Lincoln's time, and when you consider how large our population is compared to pre–Civil War days, we ought to have five parties, instead of two.

I did *Larry King Live* once with Alan Simpson, the senator from Wyoming. He was expounding about how well the two-party system had served us all these years. I sat there quietly. Finally Larry turned to me and said, "Governor, you're a member of a third party, what do you think of the two-party system?" I said, "Larry, I think the two-party system is phenomenal. After all, it gives us one more choice than Communist Russia had." Simpson couldn't seem to come up with a response to that.

Saddam Hussein had an election a couple of years before we invaded Iraq, where he was the only candidate. Imagine, in America we give you one more! Today, if they adopted our system of democracy verbatim in Iraq, like we keep saying we want, it's doomed to fail. Because Iraq already has three parties—the Sunnis, the Shiites, and the Kurds.

I like to quote the late great Jerry Garcia of the Grateful Dead, who said, "If you're made to pick the lesser of two evils, it means you're still pickin' evil." Or this perspective, which I must admit I stole in part from Pat Buchanan: It's like going into the grocery store and the only choices in the soft drink department are Coke and Pepsi. Depending on your taste buds, one is slightly sweeter than the other—but they're both colas!

We've actually had numerous third parties in the history of our republic, everything from the Anti-Masonics to the Know-Nothings to the Populists and Progressives, on up to the Dixiecrats and the Libertarians. In my lifetime alone, I've seen a number of them come and go. In the early 1970s, George Wallace was a third-party candidate. In the early 1980s, along came John Anderson. In the 1990s, there was Ross Perot. And, of course, Ralph Nader in the 2000s.

I've always advocated that anyone qualified, who so desires, can run for office. For people who say it's Nader's fault that Bush got elected, I say that's baloney. You're not picking the winner of a horse race. People voted for Nader because they wanted him to become president. When we start saying that someone like Nader shouldn't run because he'll take votes away from a Democrat or a Republican, then that's not a democracy either. Free elections mean voting your heart and your conscience.

Besides, didn't Nader bring up a lot of topics that the other two candidates wouldn't touch with a ten-foot pole? I respect Nader; he's a very intelligent and very interesting man. He's done the best he can to hold up the banner, but he also carries a certain left-wing stigma, and he's only going to go so far. At least he's out there saying some real things.

I was never able to make as much political hay out of this as I wanted, but here is how the deck gets stacked in Minnesota. State taxpayer money pays for the entire staffs of the Democratic and Republican caucuses. Those are the people who put out the propaganda, do all the political dirty work. Yet my independent party doesn't receive any such funds, and we're talking about millions of dollars. When I came in as governor and found out this situation existed, I talked about it to the press. Well, the response basically was, how dare I even bring that up?

The system locks out a third-party candidate in many ways. If you are running for a national office like the presidency, shouldn't the criteria be the same in every state to earn a place on the ballot? You'd think so. But no, I would have to fulfill fifty different criteria in fifty different states. In some states, it's so ridiculous that you must use a certain size and type of paper on which to gather your petition signatures. The number of signatures required, from state to state, is never the same, either.

It was created this way by the two parties, in order to make an independent candidate jump through as many hoops as possible. Why do you think, oftentimes when Nader would achieve success in making it onto a state's ballot, one of the parties would immediately file a challenge and tie it up in court until it was too late? Again I ask, is that the true meaning of democracy—filing suit to keep people from running for public office?

Here's what I would do. In a federal election, the same criteria should apply in every state, across the board. To get on the ballot, you would need to get an established number of signatures by a certain date—based on either a percentage of that state's population, or simply a specific number like, maybe, 25,000. Besides that, you'd only need to meet the other existing qualifications: born in the United States, be at least thiry-five years old, and so on.

The next rub is the presidential debates. First of all, we have to get the debates back into the hands of a neutral party. In 1992, when Ross Perot scared the pants off the two parties by getting almost 20 percent of the vote, that entitled him to nearly $30 million of our tax dollars if he chose to run again in '96. Shouldn't that entitlement—and the fact that he received one out of every five votes—also have automatically qualified Perot to take part in any '96 debates?

Well, that wasn't allowed. Up until that point, all presidential debates had been under the jurisdiction of the League of Women Voters. In 1996, Congress took them away from the League and formed another bureaucratic layer of government, the Federal Debate Commission. It so happens that the commission's members are not elected, but appointed, by the former heads of the Republican and Democratic national parties. In fact, two of the appointees were *themselves* the former heads of the two parties. They now determine who you get to hear in the debates.

That year, it was Bill Clinton running for reelection against Bob Dole. Dole did not want Perot in the debates, because he felt it would erode his conservative base. Clinton did not want debates at all because he was so far ahead that debates could only bring his numbers down. So, the two of them made a backroom deal. They would eliminate Perot if Clinton was allowed to say how many debates there would be, and when. They took this to the Federal Debate Commission and, of course, it was rubber-stamped. That's how we were denied seeing Perot take part in a spirited three-person debate. That year, the only two debates were held—by design—at the same time as the World Series.

Now whether or not someone can participate in debates is based upon an arbitrary polling figure. You have to be polling nationally at 15 percent. If that criteria had been applied in Minnesota, I would not have become the governor. Because at the time of the primary, I was only polling at 10 percent. But I was allowed to debate, and I proved that you could be at 10 percent and still end up winning. And I did it in a mere eight weeks.

We all know that polls can be skewed. It's all in how the questions get asked, in order to get whatever numbers they desire. Instead of the way they've rigged it, I think whether you're allowed to debate ought to be based on whether yours qualifies as a major party. If a candidate has achieved 5 percent of the vote at a national level, that would confer major-party status and entitle him or her to be part of the debates.

The way it works instead? Let me draw an analogy to playing football: The two parties get to change the rules at halftime if they desire. And the rules are, indeed, constantly changing, to benefit their team. Let's say you come to play the Democrats or Republicans, and you happen to have a great running game. They say, okay, you are allowed to run the ball once out of every four plays—but on the other three downs, you've got to pass. The rules are orchestrated to put you on the road to defeat, where it would take next to a miracle to win.

Allow me one more history lesson. For over two hundred years, America's third parties have promoted concepts and policies that eventually became crucial parts of our social and political lives. Women's right to vote, child labor laws, the forty-hour work week, unemployment insurance, the Social Security Act, and "getting tough on crime"—all these ideas were first put forward by third-party candidates.

Just because there is so much against us doesn't mean we're not effective. Because the two parties want us to disappear so badly, they will generally focus on what brought us in. In that way, a third party can carry the agenda. Remember Ross Perot, with his pie chart and his message about the deficit and balancing the budget? That's what Clinton and his opponents wound up putting at the top of their list. They wanted to prove to the people that you don't need a third party; we can take care of this problem.

Is it hopeless for an independent to get anywhere at this point? I don't think so, because, at a state level, both Angus King and I have won governor's races. It's interesting that Minnesota and Maine traditionally lead the nation in voter turnout—and those are the two states that have recently elected independent governors.

Angus and I used to have a lot of fun at the National Governors Association meetings in Washington. On the second day, when the two parties have their big caucuses in separate buildings, that kind of left poor Angus and me out in the cold. So we would take a very casual, beautiful walk down Constitution Avenue, sit down together on a park bench, and talk about our most important issues. I'd achieved so much notoriety that we had most everybody in the press corps following along. "Welcome to the Independent Governors Caucus," we told them. It was hilarious.

As Angus neared the end of his second term, the media kept asking him, "Governor, what's it going to be now, the House or the Senate?" Finally, one day, he told them, "I'm going home. I've spent eight years not doing some things that need to be done there." And he walked away. The media in Maine were as baffled as when I did the same thing in Minnesota.

Angus is a brilliant man, and an honest one. If I ever did go for president, I'd sure love to talk Angus King out of retirement to run with me.

We proved that it *can* be done. It just takes the right circumstances and, for lack of a better phrase, you've got to catch the opposition with their pants down. You've got to sneak up on them. You've got to make them think you're insignificant, not worth bothering about. You have to bring out their natural arrogance, figuring that everything is under control.

I was told that, some years later, Norm Coleman turned to a person I knew in the Republican Party when they were out to dinner one night, shook his head, and said, "What the hell *did* happen in '98?" I caught them off guard. They never dreamed it could happen.

I guess time will tell whether it could again.

TERRY: I don't think Jesse needs to do anything more in politics. I think running for president would destroy him. I don't think that they'll kill him, but that they'll do the best job of character assassination they possibly can. And they're really good at it. I just hate to see him go through it.

Whoever does win in 2008 is going to have the monumental task of spending literally his or her first four years (and maybe only four years) attempting to clean up Bush's mess. That's the part that shies me away from running. Our next president will inherit an unfinished war in Afghanistan and a complete quagmire in Iraq, not to mention what might happen in Iran in Bush's last year. The economy is more polarized than ever, the billionaires having gotten richer, and at the same time, more than 40 million Americans are trying to get by without health insurance. Call me selfish, but I would prefer to come into office with more of a clean slate and be able to try to accomplish things I'd like to do.

Another reason I don't think I could be president today is that I'm incapable of lying. Every president in my adult lifetime, except maybe Jimmy Carter, has lied to the American people. Think about LBJ and Vietnam. Nixon and Watergate. Reagan and Iran-Contra. George H.w. Bush and "No New Taxes." Clinton and Monica Lewinsky. Is that what it means now to be president of the United States—to be able to keep a straight face on TV and lie? Why have we become a country that doesn't want to hear the truth? Think about baseball for a moment: the only ballplayer telling the truth about his use of steroids was José Canseco—and he's the one who got destroyed for doing so. Jesse Ventura was a truth teller as governor of Minnesota, and there was a huge attempt to destroy me, too.

We've become what the corporations set out to turn us into—as though we're lemmings plunging suicidally into the sea. (Should I have dedicated this book to "all the lemmings?" I thought about it). There is no job security anymore. I'm seeing my friends, at age fifty, losing their jobs, left and right. And it's being done by corporate America. It's a lot cheaper to hire a twenty-year-old than to keep someone who's given you twenty-five years of loyal service. But loyalty is becoming a thing of the past in the business and work world, among both employers and employees. It's survival of the economic fittest. Look at what's been happening with the breaking of unions. It's frightening. We're in big trouble.

The definition of fascism, as Mussolini once expressed it, is a wedding between the corporation and religion. Today, we have corporate America joining forces with organized religion to control the country. I would say that we're past the point of being afraid fascism might happen. I think it *is* happening. We're beyond the warning point, just as with global warming. I still believe in humans' ability to withstand and prevail, but we're on the verge of dire and, perhaps, catastrophic consequences. And I see fascism as alive and well in the United States of America.

Many of the American people have it very cushy, and I don't exclude myself as someone who fits into that category. Because of that cushiness, no one seems to want to rock the boat at all. When will people wake up to the fact that apathy breeds bad government? Right now, I think we're living with some of the worst government imaginable. Why? Because of us. Because we're not diligent, we're not holding them accountable, everybody's waiting for their neighbor to say something. Imagine if we'd had that attitude back when we were under England's rule. We still would be a colony if people hadn't stepped forward and put themselves on the line. The sad part is, going into politics today, you have to be as mentally focused as if you're going to war—and then be prepared for every underhanded tactic you can imagine.

So I keep questioning myself. Is it worth it to put my family and me out there, to take on a force that most of the American people are willing to go along with? Somehow we've lost the concept of "We the People." The government is supposed to be us, and it's not us anymore. It's been hijacked.

Just when is somebody going to *do* something?

Or can they?

CHAPTER 16

A Character in Search of an Ending

"A little patience, and we shall see the reign of witches pass over, their spells dissolve, and the people, recovering their true sight, restore their government to its true principles. It is true that in the meantime we are suffering deeply in spirit, and incurring the horrors of a war and long oppressions of enormous public debt. . . . If the game runs sometimes against us at home we must have patience till luck turns, and then we shall have an opportunity of winning back the principles we have lost, for this is a game where principles are at stake."

—*Thomas Jefferson, 1798, after the passage of the Sedition Act*

Toward evening, I often take Dexter for a walk to the top of a sand dune about a mile from my house. I've got a spot up there where I can look due north and see not a trace of anything human. If I look to the left, I see desert and mountains. Off to the right is where the ocean meets the beach. What I most enjoy is tipping my head just enough to hear the ocean out of one ear, and the desert out of the other.

I sometimes stay there with my dog until it's just about dark. I don't think much about what's happening in America when I'm at the dune. No, my focus is more on the simple pleasures, and the unique people I've gotten a chance to know in the Baja. I've got one friend, named Fernando, who speaks decent English because he's spent the better part of his adult life hanging out with American surfers. He's a free spirit; someone who goes without everything that we in the States take for granted. His house is built with reeds and sticks and whatever else he could find, with a dirt floor. He gathers bottles from a local restaurant, so he can use the glass in a staircase he's building. I love watching Fernando survive with materials most Americans would throw out.

I also love how he met his wife, Crystal. She had just come over from Mexico City to a job in Todos Santos that didn't work out. She'd started hitchhiking on her way out of town, when Fernando picked her up. When he told me the story I laughed and said, "See? It was destiny, Fernando. You and Crystal were led to each other." In a way, Fernando reminds me of my father-in-law, because he's now taken an existing family and is becoming a father to the children. I always admire people who can do that. Fernando seems to really be enjoying the change in his life. And, as long as he's happy, that makes me happy.

An excerpt from Terry's journal: I came to Baja in the winter. What was it that made me stay here? Why did I not follow my first instincts and run back to where I came from? Why did I fall in love after a horrendous drive to get here that made me scared, furious, and so tired I felt like I wanted to sleep for days when we arrived? What kept me from jumping out of the vehicle?

It was the vista that dazzled my eyes and touched something inside me that had not yet been reached. I had no idea there was anything left inside of me to be discovered. It was not the last thing I found.

Our home is wide and deep and full of air and sunshine with ocean views to our west and rough, pointy mountains to our east. In between are ranches that reminded me of small-town middle-American family farms owned by the fourth or fifth generation men, women, and children, land that is passed down.

I spent a week unpacking, exploring, meeting my neighbors, and trying to find a reason to leave and go back to my family, grown children, and friends, to my lovely home on the lake.

I am glad I was not successful.

I love the way the beach changes everyday. I love to search the shoreline for different forms of sea life that have lost their battle with the ocean and are tossed up on the sand. The weird pieces of other people's property that end up here, like tiles, bottles, nets, and even pieces of cars! Garbage to most, interesting to ponder for some.

I love seeing the mother whales and their babies, breaching. I love to track the sea lions and dolphins with my telescope. I am especially thrilled with the fish boils, which are huge schools of sardines that form a giant ball to protect themselves from predator fish hunting them tirelessly from below while pelicans dive bomb them from above. All the while the sea that surrounds them boils and foams and travels up and down the shore until the sardines are just a small group and the predators and the pelicans are sated and spent.

I love the long winding dirt road behind our property that I walk down to the tremendous arroyo lined with rock walls ten stories high. There are cactus and agave and trees and plants of all kinds clinging to the sides of those walls and all manner of lizards, birds, rodents, and insects make their homes in them. As I walk the arroyo floor, I come upon little oases where boulders have tumbled down crevices made by rushing water to become small waterfalls and pools filled with even more plants and wildlife. Flowers attract thousands of butterflies that come here to escape the harsh snows of their homeland just like we do.

I have seen and touched and experienced so many things that I knew existed but never thought I would have a chance at trying. I wake up every day thinking, "What do I want to do today?" I go to sleep each night thinking, "How lucky I am to have this happen to me when I am still able physically and mentally to try it all."

The orange, yellow, and purple dawns inspire me, and the pink and sapphire blue evenings calm me. All the while the sea is the continuous background music that ranges from heavy metal to Bach to Sinatra playing twenty-four hours a day.

I have made friends with the local ranch families and enjoy buying fresh eggs from them that carry the remnants of the mother's body still on the shells and sometimes the remnants of the father's in the yolks. I also buy the cheese from their milk cows that is rich, creamy, and tastes of desert sage, sea salt, the earth, and the cow. The families are close, and often the grandparents are still on the property living with them. Children, there are always children. A combination of cousins and friends. The families are strong and the love runs deep and the loyalty is forever. They have family fights and sometimes do not speak but, in the end, the ties that bind are made of metal and silk and will never be broken forever.

I have a feeling of peace here that is absent in my homeland. I am not fearful here as I was there. Here we pick up families or women with children and their luggage looking for a ride, or old men from their broken-down cars, or young men get pulled out of the ditch, all of which we find on the roads into town. They open the doors to our vehicles and we find new experiences through our discussions in broken English and Español as we take them along and drop them off.

Our remote location makes neighbors stop by to let you know the propane truck is in the area or that their generator is broken down and they need help. We share trips into town for supplies or to the airport. We watch out for each other.

It is a life I remember from my childhood, seldom felt as I became an adult.

I am dreaming while I am awake, imagining while I am walking and feeling my senses expand as I go about my business of living life to the fullest in a place that allows and encourages it.

I met Robert F. Kennedy, Jr., through a mutual friend. I knew him by reputation only, as one of the leading advocates for the environment and a dynamic speaker, the second oldest son of the late senator. He and his family were coming to Cabo San Lucas for a quick vacation. We shared a mutual passion—diving—and the waters off Cabo were said to be some of the best in Baja for it. It was only a ninety-minute drive from my house to where the Kennedys were staying, and we made a date to meet around lunchtime in a gated community called the Pedregal.

I parked outside a Moorish-style house, built right into the cliffs about sixty feet above the Pacific, a house that seemed to hang in the air with views of the ocean from all sides. When Robert came out to greet us, I looked at him for a long moment. "Yeah, I can sure see the resemblance," I said. "We're about the same age, and I grew up with your father and your uncle." It was actually uncanny how much Robert looked like his father.

He called down to his wife, Mary, who was in the swimming pool with their four kids: "Honey, come up and meet the governor." We sat down at a round dining table. The twelve-year-old and nine-year-old boys especially had a lot of questions for me about wrestling. "Did you ever wrestle André the Giant?" Robert asked. I had, and told them nobody had ever been able to beat André. This launched us into a discussion about how you can tell a giant—by the hands and feet—and also the fact they don't usually live too long. André had died fairly young.

"Were you a real SEAL?" one of the boys asked. I told a few of my favorite tales from my frogman days, and pointed out to them that their grand-uncle JFK had started the Navy SEALs. Actually, Robert said, it was his father who was the impetus, because he loved all that kind of covert action stuff. Somehow I got inspired to show him and the boys the tattoos on my chest. Which prompted Robert to show one of his own, on the upper thigh. We all thought that was pretty damned funny.

"Okay," he said as we munched away on some delicious fajitas that Mary had cooked up, "we'd better head down to the dive shop or we'll be late."

Along with the oldest boy, Conor, we left the Pedregal and headed for the Cabo marina. As we neared the parking lot, Robert turned to me and asked: "What were your numbers in Minnesota?" This was politics talk, and I knew exactly what he meant.

"My numbers? Oh, the power-brokers try to pretend I didn't happen. To them, those four years were just a bad dream." Robert cracked up laughing. "But my numbers were 73 [percent approval] when I came in, and 45 was the lowest they went."

"Not bad," Robert said, and grinned at me.

We were walking toward the dive shop when I raised the fact that we'd both had private visits with Fidel Castro. "I was with him for an hour," I said.

"We were with him for four-and-a-half hours," Robert said, "starting at one o'clock in the morning!"

"Oh, well, he met with me at noon," I said. Looking back on it, there may have been a little friendly competition between us over our visits with Fidel.

The dive shop wanted to see my certification. I brought out my Navy Underwater Demolition Team card. "That will do," the man checking us in said.

So they gave us our gear, and a female guide who spoke good English, and we boarded a boat bound for Pelican Rock. We put on our tanks and went overboard. The plan was that we'd be down for about forty-five minutes, at depths as much as eighty feet. It was incredible down there. The tropical fish were abundant and beautiful. At one point, a moray eel came out from under a rock and momentarily came right toward me. That was exciting.

I was first to resurface. When Robert and Conor soon joined me on board, Robert said: "That was kind of existential." He was referring to our having gone right to the edge of the continental shelf and watched sand pour over the abyss like a waterfall.

As we all returned to shore again, I was telling a few tales about my teaching fellowship at Harvard's Kennedy School of Government.

"What did you teach?" Conor asked.

"Third-party politics," I told him, and added: "Something your dad doesn't know anything about!" Robert cracked up laughing again.

Driving back to the house, he started asking me some more personal questions. About where I lived in Minnesota and, when I said it was on a lake, whether I fished. I told him the story of Terry catching the bigger muskie. "What's your wife like?" Robert asked. I explained that Terry's health was the biggest reason that I hadn't run for governor again, but that her condition had improved immensely since we came to Baja.

Once back inside at the round table, Robert wanted to know more about my visit with Castro. So I related the whole story, including my being tailed by the CIA in Havana. Robert asked Finn, the nine-year-old, if he remembered seeing *Predator*. "The governor was

the guy with the Gatling gun," he told the boy, and Finn grinned
and said, "Oh yeah."

This got us talking about Arnold and his wife, Maria Shriver.
Robert, in fact, had been instrumental in forging Schwarzenegger's
forward-thinking environmental policies since he became California's
governor. Mary recalled how Arnold and Maria had first met at Ethel
Kennedy's tennis tournament in New York. They all knew something
was up when Maria was spotted dashing for a seat next to him on the
private bus. I recalled coaching Arnold on how to say his "I do's" on
the *Predator* set, out there in the jungle around Puerto Vallarta.

Now we got heavy into politics. We both spoke about how outraged we are concerning what's happening in America today. We
talked about the "war on terror." Robert said the Iraq War has done
nothing but *create* more terrorists. When I described myself as a
fiscal conservative who is liberal on social issues, Mary said, "That
describes Bobby, too." We seemed to be finding considerable common ground between us.

About this time, not too far offshore, we saw a spout, and then
a whale breach, landing again with a huge splash. For a little while,
we took turns on the balcony looking through a binocular telescope
at a mother humpback and her calf. "They're here early," I said. It
seemed like a good omen.

Sitting down again, I looked across at Robert and asked him,
matter-of-factly: "Do you want to run the country?"

"*What* did he say?" Mary responded.

Robert stood up. After a pause, he said quietly: "Yeah, I want to."

He added that someone with the Green Party had asked him to
consider becoming its candidate in 2008.

"Oh, don't do what Nader did!" I told him. "You should leave
the Democrats and run with me as an independent."

Was I serious? Robert looked at me quizzically.

"I'm the most powerful man in America!" I announced. "Do you know why?"

"Why?" Mary asked, wide-eyed.

"Because I'm the only one who can unite both parties against me!"

We were hot into this when Finn, who was doing headstands behind us, suddenly crashed into the ping-pong table and raised a big welt on his foot. Mary said she'd better run upstairs and get some ice.

I realized it was time to go.

First, though, I approached Robert, who was also standing on the stairs, one more time. Again I urged him to go independent.

"I *am* independent," he said. "*You* should become a Democrat."

"I'd lose all my credibility!" I exclaimed.

"We'll keep talking about it," Robert said.

On my way out the door, he came over and gave me a big bear-hug, then walked us out to my car. I confided in him that I had a secret plan, for getting on the ballot in all fifty states. "Look, if you count when Bush's father was vice president, we've had nothing but Bushes and Clintons around the White House since 1980. Twenty-seven years! That's more like a monarchy than a democracy, don't you think?"

"I never thought of that," Robert said.

"And now, in 2008, I warn you—we could end up with Hillary and Jeb!" (This was before Jeb's brother's popularity plunged to an all-time low for a sitting president.) Robert shook his head. He stood on his front step and saluted, with a big grin on his face, as I drove away.

Heading home that night, I couldn't stop thinking about it. If Robert Kennedy, Jr., ever ran for president as a Democrat, it would be no surprise to anyone. Just another Kennedy going for the brass ring. But if, because he can't stand what's happened to politics today, he left the party and ran as an independent, it would—to borrow a phrase from Muhammad Ali—shock the world.

For a minute, I thought about leaking it to the media. Jesse Ventura and Robert Kennedy, Jr., meeting in Mexico to talk about the fate of America. Then I thought better of it. I hoped I was right about this much: we'd each of us made a new friend.

Headline: JESSE VENTURA CONSIDERING 2008 WHITE HOUSE RUN

Refreshed from a semester as a visiting professor at Harvard University, former pro wrestler and Minnesota Gov. Jesse Ventura says he's considering an independent run for the White House in 2008, although he acknowledges that being leader of the free world might be too confining for him.

"That's an issue with me. I love my freedom," Ventura said in an interview with the Associated Press at his office at the John F. Kennedy School of Government. "The part that would bug me is I wouldn't be able to get up in the night and drive to the 7-11 for a Slurpee, not without them blocking off the roads, welding the manhole covers shut, and everything else that goes along with it."

Ventura has not made a firm decision on a presidential run. He is weighing the concerns of his wife, Terry, who has told him she won't go with him if he wins the White House. His solution: move the White House to Minnesota.

—Associated Press, April 15, 2004

TERRY: I'm all done with it. I won't be the First Lady this time. I just can't. If you do this, I'm staying secluded down here in Baja.

JESSE: You say you won't, but I know if push came to shove, you'd be right there. Besides, the problem is that when I come to visit, they'll destroy the place with all the helicopters. I won't be able to sneak down!

TERRY: I notice you don't even question whether or not you'll win.

JESSE: Once you become a legitimate candidate, you get Secret Service protection. And I don't go into anything to lose.

TERRY: Let me put it this way, I have no intention of being part of it, at all. I think I'd actually be more helpful to you if I wasn't involved.

JESSE: But you've softened on another point. You did admit that being vice president wouldn't be so bad, then we could live where the Gores did by the big telescope.

TERRY: Plus, then I'd get a chance to ride with the Washington, D.C. mounted park police.

JESSE: If we could just find somebody to be top dog. . . . Well, that would ease things up for me; as vice president I could be the official guy at funerals. You can't screw that up too bad.

Taking the personal and family end out of the mix, seriously, honey, can I make a difference? That will be the ultimate question that I'll ask myself. Am I just barking up a tree, or do I truly believe that my country needs me?

It's like there's a war being waged inside myself. It's also a war of my fighting to be content with simple things again. That's a dilemma. Also, do I retire in my mid-fifties? I'm done? Well, my dad did it. He reached the minimum retirement age for the city of Minneapolis, took it, and never looked back. In hindsight, I think he was smart to do that. He could have stayed on and worked another ten years and gotten more money. But he retired at fifty-five—and died at eighty-three.

TERRY: That's the other thing I think about—what if we only have twenty years left, do we really want to take four, or even maybe eight, of those years and make ourselves insane?

JESSE: You'd be open-minded enough to give me my shot. That's all I can ask for. The other battle I have is with the warrior part of me—the part that says: where would I have been today, and what opportunities would I have gotten, had it not been for the forefathers? You can't go through life waiting for the other guy to do it.

TERRY: That's what's wrong with the country right now.

JESSE: So my meeting with Vince is being arranged. I want one hour, just him and me alone in a room.

Vince McMahon, Jr., and I go way back. I'd joined his World Wrestling Federation (WWF) back in 1985. Through many ups and downs between us over the years, I've always liked Vince. He's been called wrestling's P. T. Barnum, a simply amazing showman and entrepreneur. When I was governor, he brought SummerSlam to the Target Center, and had me be the guest referee. Later, when I was teaching at Harvard, he inducted me into the Wrestling Hall of Fame. Today Vince is chairman of the board of World Wrestling Entertainment (WWE).

He's also very involved with politics. His interest began around the time I became governor of Minnesota. In July 2000, he founded WWE's Smackdown Your Vote!, a nonpartisan approach to getting young people involved in the process and registered to vote. WWE began collaborating with many other nonprofits like Rock the Vote, the Youth Vote Coalition, and the League of Women Voters. In 2003, Vince's group joined forces with Russell Simmons' Hip-Hop Summit Action Network, in an effort to get "Two Million More by 2004." They had a big impact.

Vince told me, after I won governor, "If you ever go for president, I'll back you 100 percent, with everything I've got." Now we'll see if he wants to play the game.

The scene: Vince McMahon's office at WWE headquarters in Stamford, Connecticut. Jesse Ventura sits in an easy chair across from his desk.

"Vince, you've always been a gambler. You've been P. T. Barnum on just about every stage in America. Except—I can bring you to the biggest stage out there. And that is the presidency of the United States.

"We come at it from this angle, Vince. The wrestling fans feel that they're being ignored. Just like the independent voters are. Well, this is America. America stands for freedom, a nation where anyone can run for the highest office in the land. So the WWE calls a press conference. You're going to create your own political party. The hell with the Democrats and the Republicans. The people want a WWE candidate!

"First you make this a legal political party. You run wrestling in just about every state. So you send your people out saying: do whatever it takes to get whoever we deem is going to be our candidate on the ballot. In all the states, people are collecting the signatures. As you do your various events, you have the crowd signing the petitions.

"The Democrats and the Republicans don't know what's going on. Is this real? Is it not? It's wrestling, after all. You, Vince, are of course the natural candidate. You're the leader, the brains behind it all. That's what we've got everybody thinking—up until the next WrestleMania approaches, in March of 2008.

"Shortly before that is when I come on the scene to challenge you. Hey, Vince McMahon stands for corporate America! If this guy doesn't mean special interest, who would? He's got it tattooed to his forehead! I ridicule you; this time, I get to play the good guy and you're the villain! I turn you into the Democrats and the Republicans. Jesse Ventura comes out of retirement in the Baja to dethrone Vince.

"I become the WWE's candidate. At that point, it all becomes real. No longer a gimmick. We're on the ballot in every state. And we haven't had to raise any money to get there.

"In the fall, if the two parties don't let me into their debates, then you hold your own. And if the other candidates don't show, you put up phony cardboard figures of them and make a mockery of the whole thing.

"Because we're also here to deliver the message to America: Look what we've turned into. I have every right to run. I was a mayor and know local government. I was a governor and know state government. It's a natural progression. I am qualified to be the president. I've been there at every level but the federal, and how many governors become presidents? Lots. The point being that if they won't let me in, we cry foul.

"So that's the mechanism I came up with, Vince, sitting down here in the Baja with too much time on my hands. It comes down to this: I can't beat them conventionally. I can't go into this and be competitive by doing it their way. They'll destroy me too quickly. They've got to be tricked, fooled. Then you catch them in the final six months. I honestly believe, if the timing is correct, I can win. Because I also think that, by the time we build up to WrestleMania next spring, people are really going to be sick of all these other candidates.

"That's the great thing about wrestling, it's there to create. You can take on anything, and nothing is beyond belief."

A Glimpse of the Future

"On the one hand, I was summoned by my country, whose voice I can never hear but with veneration and love, from a retreat which I had chosen with the fondest predilection, and, in my flattering hopes, with an immutable decision, as the asylum of my declining years . . ."

—*George Washington, First Inaugural Address*

Headline: VENTURA SAYS PRESIDENTIAL CANDIDACY IS "REAL"

March 2008: Before a raucous crowd at the twenty-fourth annual WrestleMania, former Minnesota governor Jesse Ventura bolted onto the stage Saturday night to announce that what many believed to be a "stunt" has become a reality: He is running on a World Wrestling Entertainment independent ticket for the presidency of the United States.

Shoving WWE promoter Vince McMahon, Jr., off to the side of the ring, Ventura declared: "This is no joke, folks, this is real! We're going beyond corporate here! We need a man of the people to run this country, and set us back on the road our forefathers envisioned for this great country of ours!"

A gathering estimated at almost 70,000 erupted in the arena. Some booed the former ring "villain," but the majority seemed to be cheering Ventura. McMahon, who most suspected was behind an ongoing effort to achieve ballot access across the nation as a gimmick, stood silently sneering across the ring. At one point, he looked poised to charge Ventura, but was restrained by his handlers.

Ventura's surprise appearance followed a battle royal between wrestlers representing both himself and the 62-year-old McMahon, a match the referee awarded to the ex-governor's contingent. Former heavyweight champion Muhammad Ali, seated at ringside, gave a thumbs-up to Ventura . . .

Headline: VENTURA SETS DATE FOR IRAQ WITHDRAWAL—THE DAY HE TAKES OFFICE

April 2008: In the first major speech of his nascent presidential campaign, former Minnesota governor Jesse Ventura said that setting a timetable for withdrawal of American troops from Iraq is not complicated. It should start happening the day the next president takes office. Which, he added, may well be him.

"In defiance of Congress, and against the will of the American people," Ventura said, "President Bush has continued to wage an illegal war in Iraq—a war launched under false pretenses that has now resulted in the deaths of more than six thousand American troops and more than one million Iraqi civilians . . ."

Ventura also pledged that, if elected, he will reopen investigations into the assassination of President Kennedy and the events surrounding the September 11th attacks. He added that he would also release all relevant information on the Iran-Contra affair, which was postponed by the current President Bush concerning the involvement of his father, George H. W. Bush.

Headline: VENTURA SPELLS OUT INDEPENDENT PLATFORM

May 2008: Describing himself as a libertarian with a small "l"—liberal on social issues, conservative on fiscal issues—ex-Minnesota governor Jesse Ventura today set forth an independent platform that included ending the "so-called war on drugs" by legalizing marijuana and bringing home all American troops from military bases around the world—"unless these countries want to compensate us for guarding their borders . . ."

Ventura also proposed radical changes in the nation's tax system, saying he would push for a constitutional amendment to replace the income tax with a national sales tax and "make the IRS the watchdog of the government, not the citizenry."

Headline: VENTURA CHALLENGES LEADING TWO-PARTY CONTENDERS TO DEBATE

June 2008: Claiming that the Republican and Democratic parties are "afraid of me" and unwilling to engage in presidential debates, popular former Minnesota governor Jesse Ventura called upon the leading candidates themselves—Hillary Clinton and Barack Obama of the Democrats, John McCain and Mike Huckabee of the Republicans—to tell the American people why they prefer to "shut me out." In what he said comes down to "the liberals versus the ideologues and demagogues," Ventura stressed that he was a candidate "from the middle, which is in truth the majority in this country . . ."

Headline: AS TWO PARTY CONVENTIONS NEAR, MAVERICK INDEPENDENT VENTURA RISES IN POLLS

July 2008: With the Democratic and Republican conventions on the horizon—and, the primaries over, with an ex-president's wife and the ex-mayor of New York City poised to battle it out in November—the independent candidacy of former Minnesota governor Jesse Ventura appears to be on the rise. In an ABC News/*New York Times* poll conducted over the weekend, many voters indicated they trust Ventura's blunt, outspoken honesty over the more status quo spokespeople from the two parties.

Now polling at 21 percent, despite having so far been kept on the sidelines during the candidates' debates, Ventura issued a statement that the latest numbers "clearly show that more and more Americans are sick and tired of men and women who need to raise millions simply to run for high office, and then become completely beholden to the big corporations and wealthy donors who make it possible for them."

While Ventura has so far raised less than a million dollars, a grassroots campaign has already managed to get his name onto the ballot in more than forty states . . .

Headline: ROBERT F. KENNEDY, JR., LEAVES DEMOCRATIC PARTY, AGREES TO JOIN VENTURA AS RUNNING MATE

August 2008: In a move that stunned the political world, Robert F. Kennedy, Jr., announced at a press conference that he is quitting the Democratic Party. An attorney and leading environmental activist, and son of the senator who was assassinated on his way to the Democratic nomination in 1968, Kennedy said: "At a time of similar crisis, when our country was locked into the terrible quagmire of the Vietnam War, my father made the painful decision to challenge President Johnson for the presidency of the United States. Today, faced with a two-party system that appears unwilling to challenge President Bush over an increasingly desperate situation in Iraq and the Middle East, I find myself forced to make an equally painful choice."

With Jesse Ventura then joining him from the audience, Kennedy revealed that he has agreed to become the running mate of the former wrestler and Minnesota governor. "It is time to break the stranglehold of the two-party system," Ventura said. "We no longer have any choice, if our Republic is to survive in the way the founders envisioned in 1776 . . ."

Headline: VENTURA-KENNEDY TICKET SURGES IN POLLS

September 2008: With young people registering to vote in apparently record numbers, the "truth-telling ticket" of Jesse Ventura and Robert F. Kennedy, Jr., now stands at a near dead-heat with the candidacies of Clinton/Obama and McCain/Huckabee.

"We need a new American revolution!" Ventura told an enthusiastic crowd estimated at more than 50,000 students, at a rally outside the University of Michigan football stadium. Kennedy spoke simultaneously in Athens, Georgia, exhorting a similarly large crowd of students to fight for an alternative energy agenda—or face a catastrophic future due to global climate change . . .

Headline: OTHER CANDIDATES BACK DOWN, INVITE VENTURA AND KENNEDY TO JOIN DEBATES

October 2008: With less than a month to go before the November election, presidential and vice presidential candidates from the Republican and Democratic parties announced in separate press conferences that they have invited independents Jesse Ventura and Robert F. Kennedy, Jr., to join in the final debate at mid-month.

While denying that public pressure bore any influence on their decision, each party headquarters has been besieged with thousands of e-mails and phone calls over the past month, urging that the American people be given an opportunity to see all of the leading contenders in action . . .

Headline: U.S. BOMBS ALLEGED NUCLEAR SITES IN IRAN

October 2008: In what President Bush called a "limited strike" aimed at eliminating Iran's nuclear weapons program, more than a hundred American fighter jets are bombarding specific targets in the Middle Eastern nation with "bunker-busting" bombs.

While leading Democratic presidential candidates offered guarded support for the long-awaited U.S. military action, independent Jesse Ventura decried the U.S. attack as a violation of international law and "a suicidal course . . ."

Headline: PRESIDENT DECLARES MARTIAL LAW AFTER "IRANIAN TERROR BOMBS" GO OFF IN FIVE CITIES

October 2008: President Bush declared martial law across the United States on Tuesday, after what he called "a rain of terror," when explosions rocked entire blocks of five American cities. The bombs, which were not nuclear, killed a still-unknown number of citizens in New York, Boston, Miami, Los Angeles, and Seattle. Initial estimates placed casualties at upwards of five thousand. The president said intelligence sources indicate that the attacks were orchestrated by the Iranian Revolutionary Guard Command, a terrorist organization.

In announcing that immediate suspension of the Constitution was warranted, the president warned that American military forces as well as private contractors would have "shoot-to-kill" orders for people intent on violating nightly curfews. The president added that, in a time of unprecedented crisis for America, dissent could not be tolerated. Rallies in support of the president's new policy took place in fundamentalist Christian churches across the nation.

Although President Bush stopped short of canceling the elections scheduled in three weeks, it is widely believed that they will not take place if martial law remains in effect . . .

Headline: LEADING PROTESTERS TO WHITE HOUSE GATES, VENTURA IS SHOT BY LONE GUNMAN

Late October 2008: Jesse Ventura, the renegade presidential candidate from Minnesota, was shot today as he led a throng of people estimated at close to 100,000 toward the gates of the White House. They were advancing on the heavily-guarded residence to protest President Bush's imposition of martial law, which has resulted in postponement of the forthcoming elections for the first time in U.S. history. Three shots rang out at 12:30 p.m., one missing the former Minnesota governor while two others lodged in his back and stomach.

While Ventura was rushed to Walter Reed Army Hospital, police captured a man who ran out from behind a fence at the nearby Executive Office Building. His weapon, a Mauser 66 sniper rifle, was found in the bushes. Identity of the assailant is still pending . . .

Headline: FORMER GOVERNOR CLINGING TO LIFE; OFFICIALS DENY SHOOTING PART OF WIDER PLOT

Early November 2008: While independent presidential candidate Jesse Ventura—in a coma for the fourth consecutive day—clung to life, with family members gathered at his bedside, a White House press spokesman denied mounting allegations that accused assassin Raul Santana was part of a wider plot.

Santana, being held without bail, is a Cuban exile said to be outraged by the former governor's "appeasing" stand toward lifting the economic boycott against Cuba while Fidel Castro remains alive. Ventura visited the island and met privately with Castro in 2002, his final year as Minnesota governor . . .

> *Last thing I remember, I was running for the door.*
> *I had to find the passage back to the place I was before.*
> *"Relax," said the night man, "We are programmed to receive.*
> *You can check out any time you like, but you can*
> *   never leave!"*
>
> *—"Hotel California," The Eagles*